The
Effects of
Nuclear War

The Effects of Nuclear War "

The Report as Originally Issued, Augmented by Two Reports Intended for the Never-Published Volume 2 and an Interview with Project Director Peter Sharfman

Gale Research Company • Book Tower • Detroit, Michigan 48226

BIBLIOGRAPHIC NOTE

This publication is based on a reprint of the publication of the same title published in 1979 by the Office of Technology Assessment through the U.S. Government Printing Office. It has been augmented by the material indicated on the contents page.

Office of Technology Assessment

The Technology Assessment Board approves the release of this report, which identifies a range of viewpoints on a significant issue facing the U.S. Congress. The views expressed in this report are not necessarily those of the Board, OTA Advisory Council, or of individual members thereof.

Library of Congress Cataloging in Publication Data

Main entry under title:

The Effects of nuclear war.

   Reprint. Originally published: Washington : Congress of the U.S., Office of Technology Assessment, 1979.
   Bibliography: p.
   1. Atomic warfare.   I. United States.   Congress. Office of Technology Assessment.
U263.E36 1984   355'.0217   84-10161
ISBN 0-8103-0999-8

Nuclear War Effects Project Staff

Lionel S. Johns, *Assistant Director*
Energy, Materials, and Global Security Division

Peter Sharfman, *National Security Group Manager and Project Director*

Jonathan Medalia *(on detail from Congressional Research Service)*

Robert W. Vining *(under contract with Systems Science and Software)*

Kevin Lewis

Gloria Proctor

Supplemental OTA Staff

Henry Kelly   Marvin Ott

Consultants

Advanced Research and Applications Corporation
Analytical Assessments Corporation
General Research Corporation
Santa Fe Corporation
Systems Science and Software

Stuart Goldman
Nan Randall
George R. Rodericks
Ronald Stivers

OTA Publishing Staff

John C. Holmes, *Publishing Officer*
Kathie S. Boss   Joanne Heming

Nuclear War Effects Project Advisory Panel

The Advisory Panel provided advice and constructive criticism throughout this project. The panel does not, however, necessarily approve, disapprove, or endorse this report. OTA assumes full responsibility for the report and the accuracy of its contents.

Contents

*Indicates that a classified version is also available to qualified requesters.

Foreword

This assessment was made in response to a request from the Senate Committee on Foreign Relations to examine the effects of nuclear war on the populations and economies of the United States and the Soviet Union. It is intended, in the terms of the Committee's request, to "put what have been abstract measures of strategic power into more comprehensible terms."

The study examines the full range of effects that nuclear war would have on civilians: direct effects from blast and radiation; and indirect effects from economic, social, and political disruption. Particular attention is devoted to the ways in which the impact of a nuclear war would extend over time. Two of the study's principal findings are that conditions would continue to get worse for some time after a nuclear war ended, and that the effects of nuclear war that cannot be calculated in advance are at least as important as those which analysts attempt to quantify.

This report provides essential background for a range of issues relating to strategic weapons and foreign policy. It translates what is generally known about the effects of nuclear weapons into the best available estimates about the impact on society if such weapons were used. It calls attention to the very wide range of impacts that nuclear weapons would have on a complex industrial society, and to the extent of uncertainty regarding these impacts.

Several years ago, OTA convened a panel of distinguished scientists to examine the effects of a limited nuclear war. The report and testimony of that panel, which were published by the Senate Foreign Relations Committee, remain valid. That panel recommended that a more thorough and comprehensive study of the effects of nuclear war be undertaken. This study is such an effort.

The Director of this assessment was Dr. Peter Sharfman, Group Manager for National Security Studies. OTA is grateful for the assistance of its Nuclear War Effects Advisory Panel, chaired by Dr. David S. Saxon, President of the University of California, and for the assistance of the Congressional Research Service, the Department of Defense, the Arms Control and Disarmament Agency, and the Central Intelligence Agency. It should be understood, however, that OTA assumes full responsibility for this report and that it does not necessarily represent the views of any of these agencies or of the individual members of the Advisory Panel.

DANIEL De SIMONE
Acting Director

Prologue

"What If the Bombs Fell?"*

Interview with Dr. Peter Sharfman, program manager for national security at the Congressional Office of Technology Assessment who supervised the study resulting in the report, "The Effects of Nuclear War."

STAMBERG: What is the most staggering piece of information in your report, *The Effects of Nuclear War?* If all Americans read it, what would be the one thing that would keep them up nights?

DR. PETER SHARFMAN: Well, the most staggering piece of information is only implicit in the report, and that is that nuclear weapons are real. They exist. I myself think that nuclear war is very unlikely. But it's possible. It could happen. And the consequences are simply beyond anything that Americans have ever experienced.

[*As a prelude to Senate debate on the Strategic Arms Limitation Treaty, the Senate Foreign Relations Committee asked the Congressional Office of Technology Assessment (OTA) to prepare a comprehensive study on the effects of nuclear war. The premise was that before making crucial decisions, policymakers had to understand what is known, and what is not known, about nuclear war.*

Dr. Peter Sharfman was program manager for national security at OTA. Sharfman and his staff were asked to think the unthinkable. What, precisely, would happen if the bombs fell? In June 1979, All Things Considered asked him to share his findings with our listeners.]

SHARFMAN continues: It's possible to calculate what the effects would be. But we found that the

*Susan Stamberg, in an interview with Peter Sharfman (originally broadcast on National Public Radio's "All Things Considered," in June, 1979), in her Every Night at Five: Susan Stamberg's "All Things Considered" Book (copyright © 1982 by National Public Radio; reprinted by permission of Pantheon Books, a Division of Random House, Inc. and National Public Radio), Pantheon Books, 1982, pp. 103-07.

effects you can't put numbers on, the ones you can't calculate, are in all probability just as important as the effects that you can calculate.

STAMBERG: What are you thinking of?

SHARFMAN: Let me give you a couple of down-to-earth examples. One is that radioactive fallout depends tremendously on the weather—which way the wind is blowing and how strong it is. We imagined that a single nuclear weapon exploded in the city of Detroit. If the wind were coming from the southwest, most of the fallout would go into Ontario, Canada, over essentially uninhabited areas. There would still be a lot of damage, but it wouldn't be devastating. But if the wind were from the northwest, the fallout would go directly over Cleveland; over Youngstown, Ohio; and over Pittsburgh. If you want to know how many people that single nuclear weapon would kill, you have to know which way the wind is going to be blowing at the exact hour the weapon is detonated.

STAMBERG: But there's no way ever to know that or to be able to control it.

SHARFMAN: That's right. We can't even predict a snowstorm a day in advance.

STAMBERG: Let's say that the wind is blowing toward Cleveland and Pittsburgh. What does it mean for the family in Columbia, Missouri, or Miami, Florida?

SHARFMAN: Imagine a big attack. Thousands of weapons detonated. Tens of millions of people would die virtually instantaneously. Additional tens of millions of people would die as a result of radioactive fallout, which is not instantaneous. Even if you get a fatal dose of radiation it takes several days for it to actually kill you. Beyond that, there would be people, millions certainly, possibly tens of millions, who would get a dose of radiation that would not immediately kill them but that would lower their bodies' resistance to other kinds of diseases. At the same time the medical facilities of the country would be largely destroyed. Most hospitals, most doctors, most medical researchers are in big cities and would have died immediately. With no factories producing antibiotics, a lot of people might die from flu or from typhoid, because they were weakened by the radiation and the medical system of the country was unable to care for them. Then you would have additional people who would be fine until the stocks of food in their immediate area ran out. The trucks that normally carry food in from the farming areas of the country wouldn't be running anymore.

STAMBERG: But the food that they would be eating would be contaminated at that point, wouldn't it?

SHARFMAN: No, not necessarily. Canned food is hard to contaminate. To get a sense of what might happen in a specific community, we asked a very good journalist named Nan Randall to come and read the materials we had been gathering—in effect, to study up on nuclear war—and then to go to Charlottesville, Virginia, and create a fictional study of what would happen if there were a nuclear war in which Charlottesville was not a target.

In the scenario she created, the nuclear attack did not come as a complete surprise to the nation. Relations between the superpowers had deteriorated to the point that citizens were deserting the cities weeks before the bombs fell.

When the sirens sounded, most of Charlottesville hurried to shelter. The sky to the east and north glowed brilliantly, following the attack on Washington and Richmond. At first no one knew how extensive the damage was—that more than 4,000 megatons had destroyed military and industrial targets, and close to 100 million U.S. citizens had been killed.

Imagine 100,000 people in shelters. That's 30,000 who are there to begin with and 70,000 refugees. They are extremely uncomfortable, to put it mildly, and probably contracting diseases of various sorts from poor sanitation. It's too hot or it's too cold. They are undergoing terrible psychological trauma, packed together and giving each other diseases. But most of them are alive.

After a couple of weeks the fallout diminishes to the point where they might as well come out. Not that it's safe. There is some statistical risk of getting cancer. But since every place in the country is going to be unsafe, you just have to come out and put up with it.

In our Charlottesville scenario, three weeks after the nuclear attack almost all the residents had returned home. The refugees could move out of shelters, but still had to camp out, waiting in endless lines for food or use of the bathrooms. Emergency authorities ordered local residents to take in refugee families. Resistance to the order was strong. In the meantime, the need for food was becoming acute. There was no refrigeration, and much food had spoiled. Food prices skyrocketed.

The number of radiation deaths increased, and mass funerals took place several times a day. The city set aside several locations for mass graves.

STAMBERG: So Charlottesville has now become a crippled population, not only decimated but crippled physically, mentally, psychologically, in all ways.

SHARFMAN: That's right. Exactly. There's another thing to consider. Apart from direct damage, a lot of people's jobs have disappeared. What's the use of owning a shoestore if you can't buy shoes to resell to people? There would probably be a mismatch between the tremendous amount that would need to be done and what the survivors would know how to do.

STAMBERG: What kind of a timetable do you put on our ability to reorganize in some way?

SHARFMAN: Well, that's the real question, of course. Social organization is really the crux of the matter. There would be surviving people. There would be surviving things. The problem would be getting them together to start the work of rebuilding. Remember that, after a few generations without machines and training, people forget how machines work. So we will have survived biologically, but our way of life is going to be unrecognizable. In several generations the U.S. could resemble a late medieval society.

STAMBERG: Is it a possibility that the actual situation might be better than the fictional Charlottesville scenario?

SHARFMAN: Sure. Or worse. I tend to think we picked a somewhat optimistic scenario. We assumed that civic spirit survives; that people for the most part treat their neighbors well; that you don't have riots or anarchy or mass looting or martial law. But you can't be sure. Remember, in a nuclear-war environment you're talking about tens of millions of people dying. In such an environment, one of the things that goes by the board is the attitude that a single human life is precious. I suppose that one of the ways you would know that the war was over, that the recovery period was over, that the survivors had gotten over the war, would be when human life could again become precious. That could take a very long time.

(Long pause)

STAMBERG: As I listen to you and become increasingly chilled by what you're saying, I feel I must ask you a personal question. What has it meant to you, working on this report? What are your dreams like these days?

SHARFMAN: Well . . . that's a hard question to answer. I guess there is a trick to doing any kind of disciplined work on an unpleasant subject. You insulate yourself. As we wrote the study, we tried to avoid drifting off into easy abstractions. You get a phrase like "a bomb would inflict a million fatalities." And I sat there with my little pencil and changed it to "a bomb would kill a million people." You have to keep reminding yourself of that. But, at the same time, killing a million people is no more comprehensible to me than it is to anybody else. And I suppose that, in a funny way, I would lose more sleep if one particular individual I knew and was attached to was simply in pain than I would at the thought of a million people whom I don't know dying. It's a strange sort of thing, but I think that's the way human psychology works, and what that means is that your gut reactions are not a sound guide to policy. That is, you can get fascinated by these weapons. You can get fascinated by the fun of trying to imagine things different. You can also get horrified, turn away in repulsion. Neither the fascination nor the repulsion is a very good guide to figuring out what would make a good foreign policy.

One way or another, ever since I was in college, I have been professionally concerned with foreign-policy matters, with issues relating to war and peace. I decided a long time ago that if war was possible, it was better to think about war and trying to understand what it is that hangs over all of us than to just try to pretend it isn't there. So I don't think that doing the study has directly affected what I dream about. You can't lie awake at night worrying about nuclear war without going nuts. What I really would hope is that, as people go about their normal business, they bear in mind that avoiding a nuclear war is important. That nuclear weapons are real. That they are serious business.

The Senate debate for which the Sharfman study was prepared didn't take place in 1980, as scheduled. In December 1979, Soviet troops moved into Afghanistan. President Carter asked the Senate to delay debate on SALT in retaliation for the Soviet action.

Chapter I
EXECUTIVE SUMMARY

Chapter I.—EXECUTIVE SUMMARY

TABLES

EXECUTIVE SUMMARY

At the request of the Senate Committee on Foreign Relations, the Office of Technology Assessment has undertaken to describe the effects of a nuclear war on the civilian populations, economies, and societies of the United States and the Soviet Union.

Nuclear war is not a comfortable subject. Throughout all the variations, possibilities, and uncertainties that this study describes, one theme is constant—a nuclear war would be a catastrophe. A militarily plausible nuclear attack, even "limited," could be expected to kill people and to inflict economic damage on a scale unprecedented in American experience; a large-scale nuclear exchange would be a calamity unprecedented in human history. The mind recoils from the effort to foresee the details of such a calamity, and from the careful explanation of the unavoidable uncertainties as to whether people would die from blast damage, from fallout radiation, or from starvation during the following winter. But the fact remains that nuclear war is possible, and the possibility of nuclear war has formed part of the foundation of international politics, and of U.S. policy, ever since nuclear weapons were used in 1945.

The premise of this study is that those who deal with the large issues of world politics should understand what is known, and perhaps more importantly what is not known, about the likely consequences if efforts to deter and avoid nuclear war should fail. Those who deal with policy issues regarding nuclear weapons should know what such weapons can do, and the extent of the uncertainties about what such weapons might do.

FINDINGS

1. **The effects of a nuclear war that cannot be calculated are at least as important as those for which calculations are attempted.** Moreover, even these limited calculations are subject to very large uncertainties.

Conservative military planners tend to base their calculations on factors that can be either controlled or predicted, and to make pessimistic assumptions where control or prediction are impossible. For example, planning for strategic nuclear warfare looks at the extent to which civilian targets will be destroyed by blast, and discounts the additional damage which may be caused by fires that the blast could ignite. This is not because fires are unlikely to cause damage, but because the extent of fire damage depends on factors such as weather and details of building construction

that make it much more difficult to predict than blast damage. While it is proper for a military plan to provide for the destruction of key targets by the surest means even in unfavorable circumstances, the nonmilitary observer should remember that actual damage is likely to be greater than that reflected in the military calculations. This is particularly true for indirect effects such as deaths resulting from injuries and the unavailability of medical care, or for economic damage resulting from disruption and disorganization rather than from direct destruction.

For more than a decade, the declared policy of the United States has given prominence to a concept of "assured destruction:" the capabilities of U.S. nuclear weapons have been described in terms of the level of damage they can surely inflict even in the most unfavorable circumstances. It should be understood that in the event of an actual nuclear war, the destruction resulting from an all-out nuclear attack would probably be far greater. In addition to the tens of millions of deaths during the days and weeks after the attack, there would probably be further millions (perhaps further tens of millions) of deaths in the ensuing months or years. In addition to the enormous economic destruction caused by the actual nuclear explosions, there would be some years during which the residual economy would decline further, as stocks were consumed and machines wore out faster than recovered production could replace them. Nobody knows how to estimate the likelihood that industrial civilization might collapse in the areas attacked; additionally, the possibility of significant long-term ecological damage cannot be excluded.

2. **The impact of even a "small" or "limited" nuclear attack would be enormous.** Although predictions of the effects of such an attack are subject to the same uncertainties as predictions of the effects of an all-out attack, the possibilities can be bounded. OTA examined the impact of a small attack on economic targets (an attack on oil refineries limited to 10 missiles), and found that while economic recovery would be possible, the economic damage and social dislocation could be immense. A review of calculations of the effects on civilian populations and economies of major counterforce attacks found that while the consequences might be endurable (since they would be on a scale with wars and epidemics that nations have endured in the past), the number of deaths might be as high as 20 million. Moreover, the uncertainties are such that no government could predict with any confidence what the results of a limited attack or counterattack would be even if there was no further escalation.

3. **It is therefore reasonable to suppose that the extreme uncertainties about the effects of a nuclear attack, as well as the certainty that the minimum consequences would be enormous, both play a role in the deterrent effect of nuclear weapons.**

4. **There are major differences between the United States and the Soviet Union that affect the nature of their vulnerability to nuclear attacks, despite the fact that both are large and diversified industrial countries.** Differences between the two countries in terms of population distribution, closeness of population to other targets, vulnerability of agricultural systems, vulnerability of cities to fire, socioeconomic system, and political system create significant asymmetries in the potential effects of nuclear attacks. Differences in civil defense preparations and in the structure of the strategic arsenals compound these asymmetries. By and large, the Soviet Union is favored by geography and by a political/economic structure geared to emergencies; the United States is favored by having a bigger and better economy and (perhaps) a greater capacity for effective decentralization. The larger size of Soviet weapons also means that they are likely to kill more people while aiming at something else.

5. **Although it is true that effective sheltering and/or evacuation could save lives, it is not clear that a civil defense program based on providing shelters or planning evacuation would necessarily be effective.** To save lives, it is not only necessary to provide shelter in, or evacuation to, the right place (and only extreme measures of dispersion would overcome the problem that the location of safe places cannot be reliably predicted), it is also necessary to provide food, water, medical supplies, sanitation, security against other people, possibly filtered air, etc. After fallout diminishes, there must be enough supplies and enough organization to keep people alive while production is being restored. The effectiveness of civil defense measures depends, among other things, on the events leading up to the attack, the enemy's targeting policy, and sheer luck.

6. **The situation in which the survivors of a nuclear attack find themselves will be quite unprecedented.** The surviving nation would be far weaker—economically, socially, and politically—than one would calculate by adding up the surviving economic assets and the numbers and skills of the surviving people. Natural resources would be destroyed; surviving equip-

ment would be designed to use materials and skills that might no longer exist; and indeed some regions might be almost uninhabitable. Furthermore, prewar patterns of behavior would surely change, though in unpredictable ways. Finally, the entire society would suffer from the enormous psychological shock of having discovered the extent of its vulnerability.

7. **From an economic point of view, and possibly from a political and social viewpoint as well, conditions after an attack would get worse before they started to get better.** For a period of time, people could live off supplies (and, in a sense, off habits) left over from before the war. But shortages and uncertainties would get worse. The survivors would find themselves in a race to achieve viability (i.e., production at least equaling consumption plus depreciation) before stocks ran out completely. A failure to achieve viability, or even a slow recovery, would result in many additional deaths, and much additional economic, political, and social deterioration. This postwar damage could be as devastating as the damage from the actual nuclear explosions.

APPROACH

The scope of this study is both broader and narrower than that of most other studies on this subject. It is broader in three respects:

1. it examines a full range of possible nuclear attacks, with attacking forces ranging in extent from a single weapon to the bulk of a superpower's arsenal;
2. it deals explicitly with both Soviet attacks on the United States and U.S. attacks on the Soviet Union; and
3. it addresses the multiple effects of nuclear war, indirect as well as direct, long term as well as short term, and social and economic as well as physical.

Those effects that cannot be satisfactorily calculated or estimated are described qualitatively. But this report's scope is narrower than most defense analyses because it avoids any consideration of military effects; although it hypothesizes (among other things) missile attacks against military targets, only the "collateral" damage such attacks would inflict on the civilian society are examined.

The approach used was to look at a series of attack "cases," (table 1) and to describe the various effects and overall impact each of them might produce. By analyzing the impact of the same attack case for both a U.S. attack on the Soviet Union and a Soviet attack on the United States, the report examines the significance of the different kinds of vulnerabilities of the two countries, and offers some insights about the consequences of the differences between the two countries' nuclear weapon arsenals. The cases were chosen primarily to investigate the effects of variations in attack size and in the kinds of targets attacked. It is believed that the analysis is "realistic," in the sense that the hypothetical attacks are possible ones. Patterns of nuclear explosions were examined that are not very different from those that, OTA believes, the existing nuclear forces would produce if the military were ordered to make attacks of the specified size on the specified targets.

Case 1: In order to provide a kind of tutorial on what happens when nuclear weapons are

Table 1.—Summary of Cases

Case	Description
1 (pp. 27-44)	Attack on single city: Detroit and Leningrad; 1 weapon, or 10 small weapons.
2 (pp. 64-80)	Attack on oil refineries, limited to 10 missiles.
3 (pp. 81-94)	Counterforce attack; includes attack only on ICBM silos as a variant.
4 (pp. 94-106)	Attack on range of military and economic targets using large fraction of existing arsenal.

For each case, the first section describes a Soviet attack on the United States, and the following section a U.S. attack on the Soviet Union.

detonated, the study describes the effects of the explosion of a single weapon. Then it examines the effects of such an explosion over a single U.S. city (Detroit) and single Soviet city (Leningrad) of comparable size. The base case was the detonation of a 1-megaton weapon (1 Mt = energy released by one million tons of TNT), since both the United States and the Soviet Union have weapons of roughly this size in their arsenals. Then, in order to look at the ways in which the specific effects and overall impact would vary if other weapons that might be available were used, the effects of a 25-Mt weapon over Detroit, the effects of a 9-Mt weapon over Leningrad, and the effects of 10 weapons of 40 kilotons (kt) each over Leningrad are described. An attempt was made to describe as well the effects of a small weapon in a large city (such as a terrorist group might set off) but was unsuccessful because the effects of such a weapon in a metropolitan setting cannot be inferred from the existing body of knowledge regarding military weapons. This is explained in the body of the report.

The casualties from such attacks could range from 220,000 dead and 420,000 injured to 2,500,000 dead and 1,100,000 injured (many of the injured would wind up as fatalities), depending on the details of the attack and the assumptions made regarding conditions. The discussion in chapter II shows how the time of day, time of year, weather conditions, size of weapon, height of burst, and preparation of the population could all make a great difference in the number of casualties resulting from such an attack. The extent of fire damage is a further uncertainty. Even if only one city is attacked, and the remaining resources of a nation are available to help, medical facilities would be inadequate to care for the injured. A further imponderable is fallout (if the attack uses a surface burst), whose effects depend on the winds.

Case 2: In order to examine the effects of a small attack on urban/industrial targets, the study examines a hypothetical attack limited to 10 SNDVs (strategic nuclear delivery vehicles, the term used in SALT to designate one missile or one bomber) on the other superpower's oil refineries. In "planning" this attack,

which is not analogous to any described in recent U.S. literature, it was hypothesized that the political leadership instructed the military to inflict maximum damage on energy production using only 10 SNDVs without regard to the extent of civilian casualties or other damage. It was assumed that the Soviets would attack such targets with SS-18 missiles (each carrying 10 multiple independently targetable reentry vehicles, or MIRVs), and that the United States would use 7 MIRVed Poseidon missiles and 3 MIRVed Minuteman III missiles.

The calculations showed that the Soviet attack would destroy 64 percent of U.S. oil refining capacity, while the U.S. attack would destroy 73 percent of Soviet refining capacity. Calculations were also made of "prompt fatalities," including those killed by blast and fallout, assuming no special civil defense measures: they showed about 5 million U.S. deaths and about 1 million Soviet deaths. The results were different for the two countries for several reasons. Soviet oil refining capacity is more concentrated than U.S. oil refining capacity, so that a small attack can reach more of it. At the same time, Soviet refineries tend to be located away from residential areas (the available data on population location deals with where people live rather than with where they work) to a greater extent than U.S. refineries. A further difference is that a limitation on the number of delivery vehicles would lead each side to use weapons with many MIRVs, so the United States would attack most of the targets with Poseidon missiles which have small warheads, while the Soviets would use SS-18 intercontinental ballistic missiles (ICBMs) which carry much larger warheads, and large warheads cause more damage to things not directly targeted (in this case, people) than do small warheads.

One can only speculate about the consequences of such extensive destruction. There would have to be drastic changes in both the U.S. and Soviet economies to cope with the sudden disappearance of the bulk of oil refining capacity. Productivity in virtually every industrial sector would decline, and some sectors would be largely wiped out. There would have to be strict allocation of the remaining available refined petroleum products. Some Soviet factory workers might end up working in the fields to replace tractors for which fuel was unavailable. The United States might have to ban commuting by automobile, forcing suburban residents to choose between moving and long walks to a bus stop. The aftermath of the war might lead to either an increase or a decrease in the amount of petroleum products required by the military. Changes in people's attitudes are impossible to predict. Calm determination might produce effective responses that would limit the damage; panic or a breakdown in civic spirit could compound the effects of the attack itself.

It is instructive to observe the asymmetries between the problems which the United States and the Soviets would face. Soviet agricultural production, which is barely adequate in peacetime, would probably decline sharply, and production rates would slow even in essential industries. However, the Soviet system is well adapted for allocating scarce resources to high-priority areas, and for keeping everybody employed even if efficient employment is unavailable. The relative wealth and freedom of the United States brings both advantages and disadvantages: while agriculture and essential industry would probably continue, there would be a staggering organizational problem in making use of resources that now depend on petroleum—one must ask what the employees of an automobile factory or a retail establishment on a highway would do if there were virtually no gasoline for cars.

A major question relating to these results is how much they could vary with changed assumptions. The figures for fatalities were based on air bursts, which would maximize destruction of the refineries. (As an excursion, U.S. fatalities were recalculated on the assumption of surface bursts, and use of the best fallout shelters within 2 miles of where each person lives. This reduced fatalities by one-third.) There was no data available on the types of Soviet residential construction in the vicinity of oil refineries: treating it parametrically gave casualty figures of about

1,500,000 if the construction is all houses, and about 800,000 if it is all apartment buildings. Perfect accuracy was assumed for missiles that are in fact somewhat inaccurate—some inaccuracy might reduce the extent of damage to the refineries, but it might well increase the number of deaths.

Case 3. In order to examine the effects on civilian populations and economies of counterforce attacks, the study examined attacks on ICBM silos and attacks on silos, bomber bases, and missile submarine bases. Such attacks have received fairly extensive study in the executive branch in recent years, so OTA surveyed a number of these studies in order to determine the range of possible answers, and the variations in assumptions that produce such a range. An unclassified summary of this survey appears as appendix D of this volume. (The complete survey, classified secret, is available separately.)

A counterforce attack would produce relatively little direct blast damage to civilians and to economic assets; the main damage would come from radioactive fallout. The uncertainties in the effects of fallout are enormous, depending primarily on the weather and on the extent of fallout sheltering which the population makes use of. The calculations made by various agencies of the executive branch showed a range in "prompt fatalities" (almost entirely deaths from fallout within the first 30 days) from less than 1 to 11 percent of the U.S. population and from less than 1 to 5 percent of the Soviet population. This shows just how great a variation can be introduced by modifying assumptions regarding population distribution and shelter.

What can be concluded from this? First, if the attack involves surface bursts of many very large weapons, if weather conditions are unfavorable, and if no fallout shelters are created beyond those that presently exist, U.S. deaths could reach 20 million and Soviet deaths more than 10 million. (The difference is a result of geography; many Soviet strategic forces are so located that fallout from attacking them would drift mainly into sparsely populated areas or into China.) Second, effective fallout sheltering (which is not necessarily the same thing as a program—this assumes people are actually sheltered and actually remain there) could save many lives under favorable conditions, but even in the best imaginable case more than a million would die in either the United States or the U.S.S.R. from a counter-force attack. Third, the "limited nature" of counterforce attacks may not be as significant as the enormous uncertainty regarding their results.

There would be considerable economic damage and disruption as a result of such attacks. Almost all areas could, in principle, be decontaminated within a few months, but the loss of so many people and the interruption of economic life would be staggering blows. An imponderable, in thinking about the process of recovery, is the extent of any lasting psychological impacts.

Case 4: In order to examine the kind of destruction that is generally thought of as the culmination of an escalatory process, the study looked at the consequences of a very large attack against a range of military and economic targets. Here too calculations that the executive branch has carried out in recent years were used. These calculations tend to assume that Soviet attacks on the United States would be a first strike, and hence use most of the Soviet arsenal, while U.S. attacks on the Soviet Union would be retaliatory strikes, and hence use only those weapons that might survive a Soviet counterforce attack. However, the difference in damage to civilian populations and economies between a "first strike" and a "second strike" seems to lie within the range of uncertainty created by other factors.

The resulting deaths would be far beyond any precedent. Executive branch calculations show a range of U.S. deaths from 35 to 77 percent (i.e., from 70 million to 160 million dead), and Soviet deaths from 20 to 40 percent of the population. Here again the range reflects the difference made by varying assumptions about population distribution and sheltering, and to a lesser extent differences in assumptions about the targeting policy of the attacker. Soviet casualties are smaller than U.S. casualties because a greater proportion of the Soviet population lives in rural areas, and because U.S. weapons (which have lower average yields) produce less fallout than Soviet weapons.

Some excursions have been run to test the effect of deliberately targeting population rather than killing people as a side effect of attacking economic and military targets. They show that such a change in targeting could kill somewhere between 20 million and 30 million additional people on each side, holding other assumptions constant.

These calculations reflect only deaths during the first 30 days. Additional millions would be injured, and many would eventually die from lack of adequate medical care. In addition, millions of people might starve or freeze during the following winter, but it is not possible to estimate how many. Chapter V attempts to calculate the further millions who might eventually die of latent radiation effects.

What is clear is that from the day the survivors emerged from their fallout shelters, a kind of race for survival would begin. One side of the race would be the restoration of production: production of food, of energy, of clothing, of the means to repair damaged machinery, of goods that might be used for trade with countries that had not fought in the war, and even of military weapons and supplies. The other side of the race would be consumption of goods that had survived the attack, and the wearing-out of surviving machines. If production rises to the rate of consumption before stocks are exhausted, then viability has been achieved and economic recovery has begun. If not, then each postwar year would see a lower level of economic activity than the year before, and the future of civilization itself in the nations attacked would be in doubt. This report cannot predict whether this race for economic viability would be won. The answer would lie in the effectiveness of postwar social and economic organization as much as in the amount of actual physical damage. There is a controversy in the literature on the subject as to whether a postattack economy would be based on centralized planning (in which case how would the necessary data and planning time be obtained?), or to individual initiative and decentralized decisionmaking (in which case who would feed the refugees, and what would serve for money and credit?).

An obviously critical question is the impact that a nuclear attack would have on the lives of those who survive it. The case descriptions discuss the possibilities of economic, political, social, and psychological disruption or collapse. However, the recital of possibilities and uncertainties may fail to convey the overall situation of the survivors, especially the survivors of a large attack that included urban-industrial targets. In an effort to provide a more concrete understanding of what a world after a nuclear war would be like, OTA commissioned a work of fiction. It appears as appendix C and presents some informed speculation about what life would be like in Charlottesville, Va., assuming that this city escaped direct damage from the attack. The kind of detail that such an imaginative account presents—detail that proved to be unavailable for a comparable Soviet city—adds a dimension to the more abstract analysis in the body of the report.

Civil Defense: Chapter III provides some basic information about civil defense measures, discusses the way in which they might mitigate the effects of nuclear attack, and discusses the uncertainties regarding their effectiveness. There is a lively controversy among experts as to the effectiveness of existing Soviet civil defense programs, and another controversy as to whether existing U.S. programs ought to be changed. The major points in dispute were identified, but no attempt was made to assess the merits of the arguments. For the purposes of this study, it was assumed that the existing civil defense programs, as described in this report, would be in effect, and that a full-scale preattack evacuation of cities (sometimes called "crisis relocation") would not take place. This assumption was made because it appeared to be the only way to describe existing vulnerabilities while avoiding predictions about the course of events leading up to a nuclear war. While both the U.S. and the Soviet Governments profess to believe that urban evacuation prior to an attack on cities would save lives, ordering such an evacuation would be a crisis management move as well as a civil defense precaution.

Long-Term Effects: While the immediate damage from the blasts would be long term in the sense that the damage could not be quickly repaired, there would be other effects which might not manifest themselves for some years after the attack. It is well established that levels of radiation too low (or too slowly absorbed) to cause immediate death or even illness will nevertheless have adverse effects on some fraction of a population receiving them. A nuclear attack would certainly produce both somatic effects (largely cancer) and genetic effects, although there is uncertainty about the numbers of victims. OTA calculated the ranges of such effects that might be produced by each of the attack cases analyzed. Cancer deaths and those suffering some form of genetic damage would run into the millions over the 40 years following the attack. For the comprehensive attack (Case 4), it appears that cancer deaths and genetic effects in a country attacked would be small relative to the numbers of immediate deaths, but that radiation effects elsewhere in the world would appear more significant. For counterforce attacks, the effects would be significant both locally and worldwide.

A 1975 study by the National Academy of Sciences (NAS)[1] addressed the question of the possibility of serious ecological damage, and concluded that while one cannot say just how such damage would occur, it cannot be ruled out. This conclusion still stands, although the NAS report may have been more alarmist about the possibility of damage to the ozone layer than recent research would support.

Table 2 summarizes the results of the case studies.

---

[1]*Long-Term Worldwide Effects of Multiple Nuclear-Weapons Detonations* (Washington, D.C.: National Academy of Sciences, 1975).

Table 2.—Summary of Effects

Case	Description	Main causes of civilian damage	Immediate deaths	Middle-term effects	Long-term effects
1 (pp. 27-44)	Attack on single city: Detroit and Leningrad; 1 weapon or 10 small weapons.	Blast, fire, & loss of infrastructure; fallout is elsewhere.	200,00-2,000,000	Many deaths from injuries; center of city difficult to rebuild.	Relatively minor.
2 (pp. 64-80)	Attack on oil refineries, limited to 10 missiles.	Blast, fire, secondary fires, fallout. Extensive economic problems from loss of refined petroleum.	1,000,000-5,000,000	Many deaths from injuries; great economic hardship for some years; particular problems for Soviet agriculture and for U.S. socioeconomic organization	Cancer deaths in millions only if attack involves surface bursts.
3 (pp. 81-94)	Counterforce attack; includes attack only on ICBM silos as a variant.	Some blast damage if bomber and missile submarine bases attacked.	1,000,000-20,000,000	Economic impact of deaths; possible large psychological impact.	Cancer deaths and genetic effects in millions; further millions of effects outside attacked countries.
4 (pp. 94-106)	Attack on range of military and economic targets using large fraction of existing arsenal.	Blast and fallout; subsequent economic disruption; possible lack of resources to support surviving population or economic recovery. Possible breakdown of social order. Possible incapacitating psychological trauma.	20,000,000-160,000,000	Enormous economic destruction and disruption. If immediate deaths are in low range, more tens of millions may die subsequently because economy is unable to support them. Major question about whether economic viability can be restored—key variables may be those of political and economic organization. Unpredictable psychological effects.	Cancer deaths and genetic damage in the millions; relatively insignificant in attacked areas, but quite significant elsewhere in the world. Possibility of ecological damage.

For each case, the first section describes a Soviet attack on the United States, and the following section a U.S. attack on the Soviet Union.

UNCERTAINTIES

There are enormous uncertainties and imponderables involved in any effort to assess the effects of a nuclear war, and an effort to look at the entire range of effects compounds them. Many of these uncertainties are obvious ones: if the course of a snowstorm cannot be predicted 1 day ahead in peacetime, one must certainly be cautious about predictions of the pattern of radioactive fallout on some unknown future day. Similar complexities exist for human institutions: there is great difficulty in predicting the peacetime course of the U.S. economy, and predicting its course after a nuclear war is a good deal more difficult. This study highlights the importance of three categories of uncertainties:

- Uncertainties in calculations of deaths and of direct economic damage resulting from the need to make assumptions about matters such as time of day, time of year, wind, weather, size of bombs, exact location of the detonations, location of people, availability and quality of sheltering, etc.

- Effects that would surely take place, but whose magnitude cannot be calculated. These include the effects of fires, the shortfalls in medical care and housing, the extent to which economic and social disruption would magnify the effects of direct economic damage, the extent of bottlenecks and synergistic effects, the extent of disease, etc.

- Effects that are possible, but whose likelihood is as incalculable as their magnitude. These include the possibility of a long downward economic spiral before viability is attained, the possibility of political disintegration (anarchy or regionalization), the possibility of major epidemics, and the possibility of irreversible ecological changes.

One major problem in making calculations is to know where the people will be at the moment when the bombs explode. Calculations for the United States are generally based on the 1970 census, but it should be borne in mind that the census data describes where people's homes are, and there is never a moment when everybody in the United States is at home at the same time. If an attack took place during a working day, casualties might well be higher since people would be concentrated in factories and offices (which are more likely to be targets) rather than dispersed in suburbs. For the case of the Soviet population, the same assumption is made that people are at home, but the inaccuracies are compounded by the unavailability of detailed information about just where the Soviet rural population lives. The various calculations that were used made varying, though not unreasonable assumptions about population location.

A second uncertainty in calculations has to do with the degree of protection available. There is no good answer to the question: "Would people use the best available shelter against blast and fallout?" It seems unreasonable to suppose that shelters would not be used, and equally unreasonable to assume that at a moment of crisis all available resources would be put to rational use. (It has been pointed out that if plans worked, people behaved rationally, and machinery were adequately maintained, there would be no peacetime deaths from traffic accidents.) The Defense Civil Preparedness Agency has concluded from public opinion surveys that in a period of severe international crisis about 10 percent of all Americans would leave their homes and move to a "safer" place (spontaneous evacuation); more reliable estimates are probably impossible, but it could make a substantial difference to the casualty figures.

A third uncertainty is the weather at the time of the attack at the various places where bombs explode. The local wind conditions, and especially the amount of moisture in the air, may make an enormous difference in the number and spread of fires. Wind conditions over a wider area determine the extent and location of fallout contamination. The time of year has a decisive effect on the damage that fallout does to agriculture—while an attack in January might be expected to do only indirect damage (destroying farm machinery or the fuel to run it), fallout when plants are young can kill them, and fallout just before harvesttime would probably make it unsafe to get the harvest in. The time of year also has direct effects on population death—the attack in the dead of winter, which might not directly damage agriculture, may lead to greater deaths from fallout radiation (because of the difficulty of improvising fallout protection by moving frozen dirt) and from cold and exposure.

The question of how rapid and efficient economic recovery would be—or indeed whether a genuine recovery would be possible at all—raises questions that seem to be beyond calculation. It is possible to calculate direct economic damage by making assumptions about the size and exact location of bomb explosions, and the hardness of economic assets; however, such calculations cannot address the issues of bottlenecks and of synergy. Bottlenecks would occur if a key product that was essential for many other manufacturing processes could no longer be produced, or (for the case of a large attack) if an entire industrial sector were wiped out. In either case, the economic loss would greatly exceed the peacetime value of the factories that were actually destroyed. There does not appear to be any reliable way of calculating the likelihood or extent of bottlenecks because economic input/output models do not address the possibility or cost of substitutions across sectors. Apart from the creation of bottlenecks, there could be synergistic effects: for example, the fire that cannot be controlled because the blast destroyed fire stations, as actually happened at Hiroshima. Here, too, there is no reliable way to estimate the likelihood of such effects: would radiation deaths of birds and the destruction of insecticide factories have a synergistic effect? Another uncertainty is the possibility of organizational bottlenecks. In the most obvious instance, it would make an enormous difference whether the President of the United States survived. Housing, defined as a place where a productive worker lives as distinct from shelter for refugees, is another area of uncertainty. Minimal housing is essential if production is to be restored, and it takes time to rebuild it if the existing housing stock is destroyed or is beyond commuting range of the surviving (or repaired) workplaces. It should be noted that the United States has a much larger and more dispersed housing stock than does the Soviet Union, but that American workers have higher minimum standards.

There is a final area of uncertainty that this study does not even address, but which could be of very great importance. Actual nuclear attacks, unlike those in this study, would not take place in a vacuum. There would be a series of events that would lead up to the attack, and these events could markedly change both the physical and the psychological vulnerability of a population to a nuclear attack. Even more critical would be the events after the attack. Assuming that the war ends promptly, the terms on which it ends could greatly affect both the economic condition and the state of mind of the population. The way in which other countries are affected could determine whether the outside world is a source of help or of further danger. The post-attack military situation (and nothing in this study addresses the effects of nuclear attacks on military power) could not only determine the attitude of other countries, but also whether limited surviving resources are put to military or to civilian use.

Moreover, the analyses in this study all assume that the war would end after the hypothetical attack. This assumption simplifies analysis, but it might not prove to be the case. How much worse would the situation of the survivors be if, just as they were attempting to restore some kind of economy following a massive attack, a few additional weapons destroyed the new centers of population and of government?

Chapter II

A NUCLEAR WEAPON OVER DETROIT OR LENINGRAD: A TUTORIAL ON THE EFFECTS OF NUCLEAR WEAPONS

Chapter II.—A NUCLEAR WEAPON OVER DETROIT OR LENINGRAD: A TUTORIAL ON THE EFFECTS OF NUCLEAR WEAPONS

A NUCLEAR WEAPON OVER DETROIT OR LENINGRAD: A TUTORIAL ON THE EFFECTS OF NUCLEAR WEAPONS

INTRODUCTION

This chapter presents a brief description of the major effects of nuclear explosions on the people and structures in urban areas. The details of such effects would vary according to weapons design, the exact geographical layout of the target area, the materials and methods used for construction in the target area, and the weather (especially the amount of moisture in the atmosphere). Thus, the reader should bear in mind that the statements below are essentially generalizations, which are subject to a substantial range of variation and uncertainty.

To convey some sense of the actual effects of large nuclear explosions on urban areas, the potential impact of explosions is described in two real cities—Detroit and Leningrad. To show how these effects vary with the size of the weapon, the effects have been calculated in each city for a variety of weapon sizes.

The descriptions and analysis assume that there is no damage elsewhere in the country. This may appear unlikely, and in the case of a surface burst it is certainly wrong, since a surface burst would generate fallout that would cause casualties elsewhere. However, isolating the effects on a single city allows the setting forth in clear terms of the direct and immediate effects of nuclear explosions. The result is a kind of tutorial in nuclear effects. Subsequent sections of this report, which deal with the effects of larger attacks, discuss the indirect effects of fallout and of economic and social disruption.

Although it is outside the scope of a discussion of "nuclear war," there has been considerable public interest in the effects of a nuclear explosion that a terrorist group might succeed in setting off in an urban area. Accordingly, a discussion of this possibility is added at the end of this chapter.

GENERAL DESCRIPTION OF EFFECTS

The energy of a nuclear explosion is released in a number of different ways:

- an explosive blast, which is qualitatively similar to the blast from ordinary chemical explosions, but which has somewhat different effects because it is typically so much larger;
- direct nuclear radiation;
- direct thermal radiation, most of which takes the form of visible light;
- pulses of electrical and magnetic energy, called electromagnetic pulse (EMP); and
- the creation of a variety of radioactive particles, which are thrown up into the air by the force of the blast, and are called radioactive fallout when they return to Earth.

The distribution of the bomb's energy among these effects depends on its size and on the details of its design, but a general description is possible.

Blast

Most damage to cities from large weapons comes from the explosive blast. The blast drives air away from the site of the explosion, producing sudden changes in air pressure (called static overpressure) that can crush objects, and high winds (called dynamic pressure) that can move them suddenly or knock them down. In general, large buildings are destroyed by the overpressure, while people and objects such as trees and utility poles are destoyed by the wind.

For example, consider the effects of a 1-megaton (Mt) air burst on things 4 miles [6 km]

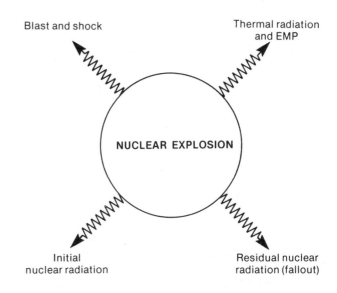

Effects of a nuclear explosion

Thermonuclear ground burst

Photo credit: U.S. Department of Energy

away. The overpressure will be in excess of 5 pounds per square inch (psi), which will exert a force of more than 180 tons on the wall of a typical two-story house. At the same place, there would be a wind of 160 mph [255 km]; while 5 psi is not enough to crush a man, a wind of 180 mph would create fatal collisions between people and nearby objects.

The magnitude of the blast effect (generally measured in pounds per square inch) diminishes with distance from the center of the explosion. It is related in a more complicated way to the height of the burst above ground level. For any given distance from the center of the explosion, there is an optimum burst height that will produce the greatest overpressure, and the greater the distance the greater the optimum burst height. As a result, a burst on the surface produces the greatest overpressure at very close ranges (which is why surface bursts are used to attack very hard, very small targets such as missile silos), but less overpressure than an air burst at somewhat longer ranges. Raising the height of the burst reduces the overpressure directly under the bomb, but widens the area at which a given smaller overpressure is produced. Thus, an attack on factories with a 1-Mt weapon might use an air burst at an altitude of 8,000 feet [2,400 m], which would maximize the area (about 28 mi² [7,200 hectares]) that would receive 10 psi or more of overpressure.

Photo credit: U.S. Air Force

Fireball from an air burst in the megaton energy range

The faintly luminous shock front seen just ahead of the fireball soon after breakaway

Table 3 shows the ranges of overpressures and effects from such a blast.

When a nuclear weapon is detonated on or near the surface of the Earth, the blast digs out a large crater. Some of the material that used to be in the crater is deposited on the rim of the crater; the rest is carried up into the air and returns to Earth as fallout. An explosion that is farther above the Earth's surface than the radius of the fireball does not dig a crater and produces negligible immediate fallout.

For the most part, blast kills people by indirect means rather than by direct pressure. While a human body can withstand up to 30

Table 3.—Blast Effects of a 1-Mt Explosion 8,000 ft Above the Earth's Surface

Distance from ground zero		Peak overpressure	Peak wind velocity (mph)	Typical blast effects
(stat. miles)	(kilometers)			
.8	1.3	20 psi	470	Reinforced concrete structures are leveled.
3.0	4.8	10 psi	290	Most factories and commercial buildings are collapsed. Small wood-frame and brick residences destroyed and distributed as debris.
4.4	7.0	5 psi	160	Lightly constructed commercial buildings and typical residences are destroyed; heavier construction is severely damaged.
5.9	9.5	3 psi	95	Walls of typical steel-frame buildings are blown away; severe damage to residences. Winds sufficient to kill people in the open.
11.6	18.6	1 psi	35	Damage to structures; people endangered by flying glass and debris.

psi of simple overpressure, the winds associated with as little as 2 to 3 psi could be expected to blow people out of typical modern office buildings. Most blast deaths result from the collapse of occupied buildings, from people being blown into objects, or from buildings or smaller objects being blown onto or into people. Clearly, then, it is impossible to calculate with any precision how many people would be killed by a given blast—the effects would vary from building to building.

In order to estimate the number of casualties from any given explosion, it is necessary to make assumptions about the proportion of people who will be killed or injured at any given overpressure. The assumptions used in this chapter are shown in figure 1. They are relatively conservative. For example, weapons tests suggest that a typical residence will be collapsed by an overpressure of about 5 psi. People standing in such a residence have a 50-percent chance of being killed by an overpressure of 3.5 psi, but people who are lying down at the moment the blast wave hits have a 50-percent chance of surviving a 7-psi overpressure. The calculations used here assume a mean lethal overpressure of 5 to 6 psi for people in residences, meaning that more than half of those whose houses are blown down on top of them will nevertheless survive. Some studies use a simpler technique: they assume that the number of people who survive in areas receiving more than 5 psi equal the number of people killed in areas receiving less than 5 psi, and hence that fatalities are equal to the number of people inside a 5-psi ring.

Direct Nuclear Radiation

Nuclear weapons inflict ionizing radiation on people, animals, and plants in two different ways. Direct radiation occurs at the time of the explosion; it can be very intense, but its range is limited. Fallout radiation is received from particles that are made radioactive by the effects of the explosion, and subsequently distributed at varying distances from the site of the blast. Fallout is discussed in a subsequent section.

For large nuclear weapons, the range of intense direct radiation is less than the range of lethal blast and thermal radiation effects. However, in the case of smaller weapons, direct radiation may be the lethal effect with the greatest range. Direct radiation did substantial damage to the residents of Hiroshima and Nagasaki.

Human response to ionizing radiation is subject to great scientific uncertainty and intense controversy. It seems likely that even small doses of radiation do some harm. To understand the effects of nuclear weapons, one must distinguish between short- and long-term effects:

- **Short-Term Effects.—**A dose of 600 rem within a short period of time (6 to 7 days) has a 90-percent chance of creating a fatal illness, with death occurring within a few weeks. (A rem or "roentgen-equivalent-man" is a measure of biological damage: a "rad" is a measure of radiation energy absorbed; a roentgen is a measure of radiation energy; for our purposes it may be assumed that 100 roentgens produce 100 rads and 100 rem.) The precise shape of the curve showing the death rate as a function of radiation dose is not known in the region between 300 and 600 rem, but a dose of 450 rem within a short time is estimated to create a fatal illness in half the people exposed to it; the other half would

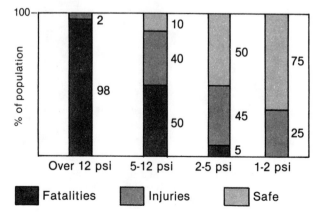

Figure 1.—Vulnerability of Population in Various Overpressure Zones

get very sick, but would recover. A dose of 300 rem might kill about 10 percent of those exposed. A dose of 200 to 450 rem will cause a severe illness from which most people would recover; however, this illness would render people highly susceptible to other diseases or infections. A dose of 50 to 200 rem will cause nausea and lower resistance to other diseases, but medical treatment is not required. A dose below 50 rem will not cause any short-term effects that the victim will notice, but will nevertheless do long-term damage.

• **Long-Term Effects.—**The effects of smaller doses of radiation are long term, and measured in a statistical way. A dose of 50 rem generally produces no short-term effects; however, if a large population were exposed to 50 rems, somewhere between 0.4 and 2.5 percent of them would be expected to contract fatal cancer (after some years) as a result. There would also be serious genetic effects for some fraction of those exposed. Lower doses produce lower effects. There is a scientific controversy about whether any dose of radiation, however small, is really safe. Chapter V discusses the extent of the long-term effects that a nuclear attack might produce. It should be clearly understood, however, that a large nuclear war would expose the survivors, however well sheltered, to levels of radiation far greater than the U.S. Government considers safe in peacetime.

Thermal Radiation

Approximately 35 percent of the energy from a nuclear explosion is an intense burst of thermal radiation, i.e., heat. The effects are roughly analogous to the effect of a 2-second flash from an enormous sunlamp. Since the thermal radiation travels at the speed of light (actually a bit slower, since it is deflected by particles in the atmosphere), the flash of light and heat precedes the blast wave by several seconds, just as lightning is seen before the thunder is heard.

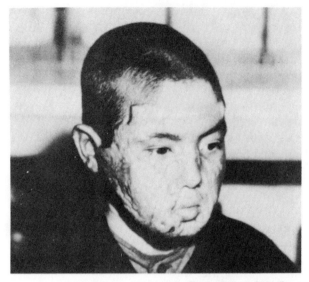

Photo credit: U.S. Air Force
Burn injuries from nuclear blasts

Photo credit: U.S. Department of Defense
The patient's skin is burned in a pattern corresponding to the dark portions of a kimono worn at the time of the explosion

The visible light will produce "flashblindness" in people who are looking in the direction of the explosion. Flashblindness can last for several minutes, after which recovery is total. A 1-Mt explosion could cause flashblindness at distances as great as 13 miles [21 km] on a clear day, or 53 miles [85 km] on a clear night. If the flash is focused through the lens of the eye, a permanent retinal burn will result. At Hiroshima and Nagasaki, there were many cases of flashblindness, but only one case of retinal burn, among the survivors. On the other hand, anyone flashblinded while driving a car could easily cause permanent injury to himself and to others.

Skin burns result from higher intensities of light, and therefore take place closer to the point of explosion. A 1-Mt explosion can cause first-degree burns (equivalent to a bad sunburn) at distances of about 7 miles [11 km], second-degree burns (producing blisters that lead to infection if untreated, and permanent scars) at distances of about 6 miles [10 km], and third-degree burns (which destroy skin tissue) at distances of up to 5 miles [8 km]. Third-degree burns over 24 percent of the body, or second-degree burns over 30 percent of the body, will result in serious shock, and will probably prove fatal unless prompt, specialized medical care is available. The entire United States has facilities to treat 1,000 or 2,000 severe burn cases; a single nuclear weapon could produce more than 10,000.

The distance at which burns are dangerous depends heavily on weather conditions. Extensive moisture or a high concentration of particles in the air (smog) absorbs thermal radiation. Thermal radiation behaves like sunlight, so objects create shadows behind which the thermal radiation is indirect (reflected) and less intense. Some conditions, such as ice on the ground or low white clouds over clean air, can increase the range of dangerous thermal radiation.

Fires

The thermal radiation from a nuclear explosion can directly ignite kindling materials. In general, ignitible materials outside the house, such as leaves or newspapers, are not surrounded by enough combustible material to generate a self-sustaining fire. Fires more likely to spread are those caused by thermal radiation passing through windows to ignite beds and overstuffed furniture inside houses. A rather substantial amount of combustible material must burn vigorously for 10 to 20 minutes before the room, or whole house, becomes inflamed. The blast wave, which arrives after most thermal energy has been expended, will have some extinguishing effect on the fires. However, studies and tests of this effect have been very contradictory, so the extent to which blast can be counted on to extinguish fire starts remains quite uncertain.

Another possible source of fires, which might be more damaging in urban areas, is indirect. Blast damage to stores, water heaters, furnaces, electrical circuits, or gas lines would ignite fires where fuel is plentiful.

The best estimates are that at the 5-psi level about 10 percent of all buildings would sustain a serious fire, while at 2 psi about 2 percent would have serious fires, usually arising from secondary sources such as blast-damaged utilities rather than direct thermal radiation.

It is possible that individual fires, whether caused by thermal radiation or by blast damage to utilities, furnaces, etc., would coalesce into a mass fire that would consume all structures over a large area. This possibility has been intensely studied, but there remains no basis for estimating its probability. Mass fires could be of two kinds: a "firestorm," in which violent inrushing winds create extremely high temperatures but prevent the fire from spreading radially outwards, and a "conflagration," in which a fire spreads along a front. Hamburg, Tokyo, and Hiroshima experienced firestorms in World War II; the Great Chicago Fire and the San Francisco Earthquake Fire were conflagrations. A firestorm is likely to kill a high proportion of the people in the area of the fire, through heat and through asphyxiation of those in shelters. A conflagration spreads slowly enough so that people in its path can escape, though a conflagration caused by a nuclear attack might take a heavy toll of those too injured to walk. Some believe that firestorms in U.S. or Soviet cities are unlikely because the density of flammable materials ("fuel loading") is too low—the ignition of a firestorm is thought to require a fuel loading of at least 8 lbs/ft² (Hamburg had 32), compared to fuel loading of 2 lbs/ft² in a typical U.S. suburb and 5 lbs/ft² in a neighborhood of two-story brick rowhouses. The likelihood of a conflagration depends on the geography of the area, the speed and direction of the wind, and details of building construction. Another variable is whether people and equipment are available to fight fires before they can coalesce and spread.

Electromagnetic Pulse

Electromagnetic pulse (EMP) is an electromagnetic wave similar to radio waves, which results from secondary reactions occurring when the nuclear gamma radiation is absorbed in the air or ground. It differs from the usual radio waves in two important ways. First, it creates much higher electric field strengths. Whereas a radio signal might produce a thousandth of a volt or less in a receiving antenna, an EMP pulse might produce thousands of volts. Secondly, it is a single pulse of energy that disappears completely in a small fraction of a second. In this sense, it is rather similar to the electrical signal from lightning, but the rise in voltage is typically a hundred times faster. This means that most equipment designed to protect electrical facilities from lightning works too slowly to be effective against EMP.

The strength of an EMP pulse is measured in volts per meter (v/m), and is an indication of the voltage that would be produced in an exposed antenna. A nuclear weapon burst on the surface will typically produce an EMP of tens of thousands of v/m at short distances (the 10-psi range) and thousands of v/m at longer distances (1-psi range). Air bursts produce less EMP, but high-altitude bursts (above 19 miles [21 km]) produce very strong EMP, with ranges of hundreds or thousands of miles. An attacker might detonate a few weapons at such altitudes in an effort to destroy or damage the communications and electric power systems of the victim.

There is no evidence that EMP is a physical threat to humans. However, electrical or electronic systems, particularly those connected to long wires such as powerlines or antennas, can undergo either of two kinds of damage. First, there can be actual physical damage to an electrical component such as shorting of a capacitor or burnout of a transistor, which would require replacement or repair before the equipment can again be used. Second, at a lesser level, there can be a temporary operational upset, frequently requiring some effort to restore operation. For example, instabilities induced in power grids can cause the entire system to shut itself down, upsetting computers that must be started again. Base radio stations are vulnerable not only from the loss of commercial power but from direct damage to electronic components connected to the antenna. In general, portable radio transmitter/receivers with relatively short antennas are not susceptible to EMP. The vulnerability of the telephone system to EMP could not be determined.

Fallout

While any nuclear explosion in the atmosphere produces some fallout, the fallout is far greater if the burst is on the surface, or at least low enough for the fireball to touch the ground. As chapter V shows in some detail, the fallout from air bursts alone poses long-term health hazards, but they are trivial compared to the other consequences of a nuclear attack. The significant hazards come from particles scooped up from the ground and irradiated by the nuclear explosion.

The radioactive particles that rise only a short distance (those in the "stem" of the familiar mushroom cloud) will fall back to earth within a matter of minutes, landing close to the center of the explosion. Such particles are unlikely to cause many deaths, because they will fall in areas where most people have already been killed. However, the radioactivity will complicate efforts at rescue or eventual reconstruction.

The radioactive particles that rise higher will be carried some distance by the wind before returning to Earth, and hence the area and intensity of the fallout is strongly influenced by local weather conditions. Much of the material is simply blown downwind in a long plume. The map shown in figure 2 illustrates the plume expected from a 1-Mt surface burst in Detroit if winds were blowing toward Canada. The illustrated plume assumed that the winds were blowing at a uniform speed of 15 mph [24 km] over the entire region. The plume would be longer and thinner if the winds were more intense and shorter and somewhat more broad if the winds were slower. If the winds were from a different direction, the plume would cover a different area. For example, a wind from the northwest would deposit enough fallout on Cleveland to inflict acute radiation sickness on those who did not evacuate or use effective fallout shelters (figure 3). Thus wind direction can make an enormous difference. Rainfall can also have a significant influence on the ways in which radiation from smaller weapons is deposited, since rain will carry contaminated particles to the ground. The areas receiving such contaminated rainfall would become "hot spots," with greater radiation intensity than their surroundings. When the radiation intensity from fallout is great enough to pose an immediate threat to health, fallout will generally be visible as a thin layer of dust.

The amount of radiation produced by fallout materials will decrease with time as the radioactive materials "decay." Each material decays at a different rate. Materials that decay rapidly give off intense radiation for a short period of time while long-lived materials radiate less intensely but for longer periods. Immediately after the fallout is deposited in regions surrounding the blast site, radiation intensities will be very high as the short-lived

materials decay. These intense radiations will decrease relatively quickly. The intensity will have fallen by a factor of 10 after 7 hours, a factor of 100 after 49 hours and a factor of 1,000 after 2 weeks. The areas in the plume illustrated in figures 2 and 3 would become "safe" (by peacetime standards) in 2 to 3 years for the outer ellipse, and in 10 years or so for the inner ellipse.

Some radioactive particles will be thrust into the stratosphere, and may not return to Earth for some years. In this case only the particularly long-lived particles pose a threat, and they are dispersed around the world over a range of latitudes. Some fallout from U.S. and Soviet weapons tests in the 1950's and early 1960's can still be detected. There are also some particles in the immediate fallout (notably Strontium 90 and Cesium 137) that remain radioactive for years. Chapter V discusses the likely hazards from these long-lived particles.

The biological effects of fallout radiation are substantially the same as those from direct radiation, discussed above. People exposed to enough fallout radiation will die, and those exposed to lesser amounts may become ill. Chapter III discusses the theory of fallout sheltering, and chapter IV some of the practical difficulties of escaping fallout from a large counterforce attack.

There is some public interest in the question of the consequences if a nuclear weapon destroyed a nuclear powerplant. The core of a power reactor contains large quantities of radioactive material, which tends to decay more slowly (and hence less intensely) than the fallout particles from a nuclear weapon explosion. Consequently, fallout from a destroyed nuclear reactor (whose destruction would, incidently, require a high-accuracy surface burst) would not be much more intense (during the first day) or widespread than "ordinary" fallout, but would stay radioactive for a considerably longer time. Areas receiving such fallout would have to be evacuated or decontaminated; otherwise survivors would have to stay in shelters for months.

Figure 2.—Main Fallout Pattern—Uniform 15 mph Southwest Wind (1-Mt Surface Burst in Detroit). (Contours for 7-Day Accumulated Dose (Without Shielding) of 3,000, 900, 300, and 90 Rem.)

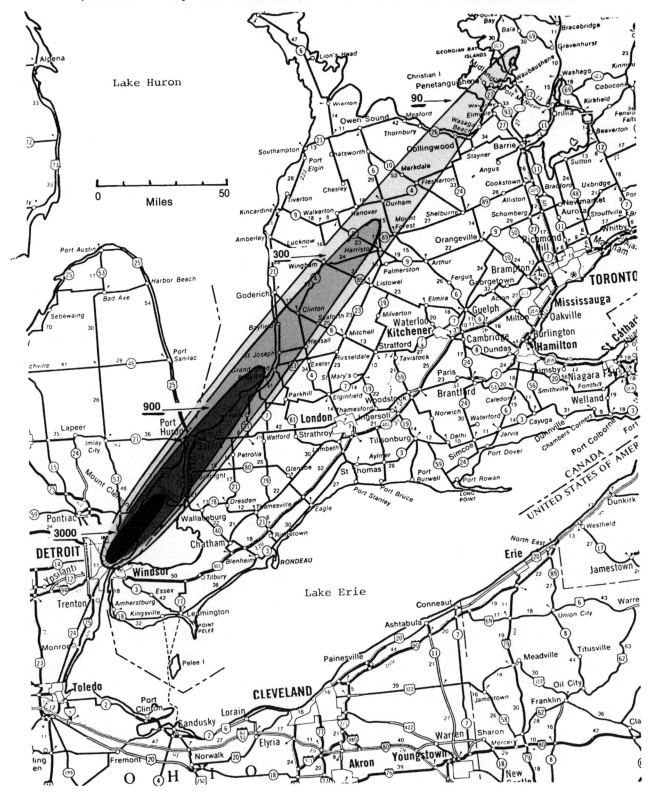

Figure 3.—Main Fallout Pattern—Uniform 15 mph Northwest Wind (1-Mt Surface Burst in Detroit).
(Contours for 7-Day Accumulated Dose (Without Shielding) of 3,000, 900, 300, and 90 Rem.)

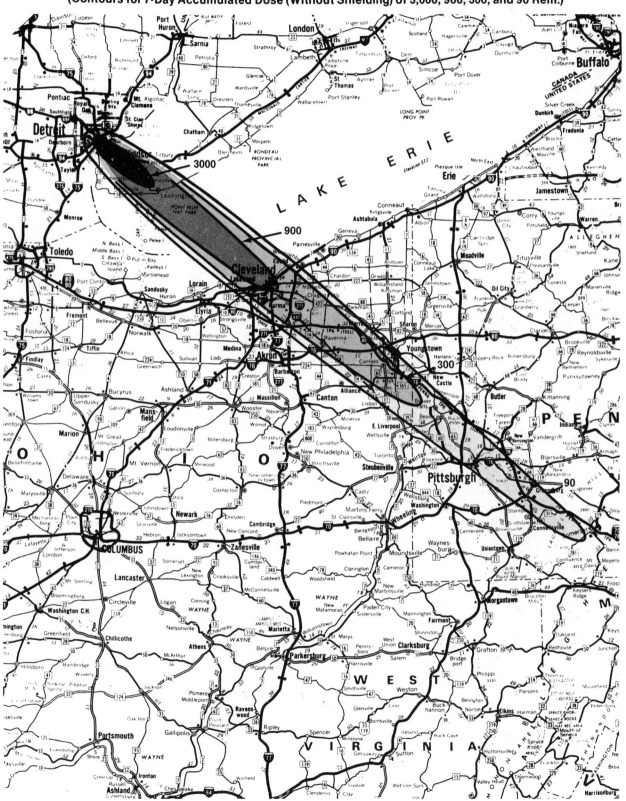

Combined Injuries (Synergism)

So far the discussion of each major effect (blast, nuclear radiation, and thermal radiation) has explained how this effect in isolation causes deaths and injuries to humans. It is customary to calculate the casualties accompanying hypothetical nuclear explosion as follows: for any given range, the effect most likely to kill people is selected and its consequences calculated, while the other effects are ignored. It is obvious that combined injuries are possible, but there are no generally accepted ways of calculating their probability. What data do exist seem to suggest that calculations of single effects are not too inaccurate for immediate deaths, but that deaths occurring some time after the explosion may well be due to combined causes, and hence are omitted from most calculations. Some of the obvious possibilities are:

- **Nuclear Radiation Combined With Thermal Radiation.**—Severe burns place considerable stress on the blood system, and often cause anemia. It is clear from experiments with laboratory animals that exposure of a burn victim to more than 100 rems of radiation will impair the blood's ability to support recovery from the thermal burns. Hence a sublethal radiation dose could make it impossible to recover from a burn that, without the radiation, would not cause death.

- **Nuclear Radiation Combined With Mechanical Injuries.**—Mechanical injuries, the indirect results of blast, take many forms. Flying glass and wood will cause puncture wounds. Winds may blow people into obstructions, causing broken bones, concussions, and internal injuries. Persons caught in a collapsing building can suffer many similar mechanical injuries. There is evidence that all of these types of injuries are more serious if the person has been ex-

posed to 300 rems, particularly if treatment is delayed. Blood damage will clearly make a victim more susceptible to blood loss and infection. This has been confirmed in laboratory animals in which a borderline lethal radiation dose was followed a week later by a blast overpressure that alone would have produced a low level of prompt lethality. The number of prompt and delayed (from radiation) deaths both increased over what would be expected from the single effect alone.

- **Thermal Radiation and Mechanical Injuries.**—There is no information available about the effects of this combination, beyond the common sense observation that since each can place a great stress on a healthy body, the combination of injuries that are individually tolerable may subject the body to a total stress that it cannot tolerate. Mechanical injuries should be prevalent at about the distance from a nuclear explosion that produces sublethal burns, so this synergism could be an important one.

In general, synergistic effects are most likely to produce death when each of the injuries alone is quite severe. Because the uncertainties of nuclear effects are compounded when one tries to estimate the likelihood of two or more serious but (individually) nonfatal injuries, there really is no way to estimate the number of victims.

A further dimension of the problem is the possible synergy between injuries and environmental damage. To take one obvious example, poor sanitation (due to the loss of electrical power and water pressure) can clearly compound the effects of any kind of serious injury. Another possibility is that an injury would so immobilize the victim that he would be unable to escape from a fire.

DETROIT AND LENINGRAD

Detroit and Leningrad are representative industrial cities large enough to warrant the use of very large weapons. Both have metropolitan populations of about 4.3 million, and both are major transportation and industrial centers.

In assessing and describing the damage, several assumptions were made that may not be realistic, but which assisted in making a clear presentation of the range of possible effects:

- There is no warning. The populations have not evacuated or sought shelter, both of which measures could reduce casualties.

- The detonations take place at night when most people are at their residences. This corresponds to the available census data about where people are, and indeed people are near their residences more than half the time.

- There is clear weather, with visibility of 10 miles [16 km].

- The air bursts are at an altitude that maximizes the area of 30 psi or more overpressure. A higher height of burst would have increased the range of 5-psi overpressure (i.e. destruction of all residences) by up to 10 percent, at the cost of less damage to very hard structures near the center of the explosion.

- No other cities are attacked, an assumption that allows for analyzing the extent of outside help that would be required, if it were available.

1 Mt on the Surface in Detroit

Physical Damage

Figure 4 shows the metropolitan area of Detroit, with Windsor, Canada, across the river to the southeast and Lake St. Clair directly east. The detonation point selected is the intersection of I-75 and I-94, approximately at the civic center and about 3 miles [5 km] from the Detroit-Windsor tunnel entrance. Circles are drawn at the 12-, 5-, 2-, and 1-psi limits.

The 1-Mt explosion on the surface leaves a crater about 1,000 feet [300 m] in diameter and 200 feet [61 m] deep, surrounded by a rim of highly radioactive soil about twice this diameter thrown out of the crater. Out to a distance of 0.6 miles [1 km] from the center there will be nothing recognizable remaining, with the exception of some massive concrete bridge abutments and building foundations. At 0.6 miles some heavily damaged highway bridge sections will remain, but little else until 1.3 miles [2.1 km], where a few very strongly constructed buildings with poured reinforced concrete walls will survive, but with the interiors totally destroyed by blast entering the window openings. A distance of 1.7 miles [2.7 km] (12-psi ring) is the closest range where any significant structure will remain standing.

Of the 70,000 people in this area during nonworking hours, there will be virtually no survivors. (See table 4.) Fatalities during working hours in this business district would undoubtedly be much higher. The estimated daytime population of the "downtown" area is something over 200,000 in contrast to the census data of about 15,000. If the attack occurred during this time, the fatalities would be increased by 130,000 and injuries by 45,000 over the estimates in table 4. Obviously there would be some reduction in casualties in outlying residential areas where the daytime population would be lower.

In the band between the 1.7- and the 2.7-mile (5 psi) circles, typical commercial and residential multistory buildings will have the walls completely blown out, but increasingly at the greater distances the skeletal structure will remain standing.

Individual residences in this region will be totally destroyed, with only foundations and basements remaining, and the debris quite uniformly distributed over the area. Heavy industrial plants will be destroyed in the inner part of the ring, but some industry will remain functional towards the outer edge. The debris depth that will clutter the streets will naturally

Photo credit: Detroit News by Steve Thorpe, 1979

Skyline of Detroit, Mich.

Figure 4.—Detroit 1-Mt Surface Burst

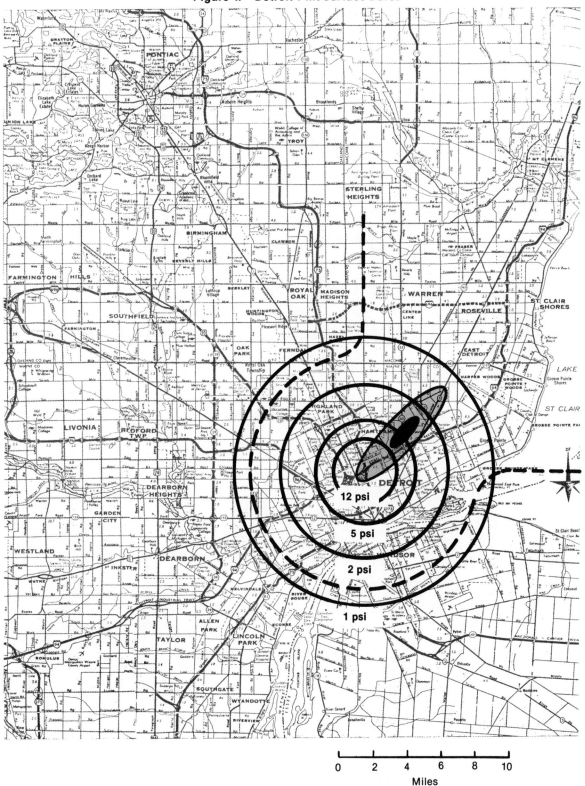

12 psi

5 psi

2 psi

1 psi

0   2   4   6   8   10
Miles

Photo credit: Nuclear Defense Agency

Damage to unreinforced brick house (5-psi overpressure)

Table 4.—Casualty Estimates
(in thousands)

Region (mi)	Area (mi²)	Population	Fatalities	Injuries	Uninjured
0-1.7	9.1	70	70	0	0
1.7-2.7	13.8	250	130	100	20
2.7-4.7	46.5	400	20	180	200
4.7-7.4	102.6	600	0	150	450

depend on both the building heights and how close together they are spaced. Typical depths might range from tens of feet in the downtown area where buildings are 10 to 20 stories high, down to several inches where buildings are lower and streets broader in the sector to the west and north. In this band, blast damage alone will destroy all automobiles, while some heavier commercial vehicles (firetrucks and repair vehicles) will survive near the outer edges. However, few vehicles will have been sufficiently protected from debris to remain useful. The parking lots of both Cobb Field and Tiger Stadium will contain nothing driveable.

In this same ring, which contains a nighttime population of about 250,000, about half will be fatalities, with most of the remainder being injured. Most deaths will occur from collapsing buildings. Although many fires will be started, only a small percentage of the buildings are likely to continue to burn after the blast wave passes. The mechanics of fire spread in a heavily damaged and debris strewn area are not well understood. However, it is probable that fire spread would be slow and there would be no firestorm. For unprotected people, the initial nuclear radiation would be lethal out to 1.7 miles [2.7 km], but be insignificant in its prompt effects (50 rems) at 2.0 miles [3.2 km]. Since few people inside a 2-mile ring will survive the blast, and they are very likely to be in strong buildings that typically have a 2- to 5-protection factor, the additional fatalities and injuries from initial radiation should be small compared to other uncertainties.

The number of casualties from thermal burns depends on the time of day, season, and atmospheric visibility. Modest variations in these factors produce huge changes in vulnerability to burns. For example, on a winter night

less than 1 percent of the population might be exposed to direct thermal radiation, while on a clear summer weekend afternoon more than 25 percent might be exposed (that is, have no structure between the fireball and the person). When visibility is 10 miles [16 km], a 1-Mt explosion produces second-degree burns at a distance of 6 miles [10 km], while under circumstances when visibility is 2 miles [3 km], the range of second-degree burns is only 2.7 miles [4.3 km]. Table 5 shows how this variation could cause deaths from thermal radiation to vary between 1,000 and 190,000, and injuries to vary between 500 and 75,000.

In the band from 2.7 to 4.7 miles [4.4 to 7.6 km] (2 psi), large buildings will have lost windows and frames, interior partitions, and, for those with light-walled construction, most of the contents of upper floors will have been blown out into the streets. Load-bearing wall buildings at the University of Detroit will be severely cracked. Low residential buildings will be totally destroyed or severely damaged. Casualties are estimated to be about 50 percent in this region, with the majority of these injured. There will still be substantial debris in the streets, but a very significant number of cars and trucks will remain operable. In this zone, damage to heavy industrial plants, such as the Cadillac plant, will be severe, and most planes and hangars at the Detroit City Airport will be destroyed.

In this ring only 5 percent of the population of about 400,000 will be killed, but nearly half will be injured (table 4). This is the region of the most severe fire hazard, since fire ignition and spread is more likely in partly damaged buildings than in completely flattened areas. Perhaps 5 percent of the buildings would be initially ignited, with fire spread to adjoining buildings highly likely if their separation is less than 50 feet [15 m]. Fires will continue to spread for 24 hours at least, ultimately destroying about half the buildings. However, these estimates are extremely uncertain, as they are based on poor data and unknown weather conditions. They are also made on the assumption that no effective effort is made by the uninjured half of the population in this region to prevent the ignition or spread of fires.

As table 5 shows, there would be between 4,000 and 95,000 additional deaths from thermal radiation in this band, assuming a visibility of 10 miles [16 km]. A 2-mile [3 km] visibility would produce instead between 1,000 and 11,000 severe injuries, and many of these would subsequently die because adequate medical treatment would not be available.

In the outermost band (4.7 to 7.4 miles [7.6 to 11.9 km]) there will be only light damage to commercial structures and moderate damage to residences. Casualties are estimated at 25 percent injured and only an insignificant number killed (table 4). Under the range of conditions displayed in table 5, there will be an additional 3,000 to 75,000 burn injuries requiring specialized medical care. Fire ignitions should be comparatively rare (limited to such kindling material as newspaper and dry leaves) and easily controlled by the survivors.

Whether fallout comes from the stem or the cap of the mushroom is a major concern in the general vicinity of the detonation because of the time element and its effect on general emergency operations. Fallout from the stem starts building after about 10 minutes, so during the first hour after detonation it represents the prime radiation threat to emergency crews. The affected area would have a radius of about 6.5 miles [10.5 km] (as indicated by the dashed circle on figure 4) with a hot-spot a distance downwind that depends on the wind velocity. If a 15-mph wind from the southwest is assumed, an area of about 1 mi² [260 hectares]—the solid ellipse shown—would cause an average exposure of 300 rems in the first hour to people with no fallout protection at all. The larger toned ellipse shows the area of 150 rems in the first hour. But the important feature of short-term (up to 1 hour) fallout is the relatively small area covered by life-threatening radiation levels compared to the area covered by blast damage.

Starting in about an hour, the main fallout from the cloud itself will start to arrive, with some of it adding to the already-deposited local stem fallout, but the bulk being distributed in an elongated downwind ellipse. Figures 2 and 3 show two fallout patterns, differing only in the direction of the wind. The

Table 5.—Burn Casualty Estimates
(1 Mt on Detroit)

Distance from blast (mi)	Survivors of blast effects	Fatalities (eventual)		Injuries	
		2-mile visibility	10-mile visibility	2-mile visibility	10-mile visibility
(1 percent of population exposed to line of sight from fireball)					
0-1.7	0	0	0	0	0
1.7-2.7	120,000	1,200	1,200	0	0
2.7-4.7	380,000	0	3,800	500	0
4.7-7.4	600,000	0	2,600	0	3,000
Total (rounded) . .		1,000	8,000	500	3,000
(25 percent of population exposed to line of sight from fireball)					
0-1.7	0	0	0	0	0
1.7-2.7	120,000	30,000	30,000	0	0
2.7-4.7	380,000	0	95,000	11,000	0
4.7-7.4	600,000	0	66,000	0	75,000
Total (rounded) . .		30,000	190,000	11,000	75,000

These calculations arbitrarily assume that exposure to more than 6.7 cal/cm² produces eventual death, and exposure to more than 3.4 cal/cm² produces a significant injury, requiring specialized medical treatment.

contours marked are the number of rems received in the week following the arrival of the cloud fallout, again assuming no fallout protection whatever. Realistic patterns, which will reflect wind shear, a wider crosswind distribution, and other atmospheric variabilities, will be much more complex than this illustration.

Infrastructure Status

As a complement to the preceding description of physical destruction, the status of the various infrastructure elements of the Detroit metropolitan area, and the potential for their recovery, can be addressed. The reader should understand that this tutorial considers Detroit to be the only damaged area in the United States, that there is no other threat that would prevent survivors and those in surrounding areas from giving all possible aid, and that Federal and State governments will actively organize outside assistance.

The near half-million injured present a medical task of incredible magnitude. Those parts of Wayne, Macomb, and Oakland counties shown on the map have 63 hospitals containing about 18,000 beds. However, 55 percent of these beds are inside the 5-psi ring and thus totally destroyed. Another 15 percent in the 2- to 5-psi band will be severely damaged, leaving 5,000 beds remaining outside the region of significant damage. Since this is only 1 percent of the number of injured, these beds are incapable of providing significant medical assistance. In the first few days, transport of injured out of the damaged area will be severely hampered by debris clogging the streets. In general, only the nonprofessional assistance of nearby survivors can hope to hold down the large number of subsequent deaths that would otherwise occur. Even as transportation for the injured out of the area becomes available in subsequent days, the total medical facilities of the United States will be severely overburdened, since in 1977 there were only 1,407,000 hospital beds in the whole United States. Burn victims will number in the tens of thousands; yet in 1977 there were only 85 specialized burn

centers, with probably 1,000 to 2,000 beds, in the entire United States.

The total loss of all utilities in areas where there has been significant physical damage to the basic structure of buildings is inevitable. The electric power grid will show both the inherent strength and weakness of its complex network. The collapse of buildings and the toppling of trees and utility poles, along with the injection of tens of thousands of volts of EMP into wires, will cause the immediate loss of power in a major sector of the total U.S. power grid. Main electrical powerplants (near Grosse Point Park to the east, and Zug Island to the south) are both in the 1-psi ring and should suffer only superficial damage. Within a day the major area grid should be restored, bringing power back to facilities located as close to the blast as the 1-psi ring. Large numbers of power-line workers and their equipment brought in from the surrounding States will be able to gradually restore service to surviving structures in the 1- to 2-psi ring over a period of days.

The water distribution system will remain mostly intact since, with the exception of one booster pumping station at 2 psi (which will suffer only minor damage), its facilities are outside the damaged area. However, the loss of electric power to the pumps and the breaking of many service connections to destroyed buildings will immediately cause the loss of all water pressure. Service to the whole area will be restored only when the regional power grid is restored, and to the areas of light and intermediate damage only as valves to broken pipes can be located and shut off over a period of days. There will be only sporadic damage to buried mains in the 2- to 5-psi region, but with increasing frequency in the 5- to 12-psi region. Damaged sections near the explosion center will have to be closed off.

The gas distribution system will receive similar damage: loss of pressure from numerous broken service connections, some broken mains, particularly in the 5- to 12-psi ring, and numerous resulting fires. Service will be slowly restored only as utility repairmen and service equipment are brought in from surrounding areas.

Rescue and recovery operations will depend heavily on the reestablishment of transportation, which in Detroit relies on private cars, buses, and commercial trucks, using a radial interstate system and a conventional urban grid. Since bridges and overpasses are surprisingly immune to blast effects, those interstate highways and broad urban streets without significant structures nearby will survive as far in as the 12-psi ring and can be quickly restored to use on clearing away minor amounts of debris. However, the majority of urban streets will be cluttered with varying quantities of debris, starting with tree limbs and other minor obstacles at 1 psi, and increasing in density up to the 12-psi ring, where all buildings, trees, and cars will be smashed and quite uniformly redistributed over the area. It could take weeks or months to remove the debris and restore road transportation in the area.

The Detroit city airport, located in the middle of the 2- to 5-psi ring, will have essentially all of its aircraft and facilities destroyed. Usually runways can be quickly restored to use following minor debris removal but, in this particular example with the southwest wind, the airport is the center of the fallout hot spot from the dust column as well as of the intensive fallout from the cloud. Thus, cleanup efforts to restore flight operations could not commence for 2 weeks at the earliest, with the workers involved in the cleanup receiving 100 rems accumulated during the third week. The Detroit Metropolitan Wayne County Airport and the Willow Run Airport are far outside the blast effects area and would be available as soon as the regional power grid electric service was restored.

The main train station, near the Detroit-Windsor highway tunnel, would have suffered major damage (5 psi), but since few people commute to the downtown area by train, its loss would not be a major factor in the overall paralysis of transportation. The surrounding industry depends heavily on rail transportation, but rail equipment and lines will usually survive wherever the facilities they support survive.

Most gasoline fuel oil tanks are located out beyond Dearborn and Lincoln Park and, at 16 miles from the detonation, will have suffered no damage. Arrival of fuel should not be impeded, but its distribution will be totally dependent on cleanup of streets and highways.

The civil defense control center, located just beyond the Highland Park area in the 1- to 2-psi ring, should be able to function without impairment. Commercial communications systems (television and base radio transmitters) will be inoperable both from the loss of commercial power in the area and, for those facilities in the blast area, from EMP. Those not blast damaged should be restored in several days. In the meantime, mobile radio systems will provide the primary means of communicating into the heavily damaged areas. The telephone system will probably remain largely functional in those areas where the lines have survived structural damage in collapsing buildings, or street damage in areas where they are not buried.

Radioactive Fallout

The extent and location of radioactive fallout will depend on weather conditions, especially the speed and direction of the wind. Figures 2 and 3 show how a uniform wind velocity of 15 mph could distribute fallout either over sparsely populated farming areas in Canada if the wind is from the southwest, or over Cleveland and Youngstown, Ohio, and Pittsburgh, Pa., if the wind is from the northwest. It should not be forgotten that these fallout patterns are idealized—such neat elipses would occur in reality only with an absolutely constant wind and no rain.

No effort was made to calculate the deaths, injuries, or economic losses that might result from such fallout patterns. However, the possibilities are instructive:

• The onset of fallout would depend on wind velocity and distance from the explosion and it would be most dangerous during the first few days. In the case of an attack on a single city (using a surface burst, as our example does), people living downwind would probably evacuate. Those who neither evacuated nor found adequate fallout shelters would be subjected to dangerous levels of radiation: people in the inner contour would receive a fatal dose within the first week; people in the next contour out would contract very severe radiation sickness if they stayed indoors and would probably receive a fatal dose if they spent much time outdoors; people in the next contour out would contract generally nonfatal radiation sickness, with increased hazards of deaths from other diseases. People in the outer contour (90 roentgens in the first week) would suffer few visible effects, but their life expectancy would drop as a result of an increased risk of eventual cancer.

- As time passes, the continuing decay of fallout radiation could be accelerated by decontamination. Some decontamination takes place naturally, as rain washes radioactive particles away, and as they are leached into the soil which attenuates the radiation. It is also possible to take specific measures to speed decontamination. Presumably evacuees would not move back into a contaminated area until the effects of time and decontamination had made it safe.

- A limiting case is one in which no significant decontamination takes place, and areas receiving fallout become safe only when the radioactive particles have decayed to safe levels. Decay to a level of 500 millirems per year would require 8 to 10 years for the inner contour (3,000 roentgens in the first week); 6 years or so for the next contour (900 roentgens in the first week); 3 to 4 years for the next contour (300 roentgens in the first week); and about 3 years for the outer contour (90 roentgens in the first week).

- Natural processes could concentrate some radioactive particles, and those that entered the food chain could pose an additional hazard.

Summary

It should be emphasized that there are many uncertainties in the assumptions underlying the description of the results of a 1-Mt surface burst in Detroit. Nevertheless, several salient features stand out:

- seventy square miles of property destruction (2 psi),
- a quarter-of-a-million fatalities, plus half a million injuries,
- additional damage from widespread fires,
- casualties could have been greatly reduced by an alert and informed population, and
- rescue and recovery operations must be organized and heavily supported from outside the area (food, medical, utility restoration, and cleanup).

1-Mt Air Burst on Detroit

For comparison, the same 1-Mt nuclear weapon was assumed to have been air burst at an altitude of 6,000 feet [1.8 km] over the same interstate intersection as used in the preceding ground burst discussion. This altitude will maximize the size of the 30-psi circle, but the radius of the 5-psi circle that results will be only 10 percent smaller than what would have resulted from a height of burst raised to the 5-psi optimized value. There will be several significant differences in this case.

- The sizes of the rings of pressure damage will be larger.
- The range of thermal burns and fire starts will also increase.
- There will be no significant fallout.
- There will be no crater.
- The strongest structures may partly survive even directly under the blast.

Figure 5 shows the corresponding pressure circles and figure 6 (second column) illustrates that the number of fatalities nearly doubled, and the number of injured have greatly increased. At the same time, damage to major in-

Figure 5.—Detroit 1-Mt Air Burst

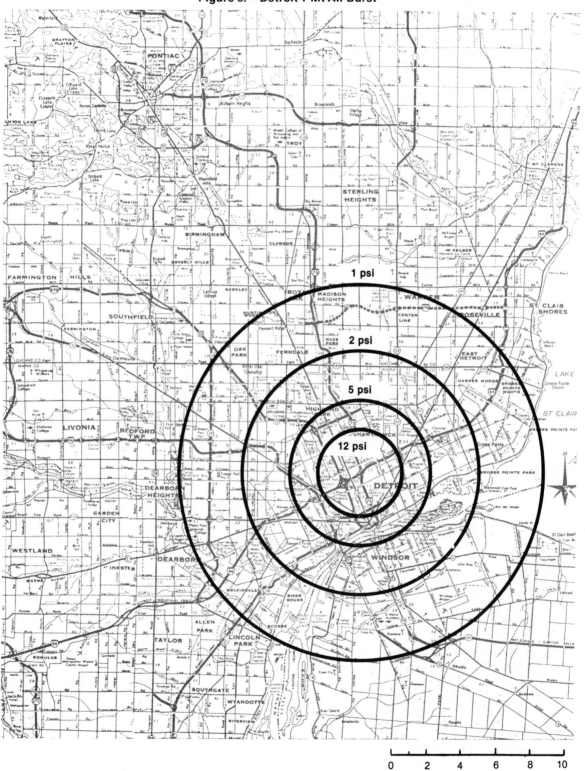

Figure 6.—Casualties (thousands)

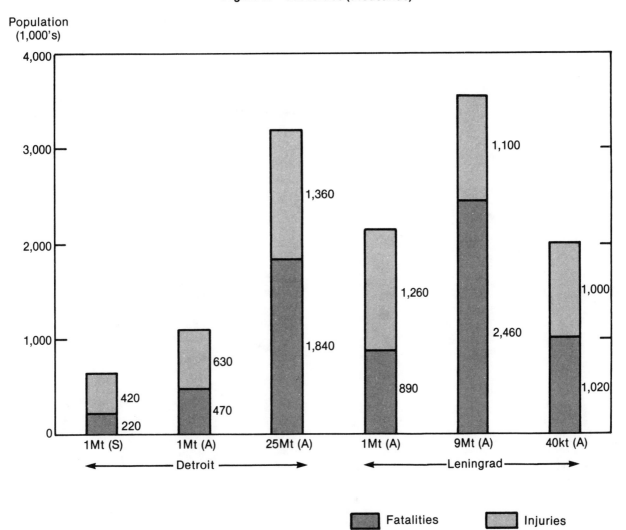

dustrial facilities is becoming significant, with the Chrysler plant in the middle of the 2- to 5-psi band, and the Ford River Rouge plant in the 1- to 2-psi band.

25-Mt Air Burst on Detroit

For 25 Mt, we assumed a burst altitude of 17,500 feet [5.3 km], over the same detonation point. Figure 7 shows the 12-, 5-, and 2-psi rings, but the 1-psi ring at 30.4 miles [48.9 km] is completely off the map. It is obvious that damage and casualties would be increased even further had the detonation point been moved about 5 miles [8 km] to the northwest. But even without this shift, it is clear that the whole metropolitan area has been heavily damaged by the explosive power of this huge weapon. The casualties are again shown on figure 6 (column 3). The contrasts to the 1-Mt surface burst are stark:

- There will be very few survivors (1.1 million available to assist the much more numerous casualties—3.2 million). This is in contrast to the 1-Mt surface burst in which 3.7 million survivors were potentially available to assist the 640,000 casualties.

Figure 7.—Detroit 25-Mt Air Burst

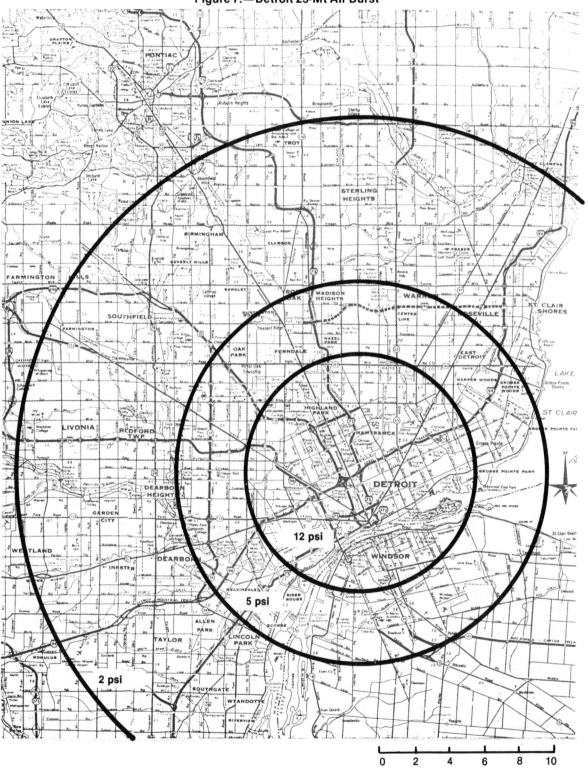

12 psi

5 psi

2 psi

0   2   4   6   8   10

Miles

- There will be virtually no habitable housing in the area.
- Essentially all heavy industry will be totally destroyed.

As a result, rescue operations will have to be totally supported from outside the area, with evacuation of the 1.2 million survivors the only feasible course. Recovery and rebuilding will be a very long-term, problematical issue.

Leningrad

Leningrad is a major industrial and transportation center built on the low-lying delta where the Neva River enters the Gulf of Finland. The older part of the city is built on the delta itself, with the newer residential sections leapfrogging industrial sections, primarily to the south and southwest (figure 8). The residential and commercial (but not industrial) areas are shown on the map.

The major difference between housing in Leningrad and that in Detroit is that Leningrad suburbs contain very few single-family residences. In the older part of Leningrad, the buildings have masonry load-bearing walls and wooden interior construction and are typically six to eight stories, reflecting the early code that only church spires could be higher than the Tsar's Winter Palace. The post-World War II housing construction is 10- to 12-story apartments having steel frames and precast concrete walls, with the buildings comfortably spaced on wide thoroughfares in open parklike settings.

Since actual population density data for Leningrad was unavailable, simplifying demographic assumptions are used. The assumed populated areas are shown in figure 9, broken down into 1-km [0.6 mile] squares. The stated area of Leningrad is 500 km² [193 mi²]. Since the shaded squares cover 427 km² [165 mi²], it is assumed that the remaining areas are relatively uninhabited at night. It has also been assumed that in these inhabited areas the population density is uniform at 10,000 per km², because although the building density is lower in the newer apartment areas, the build-

ings themselves are generally higher. Thus, the population density does not drop off as it does in the U.S. suburbs of predominately single-family houses.

1-Mt and 9-Mt Air Bursts on Leningrad

The Leningrad apartments described are likely to have their walls blown out, and the people swept out, at about 5 psi, even though the remaining steel skeleton will withstand much higher pressures. Thus, although the type of construction is totally different from Detroit, the damage levels are so similar that the same relationship between overpressure and casualties is assumed (figure 1, p. 19).

The 1-Mt and 9-Mt air burst pressure rings are shown in figures 10 and 11. Note that for the 9-Mt case the 1-psi ring falls completely off the map, as was the case for 25 Mt on Detroit. The calculated casualties are illustrated on figure 6 (columns 4 and 5), and are about double those for Detroit for the comparable 1-Mt case. This results directly from the higher average population density. Other contrasts between the cities can be noted; in Leningrad:

- People live close to where they work. In general, there is no daily cross-city movement.
- Buildings (except in the old part of the city) are unlikely to burn.
- Apartment building spacing is so great as to make fire spread unlikely, even though a few buildings would burn down.
- There will be much less debris preventing access to damaged areas.
- Transportation is by rail to the outlying areas, and by an excellent metro system within the city.
- There is only one television station—in the middle of the city—so mass communications would be interrupted until other broadcasting equipment was brought in and set up.

Ten 40-kt Air Bursts on Leningrad

Figure 12 shows one possible selection of burst points, set to have the 5-psi circles

Figure 8.—Leningrad—Commercial and Residential Sections

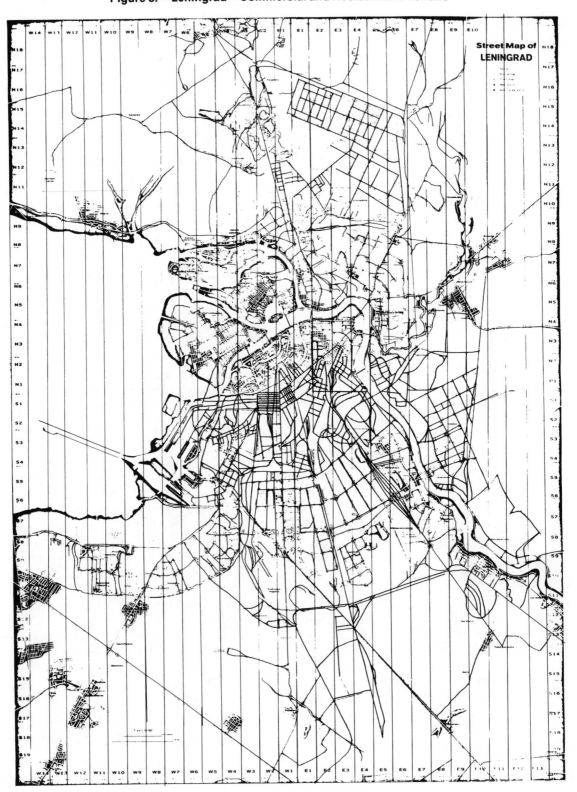

Figure 9.—Leningrad—Populated Area

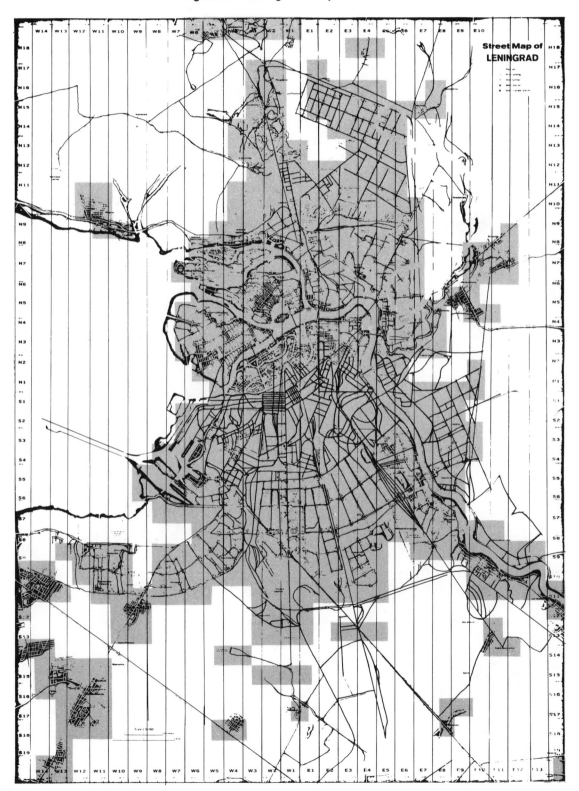

Figure 10.—Leningrad 1-Mt Air Burst

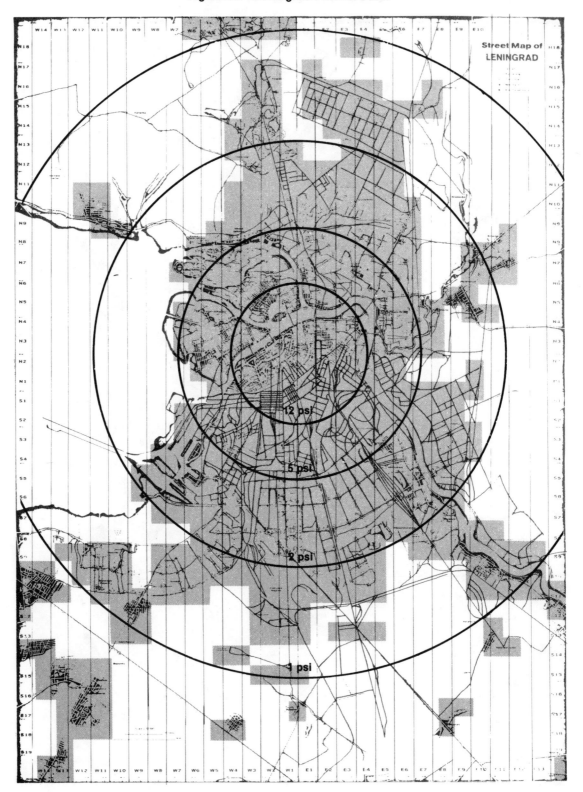

Figure 11.—Leningrad 9-Mt Air Burst

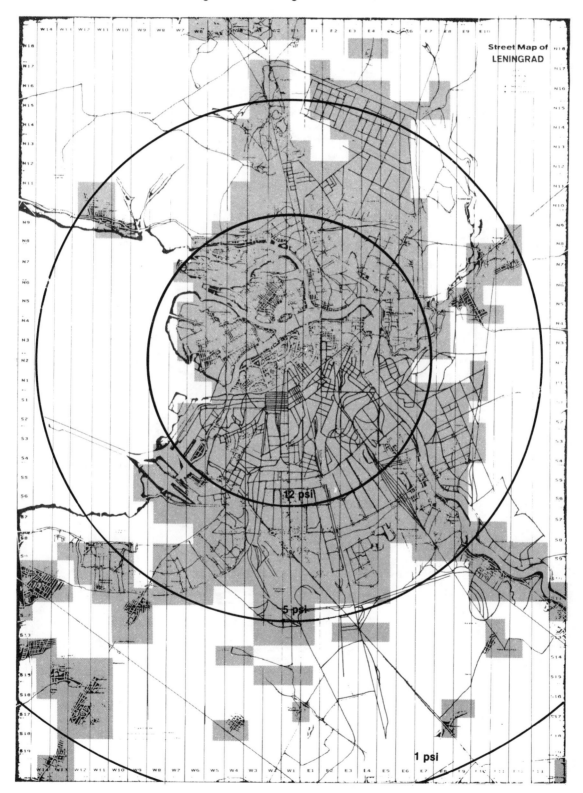

Figure 12.—Leningrad Ten 40-kt Air Burst

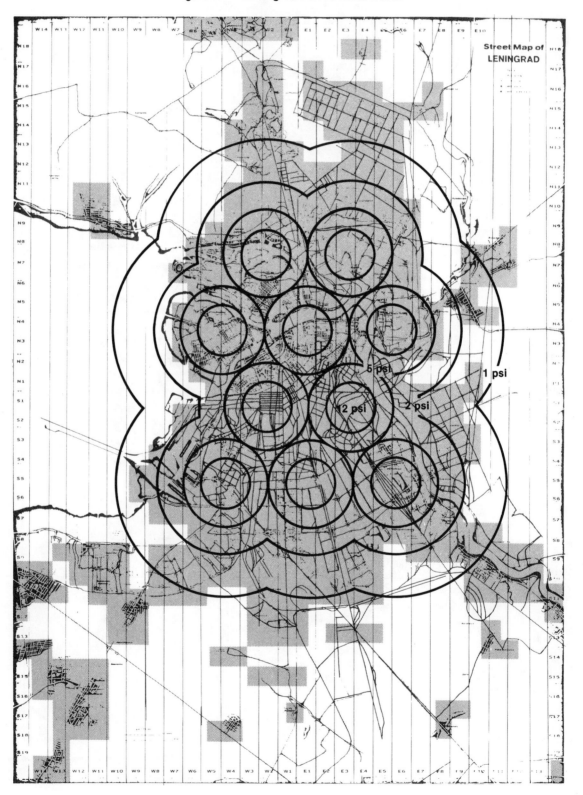

touching, and with only the envelope of the 2- and 1-psi rings shown. Since this is an effects discussion only, it is assumed that this precise pattern can be achieved. The errors arising from neglecting the overlap of the 2- to 5-psi bands will be negligible compared to uncertainties in population distribution and structural design. Casualty estimates are shown in the righthand column of figure 6 (p. 37). Note

that fatalities are only slightly greater than for the 1-Mt case, which corresponds well to the equivalent megatonage (1.17 Mt) of the ten 40-kiloton (kt) weapons. However, the number of injured are considerably smaller because they primarily occur in the 2- to 5-psi band, which is much smaller for the 40-kt pattern than for the single 1-Mt case.

1-KT TERRORIST WEAPON AT GROUND LEVEL

To this point this chapter has addressed nuclear effects from current strategic weapon systems. Another nuclear weapon of concern is one constructed by terrorists and detonated in a major city.* A terrorist group using stolen or diverted fission material, having general technical competence but lacking direct weapon design experience, could probably build a weapon up to several kilotons. This weapon would be large and heavy, certainly not the often-discussed "suitcase bomb," so is likely to be transported in a van or small truck, with threatened detonation either in the street or the parking garage of a building.

Because of the locations and yield of this weapon, its effects will be much less devasting than those of high-yield, strategic weapons. The range and magnitude of all the nuclear effects will be greatly reduced by the low yields; in addition, the relative range of lethal effects will be changed. At high yields, blast and thermal burn reach out to greater distances than does the initial nuclear radiation. At 1 kt the reverse is true; for example, 5-psi overpressure occurs at 1,450 feet [442 m], while 600 rems of initial radiation reaches out to 2,650 feet [808 m]. For the 1-Mt surface burst, 5 psi occurred at 2.7 miles and 600 rems at 1.7 miles.

In addition to these changes in range, the highly built-up urban structure in which the weapon is placed will significantly modify the resulting nuclear environment. This occurs

*OTA report on "Nuclear Proliferation and Safeguards," U.S. Government Printing Office, June 1977, pp. 121-122.

when the lethal range of effects shrink to such an extent that they are comparable to the size of urban structures. It is indeed reasonable to expect that the blast effects of a small weapon (5 psi at a range of only 1,450 feet) will be severely influenced by nearby structures having comparable dimensions. Preliminary calculations have confirmed this. For example, suppose a device is detonated in a van parked alongside a 1,000-foot high building in the middle of the block of an urban complex of rather closely spaced streets in one direction and more broadly spaced avenues in the other direction. Whereas the 2.5-psi ring would have a radius of 2,100 feet [640 m] detonated on a smooth surface, it is found that this blast wave extends to 2,800 feet [850 m] directly down the street, but to only 1,500 feet [460 m] in a random direction angling through the built-up blocks. These calculations have been made by many approximating factors which, if more accurately represented, would probably lead to an even greater reduction in range.

Other weapons effects will be similarly modified from those predicted on the basis of a relatively open target area. In the case of initial nuclear radiation, a lethal 600 rem would be expected to extend to 2,650 feet [808 m] from 1 kt. Because of the great absorption of this radiation as it passes through the multiple walls of the several buildings in a block, it is expected that 600 rems will reach out no further than 800 feet [245 m], thus covering an area only one-tenth as great. The thermal radiation will affect only those directly exposed up and down the street, while the majority of people will be protected by buildings. For the same reason directly initiated fires will be insignificant, but the problem of secondary fires starting from building damage will remain. The local fallout pattern also will be highly distorted by the presence of the buildings. The fireball, confined between the buildings, will be blown up to a higher altitude than otherwise expected, leading to reduced local fallout but causing broadly distributed long-term fallout.

In summary, the ranges of nuclear effects from a low-yield explosion in the confined space of an urban environment will differ significantly from large yield effects, but in ways that are very difficult to estimate. Thus the numbers of people and areas of buildings affected are very uncertain. However, it appears that, with the exception of streets directly exposed to the weapon, lethal ranges to people will be smaller than anticipated and dominated by the blast-induced collapse of nearby buildings.

Chapter III
CIVIL DEFENSE

Chapter III.—CIVIL DEFENSE

CIVIL DEFENSE

INTRODUCTION

Effective civil defense measures have the potential to reduce drastically casualties and economic damage in the short term, and to speed a nation's economic recovery in the long term. Civil defense seeks to preserve lives, economic capacity, postattack viability, and preattack institutions, authority, and values. The extent to which specific civil defense measures would succeed in doing so is controversial.

Some observers argue that U.S. civil defense promotes deterrence by increasing the credibility of U.S. retaliation and by reducing any Soviet "destructive advantage" in a nuclear war. Others, however, argue that a vigorous civil defense program would induce people to believe that a nuclear war was "survivable" rather than "unthinkable," and that such a change in attitude would increase the risk of war.

CIVIL DEFENSE MEASURES

Civil defense seeks to protect the population, protect industry, and improve the quality of postattack life, institutions, and values. This section considers several measures that support these goals.

Population Protection

People near potential targets must either seek protective shelter or evacuate from threatened areas to safer surroundings; if not at risk from immediate effects, they must still protect themselves from fallout. Both forms of protection depend on warning, shelter, supplies, life-support equipment (e.g., air filtration, toilets, communication devices), instruction, public health measures, and provision for rescue operations. In addition, evacuation involves transportation. This section examines each form of protection.

Blast Shelters

Some structures, particularly those designed for the purpose, offer substantial protection against direct nuclear effects (blast, thermal radiation, ionizing radiation, and related effects such as induced fires). Since blast is usually the most difficult effect to protect against, such shelters are generally evaluated on blast resistance, and protection against other direct effects is assumed. Since most urban targets can be destroyed by an overpressure of 5 to 10 psi, a shelter providing protection against an overpressure of about 10 psi is called a blast shelter, although many blast shelters offer greater protection. Other shelters provide good protection against fallout, but little resistance to blast—such "fallout shelters" are disccused in the next section. Blast shelters generally protect against fallout, but best meet this purpose when they contain adequate life-support systems. (For example, a subway station without special provisions for water and ventilation would make a good blast shelter but a poor fallout shelter.)

Nuclear explosions produce "rings" of various overpressures. If the overpressure at a given spot is very low, a blast shelter is unnecessary; if the overpressure is very high (e.g., a direct hit with a surface burst), even the best blast shelters will fail. The "harder" the blast shelter (that is, the greater the overpressure it can resist), the greater the area in which it could save its occupants' lives. Moreover, if the weapon height of burst (HOB) is chosen to maximize the area receiving 5 to 10 psi, only a very small area (or no area at all) receives more than 40 to 50 psi. Hence, to attack blast shelters of 40 to 50 psi (which is a reasonably attainable hardness), weapons must be detonated at a lower altitude, reducing the area over which buildings, factories, etc., are destroyed.

The costs of blast shelters depend on the degree of protection afforded and on whether the shelter is detached or is in a building constructed for other purposes. However, a large variation in costs occurs between shelters added to existing buildings and those built as part of new construction. The installation of shelters in new construction, or "slanting," is preferable, but it could take as long as 20 years for a national policy of slanting to provide adequate protection in cities.

An inexpensive way to protect population from blast is to use existing underground facilities such as subways, where people can be located for short periods for protection. If people must remain in shelters to escape fallout, then life-support measures requiring special preparation are needed.

Other lethal nuclear effects cannot be overlooked. Although, as noted above, blast shelters usually protect against prompt radiation, the shelters must be designed to ensure that this is the case.

Another problem is protection against fallout. If a sheltered population is to survive fallout, two things must be done. First, fallout must be prevented from infiltrating shelters through doors, ventilation, and other conduits. Other measures to prevent fallout from being tracked or carried into a shelter must also be taken. More important, the shelter must enable its occupants to stay inside as long as outside radiation remains dangerous; radiation doses are cumulative and a few brief exposures to outside fallout may be far more hazardous than constant exposure to a low level of radiation that might penetrate into a shelter.

Since radiation may remain dangerous for periods from a few days to several weeks, each shelter must be equipped to support its occupants for at least this time. Requirements include adequate stocks of food, water, and necessary medical supplies, sanitary facilities, and other appliances. Equipment for controlling temperature, humidity, and "air quality" standards is also critical. With many people enclosed in an airtight shelter, temperatures, humidity, and carbon dioxide content increase, oxygen availability decreases, and fetid materials accumulate. Surface fires, naturally hot or humid weather, or crowded conditions may make things worse. If unregulated, slight increases in heat and humidity quickly lead to discomfort; substantial rises in temperature, humidity, and carbon dioxide over time could even cause death. Fires are also a threat to shelterees because of extreme temperatures (possibly exceeding 2,000° F) and carbon monoxide and other noxious gases. A large fire might draw oxygen out of a shelter, suffocating shelterees. World War II experience indicates that rubble heated by a firestorm may remain intolerably hot for several days after the fire is put out.

Fallout Shelters

In the United States, fallout shelters have been identified predominantly in urban areas (by the Defense Civil Preparedness Agency (DCPA) shelter survey), to protect against fallout from distant explosions, e.g., a Soviet attack on U.S. intercontinental ballistic missiles (ICBMs). On the other hand, Soviet fallout shelters are primarily intended for the rural population and an evacuated urban population.

Fallout protection is relatively easy to achieve. Any shielding material reduces the radiation intensity. Different materials reduce the intensity by differing amounts. For example, the thickness (in inches) of various substances needed to reduce gamma radiation by a factor of 10 is: steel, 3.7; concrete, 12; earth, 18; water, 26; wood, 50. Consider an average home basement that provides a protection factor (PF) of 10 (reduces the inside level of radiation to one-tenth of that outside). Without additional protection, a family sheltered here could still be exposed to dangerous levels of radiation over time. For example, after 7 days an accumulated dose of almost 400 rems inside the basement would occur if the radiation outside totaled 4,000 roentgens. This could be attenuated to a relatively safe accumulation of 40 rems, if about 18 inches of dirt could be piled against windows and exposed walls before the fallout begins. Thirty-six inches of dirt would reduce the dose to a negligible level of 4 rems (400 ÷ 100). Thus, as DCPA notes, "fallout protection is as cheap as dirt." Moving dry, unfrozen earth to increase the protection in a fallout shelter requires considerable time and effort, if done by hand. A cubic foot of earth weighs about 100 lbs; a cubic yard about 2,700 lbs. Given time, adequate instructions, and the required materials, unskilled people can convert home basements into effective fallout shelters.

The overall effectiveness of fallout shelters, therefore, depends on: (a) having an adequate shelter—or enough time, information, and materials to build or improve an expedient shelter; (b) having sufficient food, water, and other supplies to enable shelterees to stay sheltered until the outside fallout decays to a safe level (they may need to remain in shelters for periods ranging from a few days to over 1 month, depending on fallout intensity); and (c) entering the shelter promptly before absorbing much radiation. (An individual caught by fallout before reaching shelter could have difficulty entering a shelter without contaminating it.)

Over the years, home fallout shelters have received considerable attention, with the Government distributing plans that could be used to make home basements better shelters. Such plans typically involve piling dirt against windows and (if possible) on floors above the shelter area, stocking provisions, obtaining radios and batteries, building makeshift toilets, and so forth. Such simple actions can substantially increase protection against radiation and may slightly improve protection against blast. How-

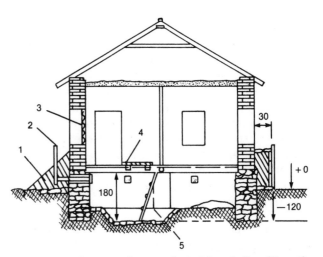

Basement of a stone house adapted for shelter: (1) earth embankment; (2) exhaust duct; (3) curtains on windows; (4) airtight hatch; (5) recessed pit. Material requirements: lumber, 0.5 m³; nails, 1 kg; earth, 3 to 5 m³; labor, 15 to 29 hours (man-hours).

ever, few homes in the South and West have basements.

With adequate time, instructions, and materials, an "expedient" shelter offering reasonable radiation protection can be constructed. This is a buried or semiburied structure, shielded from radiation by dirt and other common materials. Expedient shelter construction figures prominently in Soviet civil defense planning.

Evacuation

Evacuation is conceptually simple: people move from high-risk to low-risk areas. In effect, evacuation (or crisis relocation) uses safe distances for protection from immediate nuclear effects. The effectiveness of crisis relocation is highly scenario-dependent. If relocated people have time to find or build shelters, if the areas into which people evacuate do not become new targets, and if evacuated targets are attacked, evacuation will save many lives.

Although evacuating is far less costly per capita than constructing blast shelters, planning and implementing an evacuation is difficult. First, people must be organized and transported to relocation areas. This is a staggering logistics problem. Unless people are assigned to specific relocation areas, many areas could be overwhelmed with evacuees, causing severe health and safety problems. Unless private transportation is strictly controlled, monumental traffic jams could result. Unless adequate public transportation is provided, some people would be stranded in blast areas. Unless necessary supplies are at relocation areas, people might rebel against authority. Unless medical care is distributed among relocation areas, health problems would multiply.

Once evacuated, people must be sheltered. They might be assigned to existing public shelters or to private homes with basements suitable for shelter. If materials are available and time permits, new public shelters could be built. Evacuees require many of the same life-support functions described previously under fallout shelters; providing these in sufficient quantity would be difficult.

Evacuation entails many unknowns. The time available for evacuation is unknown, but extremely critical. People should be evacuated to areas that will receive little fallout, yet fallout deposition areas cannot be accurately predicted in advance. Crisis relocation could increase the perceived threat of nuclear war and this might destablize a crisis.

Whether people would obey an evacuation order depends on many factors, especially public perception of a deteriorating international crisis. If an evacuation were ordered and people were willing to comply with it, would time allow compliance? If the attack came while the evacuation is underway, more people might die than if evacuation had not been attempted. Sufficiency of warning depends on circumstances; a U.S. President might order an evacuation only if the Soviets had started one. In this case, the United States might have less evacuation time than the Soviets. The abundance of transportation in the United States could in theory permit faster evacuation, but panic, traffic jams, and inadequate planning could nullify this advantage. Disorder and panic, should they occur, would impede evacuation.

The success of evacuation in the United States would likely vary from region to region. Generally, evacuation requires little planning in sparsely populated areas. In some areas, especially the Midwest and South, evacuation is feasible but requires special planning because fallout from attacks on ICBMs might mean longer evacuation distances. Evacuation from the densely populated Boston-to-Washington and Sacramento-to-San Diego corridors, with their tens of millions of people and limited relocation areas, may prove impossible.

The Soviet Union reportedly has plans for large-scale evacuation of cities, and recent debate on its effectiveness has stimulated discussion of a similar plan, known as "crisis relocation" for the United States. Some key considerations are:

- Tactical warning of a missile attack does not give enough time for an evacuation. Evacuation plans thus assume that an intense crisis will provide several days' strategic warning of an attack, and that the leadership would make use of this warning.

- Unlike in-place blast sheltering, peacetime expenditures on evacuation are relatively small, since most expenditures occur only when a decision has been reached to implement plans.

- Evacuation involves considerably more preattack planning than a shelter-based civil defense plan, as logistical and other organizational requirements for moving millions of people in a few days are much more complex. Plans must be made to care for the relocated people. People must know where to go. Transportation or evacuation routes must be provided. A recent survey of the U.S. population revealed that many would spontaneously evacuate in a severe crisis, which could interfere with a planned evacuation.

Some U.S. analysts argue that detailed Soviet evacuation plans, together with evidence of practical evacuation preparations, indicate a reasonable evacuation capability. Others claim that actual Soviet capabilities are far less than those suggested in official plans and that, in particular, an actual evacuation under crisis conditions would result in a mixture of evacuation according to plan for some, delay for others, and utter chaos in some places. In any case, a large evacuation has never been attempted by the United States. The extent of Soviet evacuation exercises is a matter of controversy.

Crisis relocation of large populations would have major economic impacts. These are the subject of a current DCPA study in which the Treasury, Federal Reserve Board, and Federal Preparedness Agency are participating. Results to date indicate that economic impacts of relocation, followed by crisis resolution and return of evacuees, could continue for 1 to 3 years, but that appropriate Government policies could significantly reduce such impacts. If blast shelters for key workers are built in risk areas, and if workers are willing to accept the risks, essential industries could be kept functioning while most people were in relocation areas. Such a program would substantially reduce the economic impacts of an extended crisis relocation.

Protection of Industry and Other Economic Resources

Efforts to preserve critical economic assets, and thereby accelerate postattack recovery, could take several forms. For example, if there is warning, railroad rolling stock might be moved from urban classification yards into rural locations, perhaps saving many cars and their cargo. Some industrial equipment and tooling might be protected by burial and sandbagging. Other industrial facilities, such as petroleum refineries and chemical plants, may be impossible to protect. Industrial defense measures include measures to make buildings or machinery more resistant to blast pressure (hardening), dispersal of individual sites and of mobile assets (e.g., transport, tools, equipment, fuel), proliferation of "redundant" and complementary capabilities, and plans to minimize disruption to an economy and its components in wartime by coordinated shutdown of

industrial processes, speedy damage control, and plant repair.

There is no practicable way to protect an industrial facility that is targeted by a nuclear weapon with 1980's accuracy. Protective measures might, however, be helpful at industrial facilities that are not directly targeted, but that are near other targets.

Some equipment within structures can be protected against blast, fire, and debris with suitable measures. Other equipment, especially costly and critical equipment, and finished products, can be sheltered in semiburied structures and other protective facilities. A recent study[1] demonstrated that special hardening measures could save some machinery at blast overpressures higher than necessary to destroy the building in which the machinery is housed. However, it is unknown whether the amount of equipment that could actually be protected would make much difference in recovery.

Another method of protecting industrial capabilities is the maintenance of stockpiles of critical equipment or of finished goods. Stockpiling will not provide a continuing output of the stockpiled goods, but could ensure the availability of critical items until their production could be restarted. Stockpiles can obviously be targeted if their locations are known, or might suffer damage if near other potential targets.

Finally, dispersal of industry, both within a given facility consisting of a number of buildings and between facilities, can decrease damage to buildings from weapons aimed at other buildings. A Soviet text on civil defense notes that:

Measures may be taken nationally to limit the concentration of industry in certain regions. A rational and dispersed location of industries in the territories of our country is of great national economic importance, primarily from the standpoint of an accelerated economic development, but also from the stand-

---

[1]T. K. Jones, "Industrial Survival and Recovery After Nuclear Attack: A Report to the Joint Committee on Defense Production, U.S. Congress" (Seattle, Wash.: The Boeing Aerospace Co., November 1976).

point of organizing protection from weapons of mass destruction.[2]

However, there is little evidence that the U.S.S.R. has adopted industrial dispersion as national policy. Despite reports of Soviet industrial decentralization over the last decade or so, Soviet industry appears more concentrated than ever. An excellent example is the Kama River truck and auto facility, a giant complex the size of Manhattan Island where about one-fifth of all Soviet motor vehicles is produced. Clearly, Soviet planners have chosen industrial efficiency and economies of scale over civil defense considerations. Sim-

ilarly, the United States has no directed policy of decentralization, and other facts suggest that nuclear war is not a significant civil planning determinant. There are those who reason that this "disregard" for many of the consequences of nuclear war indicates that policymakers believe nuclear war is a very low possibility.

Planning for Postattack Activities

The economic and social problems following a nuclear attack cannot be foreseen clearly enough to permit drafting of detailed recovery plans. In contrast, plans can be made to preserve the continuity of government, and both the United States and the Soviet Union surely have such plans.

---

[2]P. T. Egorov, I. A. Shlyakov, and N. I. Alabin, *Civil Defense*. Translated by the Scientific Translation Service (Springfield, Va.: Department of Commerce, National Technical Information Service, December 1973), p. 101.

U.S. AND SOVIET CIVIL DEFENSE

U.S. Civil Defense

U.S. attitudes have been ambivalent toward civil defense ever since the Federal Civil Defense Act of 1950 responded to the first Soviet test of atomic bombs in 1949. Indeed, much of the U.S. civil defense was a reaction to external factors rather than part of a carefully-thought-through program. The "duck and cover" program and the evacuation route program, both of the early 1950's, responded to the threat of Soviet atomic bombs carried by manned bombers. Lack of suitable protection against fire and blast led to plans for rapid evacuation of cities during the several hours separating radar warning and the arrival of Soviet bombers.

The first Soviet test of thermonuclear weapons in 1953 necessitated changes in these plans. The much higher yield of these weapons meant that short-distance evacuations and modestly hard blast shelters in cities were ineffective for protecting people, and that simply "ducking" in school corridors, while perhaps better than nothing, was not part of a serious civil defense plan. H-bombs also raised the

specter of radioactive fallout blanketing large areas of the country. Previously, civil defense could be conceptualized as moving people a short distance out of cities, while the rest of the country would be unscathed and able to help the target cities. Fallout meant that large areas of the country—the location of which was unpredictable—would become contaminated, people would be forced to take shelter in those areas, and their inhabitants, thus pinned down, would be unable to offer much help to attacked cities for several weeks.

The advent of ICBMs necessitated further changes. Their drastically reduced warning times precluded evacuations on radar warning of attack.

With previous plans made useless by advances in weapons technology, the United States cast around for alternative plans. One approach was to identify and stock fallout shelters, while recognizing the impracticability of protecting people from blast. After the Berlin crisis of 1961, the President initiated a program to provide fallout shelters for the entire population. The National Shelter Survey

Program was commenced on a crash basis. The President proposed:

1. the survey, identification, and stocking of existing shelters;
2. the subsidization of fallout shelter installation in new construction; and
3. the construction of single-purpose fallout shelters where these were needed.

Only the first step in this program was authorized. The Government also urged people to build home fallout shelters.

The civil defense program was broadened in the early 1970's to include preparedness for peacetime as well as wartime disasters. The 1970's also saw a new emphasis on operational capabilities of all available assets, including warning systems, shelters, radiological detection instruments and trained personnel, police and fire-fighting forces, doctors and hospitals, and experienced management. This development program was called On-Site Assistance.

In the mid-1970's, contingency planning to evacuate city and other high-risk populations during a period of severe crisis was initiated.

At present, U.S. civil defense has the following plans and capabilities:

Organization.—The Federal civil defense function has been repeatedly reorganized since the Federal Civil Defense Act of 1950. The most recent organization gave prime responsibility for civil defense to the Defense Civil Preparedness Agency (DCPA), housed in the Defense Department. The Federal Preparedness Agency (FPA) in the General Services Administration conducts some planning for peacetime nuclear emergencies, economic crises, continuity of Government following a nuclear attack, and other emergencies. The Federal Disaster Assistance Administration (FDAA), in the Department of Housing and Urban Development, is concerned with peacetime disaster response. In 1978, Congress assented to a Presidential proposal to reorganize civil defense and peacetime disaster functions into a single agency, the Federal Emergency Management Agency, which will incorporate DCPA, FPA, FDAA, and other agencies.

Civil Protection.—The United States is looking increasingly at crisis relocation (CR), under which city-dwellers would move to rural "host" areas when an attack appeared likely. CR would require several days of warning, so it would be carried out during a crisis rather than on radar warning of missile launch. The United States has conducted surveys to identify potential fallout shelters in host areas, and blast and fallout shelters in risk areas. Through FY 1971, about 118,000 buildings had been marked as shelters; about 95,000 other buildings have been identified as potential shelters but have not been marked. Marking would be done in crises. In the early 1960's, the Federal Government purchased austere survival supplies for shelters. The shelf life of these supplies has expired; shelter stocking is now to be accomplished during a crisis.

Direction and Control.—The Federal Government has several teletype, voice, and radio systems for communicating in crises between DCPA, FDAA, and FPA headquarters, regional offices, States, and Canada. State and local governments are planning to integrate communication systems into this net. DCPA has eight regions, each with emergency operating centers (EOCs). Six of these centers are hardened against nuclear blast. Forty-three States have EOCs, and EOCs with fallout protection are operational or under development in locales including about half the population.

Attack Warning.—Warning can be passed over the National Warning System to over 1,200 Federal, State, and local warning points, which operate 24 hours a day. Once warning has reached local levels, it is passed to the public by sirens or other means. Almost half of the U.S. population is in areas that could receive outdoor warning within 15 minutes of the issue of a national warning. Dissemination of warning to the public, however, is inadequate in many places.

Emergency Public Information.—Fallout protection, emergency power generators, and remote units have been provided for radio stations in the Emergency Broadcast System, to permit broadcast of emergency information under fallout conditions. About a third of the stations are in high-risk areas and could be destroyed by blast. A program has been initiated to protect 180 stations from electromagnetic pulse (EMP). About one-third of the more than 5,000 localities participating in the civil defense program have reported development of plans to provide the public with information in emergencies.

Radiological Defense. — This function encompasses radiological detection instruments, communication, plans and procedures, and personnel trained to detect and evaluate radiological hazards. Between FY 1955-74, the Federal Government had procured about 1.4 million rate meters, 3.4 million dose meters, and related equipment. Effective radiological defense would require an estimated 2.4 million people to be trained as radiological monitors in a crisis.

Citizen Training.—The civil defense program once provided substantial training for the public at large, but crisis training via news media must now be relied on to educate citizens on hazards and survival actions. DCPA offers classroom and home study training for civil defense personnel.

Several points emerge from this discussion:

1. On paper, civil defense looks effective. The United States has more than enough identified fallout shelter spaces for the entire population, which include underground parking, subways, tunnels, and deep basement potential blast shelters. The United States has a vast network of highways and vehicles; every holiday weekend sees a substantial urban evacuation. CB and other radios can aid communication after an attack. The United States has enormous resources (food, medical supplies, electrical-generating capability, etc.) beyond the minimum needed for survival.
2. However, no one at all thinks that the United States has an effective civil defense.

3. U.S. civil defense capability is weakened because some elements are in place while others are not or have not been maintained. Shelters will not support life if their occupants have no water. Evacuation plans will save fewer people if host areas have inadequate shelter spaces and supplies, or if people are poorly distributed among towns.
4. Faced with drastic technological change, moral and philosophical questions about the desirability of civil defense, and budgetary constraints, Federal plans have been marked by vacillation, shifts in direction, and endless reorganization.

Soviet Civil Defense

Soviet civil defense has faced the same technical challenges as the United States—atomic bombs, hydrogen bombs, fallout, ICBMs, limited warning, and so on. The Soviet Union has consistently devoted more resources to civil defense than has the United States, and has been more willing to make and follow long-term plans. However, it is not known how Soviet leaders evaluate the effectiveness of their civil defense.

The Soviet civil defense organization is a part of the Ministry of Defense and is headed by Deputy Minister Colonel-General A. Altunin. Permanent full-time staff of the organization is believed to number over 100,000. Some civil defense training is compulsory for all Soviet citizens, and many also study first aid. There has also been a large shelter-building program.

The Soviets reportedly have an extensive urban evacuation plan. Each urban resident is assigned to a specific evacuation area, located on collective farms; each farmer has instructions and a list of the people he is to receive. If fallout protection is not available, it is planned that simple expedient shelters would be constructed quickly. Soviet plans recommend that shelters be located at least 40 km [25 miles] from the city district to provide sufficient protection against the effects of a 1-Mt weapon exploding at a distance of 10 to 20 km [6 to 12 miles].

In July 1978, the Central Intelligence Agency (CIA) released its unclassified study, "Soviet Civil Defense."[3] In brief, the report finds that Soviet civil defense is "an ongoing nationwide program under military control." It notes several motivations for the Soviet program: the traditional Soviet emphasis on homeland defense, to convince potential adversaries they cannot defeat the Soviet Union, to increase Soviet strength should war occur, to help maintain the logistics base for continuing a war effort following nuclear attack, to save people and resources, and to promote postattack recovery. It observes that Soviet civil defense "is not a crash effort, but its pace increased beginning in the late 1960's." It points to several difficulties with the Soviet program: bureaucratic problems, apathy, little protection of economic installations, and little dispersal of industry.

According to the report, the specific goals of Soviet civil defense are to protect the leadership, essential workers, and others, in that priority order; to protect productivity; and to sustain people and prepare for economic recovery following an attack. In assessing Soviet efforts to meet these goals, the CIA found:

> The Soviets probably have sufficient blast-shelter space in hardened command posts for virtually all the leadership elements at all levels (about 110,000 people)... Shelters at key economic installations could accommodate about 12 to 24 percent of the total work force...
>
> A minimum of 10 to 20 percent of the total population in urban areas (including essential workers) could be accommodated at present in blast-resistant shelters...
>
> The critical decision to be made by the Soviet leaders in terms of sparing the population would be whether or not to evacuate cities. Only by evacuating the bulk of the urban population could they hope to achieve a marked reduction in the number of urban casualties. An evacuation of urban areas could probably be accomplished in two or three

days, with as much as a week required for full evacuation of the largest cities...

> Soviet measures to protect the economy could not prevent massive industrial damage...
>
> (Regarding postattack recovery), the coordination of requirements with available supplies and transportation is a complex problem for Soviet planners even in peacetime, let alone following a large-scale nuclear attack.

Assessing the effectiveness of Soviet civil defense, the CIA study found that a worst case attack could kill or injure well over 100 million people, but many leaders would survive; with a few days for evacuation and shelter, casualties could be reduced by more than 50 percent; and with a week for preattack planning, "Soviet civil defenses could reduce casualties to the low tens of millions."

The U.S. Arms Control and Disarmament Agency (ACDA) released "An Analysis of Civil Defense in Nuclear War" in December 1978.[4] This study concluded that Soviet civil defense could do little to mitigate the effects of a major attack. Blast shelters might reduce fatalities to 80 percent of those in an unsheltered case, but this could be offset by targeting additional weapons (e.g., those on bombers and submarines that would be alerted during a crisis) against cities. Evacuation might reduce fatalities to a range of 25 million to 35 million, but if the United States were to target the evacuated population, some 50 million might be killed. Furthermore, civil defense could do little to protect the Soviet economy, so many evacuees and millions of injured could not be supported after the attack ended.

The sharp disagreement about Soviet civil defense capability revolves around several key issues:

Can the Soviets follow their stated civil defense plans? Some believe that the Soviets would fill their urban blast shelters to maximum occupancy rather than leave unevacuated people without protection and would evacuate all persons for whom no urban shelter spaces

---

[3]*Soviet Civil Defense* (Washington, D.C.: Director of Central Intelligence, July 1978), the text quotation below is from pp. 2-3.

[4]"An Analysis of Civil Defense in Nuclear War" (Washington, D.C.: U.S. Arms Control and Disarmament Agency, December 1978).

were available. Others believe that administrative confusion and other difficulties might render the Soviets far more vulnerable in practice.

How widely would evacuees be dispersed? It is obvious that the more widely dispersed an urban population is, the fewer casualties an attack on cities will produce. It is equally obvious that the more time there is for an evacuation, the more widely people can disperse. Nevertheless, there is great uncertainty over how well an evacuation would perform in practice. A Boeing study estimates that if urban dwellers walked for a day away from the cities, the population of cities would be more or less distributed over a circle of radius 30 miles [48.3 km].[5] If they did not dig shelters, a U.S. attack would kill about 27 percent of the Soviet population; if they dug expedient shelters, the attack would kill about 4 percent. If the Soviets fully implemented their evacuation plans but the evacuees were not protected from fallout, then 8 percent of the total population would die; if they constructed hasty shelters, 2 percent would die. ACDA, however, argues that even if the Soviet Union is totally successful in implementing its evacuation, the United States could, if the objective is to kill people, use its reserve weapons against the evacuated population and ground burst its weapons, thus inflicting from 70 million to 85 million fatalities.

How well would evacuees be protected from fallout? Some believe that Soviet evacuees could be fully protected against very high radiation levels if they are allowed a 1- to 2-week preattack "surge" period. (Tests conducted by the Oak Ridge National Laboratory have shown, for example, that American families can construct adequate fallout shelters in 24 to 36 hours, if they are issued the necessary tools and instructions.)[6] The ACDA study assumes that from one-third to two-thirds of the evacuees would have little protection against fallout. The two cases are not necessarily exclusive, since the ability to dig in depends on assumptions, especially time available for preparations before an attack. Some assume a lengthy and deepening crisis would precede nuclear strikes. Others believe that error or miscalculation would lead to nuclear war, leaving the United States or the Soviet Union unprepared and not having ordered evacuation. In addition, should an attack occur when the earth is frozen or muddy, construction of expedient shelters would be difficult.

How effective is Soviet industrial hardening? Soviet civil defense manuals provide instructions for the last-minute hardening of key industrial equipment in order to protect it from blast, falling debris, and fires. A considerable controversy has developed in the United States as to how effective such a program would be. The Boeing Company and the Defense Nuclear Agency carried out a number of tests that led them to conclude that "techniques similar to those described in Soviet Civil Defense manuals for protecting industrial equipment appear to hold great promise for permitting early repair of industrial machinery and its restoration to production."[7] Others have challenged this conclusion: for example, the ACDA civil defense study concluded that "attempts to harden above-ground facilities are a futile exercise, and that even buried facilities which are targeted cannot survive."

To understand this issue, one must recognize that it is virtually impossible to harden an economic asset so that it would survive if it were directly targeted. By lowering the height of burst, the maximum overpressure can be increased (at a small sacrifice to the area covered by moderate overpressures), and even missile silos can be destroyed by sufficiently accurate weapons. However, many economic targets are relatively close together (for example, separate buildings in a single factory), and it is possible and efficient to aim a single

---

[5]T. K. Jones, "Effect of Evacuation and Sheltering on Potential Fatalities From a Nuclear Exchange" (Seattle, Wash.: The Boeing Aerospace Co., 1977).

[6]S. J. Condie, et al., "Feasibility of Citizen Construction of Expedient Fallout Shelters" (Oak Ridge, Tenn.: Oak Ridge National Laboratory, August 1978). See also R. W. Kindig, "Field Testing and Evaluation of Expedient Shelters" (Denver, Colo.: University of Colorado, February 1978).

[7]Edwin N. York, *Industrial Survival/Recovery* (Seattle, Wash.: The Boeing Aerospace Co., undated).

weapon so that it destroys a number of targets at once. If each target is adequately hardened, then the attacker must either increase the number or yield of weapons used, or else accept less damage to the lower priority targets. However, the practicability of hardening entire installations to this extent is questionable, and the more likely measure would be to harden key pieces of machinery. The uncertainties about the Soviet program include the following:

- How much hardening could be done in the days before an attack?

- Would the United States target additional or larger weapons to overcome the effects of hardening?

- To what extent would the survival of the most important pieces of machinery in the less important Soviet factories contribute to economic recovery?

CONCLUDING NOTE

These pages have provided a brief description of civil defense as it might affect the impact of nuclear war. However, no effort has been made to answer the following key questions:

- Would a civil defense program on a large scale make a big difference, or only a marginal difference, in the impact of a nuclear war on civil society?

- What impact would various kinds of civil defense measures have on peacetime diplomacy or crisis stability?
- What civil defense measures would be appropriate if nuclear war were considered likely in the next few years?
- What kind and size of civil defense program might be worth the money it would cost?

THREE ATTACK CASES

Chapter IV.—THREE ATTACK CASES

THREE ATTACK CASES

OVERVIEW

The following pages present descriptions of three "cases" of nuclear attacks. (The tutorial on nuclear effects—chapter II—was the first of our four cases.) As mentioned in the *Executive Summary*, these cases do not necessarily represent "probable" kinds of nuclear attacks; they were chosen rather to shed light on the way in which different types of attacks could have differing effects on the civilian population, economy, and society. Moreover, each case is considered in isolation—events that could lead up to such an attack are deliberately ignored (because their prediction is impossible), and it is assumed (although that assumption is questionable at best) that the attack described is not followed by further nuclear attacks.

Each case considers first a Soviet attack on the United States, and then a U.S. attack on the Soviet Union. These attacks are similar in that they attack similar target sets, but different in detail because both the weapons available to the attacker and the geography of the victim are different. It should be emphasized that this discussion is not suggesting that in the real world an attack would be followed by a mirror-image retaliation; rather, it is looking at similar attacks so as to highlight the asymmetries in the ways in which the United States and the Soviet Union are vulnerable. To save space, it is assumed that the reader will read the Soviet attack on the United States in each case before turning to the U.S. attack on the Soviet Union, and repetition has been minimized.

The analyses that follow are much more like sketches than detailed portraits. Precise prediction of the future of the United States or the Soviet Union is impossible even without taking into account something as unprecedented as a nuclear attack. A detailed study would say more about the assumptions used than about the impact of nuclear war. What is possible, and what this report tries to do, is to indicate the kinds of effects that would probably be most significant, and to comment on the major uncertainties.

The following pages discuss the impact on civilian societies of:

- A limited attack on industrial targets. For this case the hypothesis was an attack that would be limited to 10 strategic nuclear delivery vehicles (SNDVs) (i.e., 10 missiles or bombers, in this case Soviet SS-18 intercontinental ballistic missiles (ICBMs), and U.S. Poseidon submarine-launched ballistic missiles (SLBMs), and Minuteman III ICBMs), and that would be directed at the oil refining industry. Oil refining was chosen as the hypothetical target because it is vital, vulnerable, and concentrated in both countries. It is assumed that the attack would be planned without any effort either to minimize or to maximize civilian casualties.

- A large counterforce attack. The possibilities considered included both an attack on ICBM silos only (a case that has gained some notoriety as a result of assertions by some that the United States may become vulnerable to such an attack) and an attack on silos, missile submarine bases, and bomber bases (which some characterize as the least irrational way to wage a strategic nuclear war). The analysis draws on several previous studies that made varying assumptions about attack design, weapon size, targets attacked, and vulnerability of the population; the ways in which variations in these assumptions affect the calculations of estimated fatalities are discussed.

• A large attack against a range of military and economic targets. This attack is intended to approximate "the ultimate deterrent"—the climax of an escalation process. The description of the results of this attack draws upon several previous studies that made differing assumptions about the number of weapons used and the precise choice of targets, but such variations are useful in indicating the range of possibilities. However, deliberate efforts to kill as many people as possible are not assumed, which would lead to more immediate deaths (perhaps 10 million to 20 million more) than targeting economic and military facilities.

CASE 2: A SOVIET ATTACK ON U.S. OIL REFINERIES

This case is representative of a kind of nuclear attack that, as far as we know, has not been studied elsewhere in recent years—a "limited" attack on economic targets. This section investigates what might happen if the Soviet Union attempted to inflict as much economic damage as possible with an attack limited to 10 SNDVs, in this case 10 SS-18 ICBMs carrying multiple independently targetable reentry vehicles (MIRVs). An OTA contractor designed such an attack, operating on instructions to limit the attack to 10 missiles, to create hypothetical economic damage that would take a very long time to repair, and to design the attack without any effort either to maximize or to minimize human casualties. (The contractor's report is available separately.) The Department of Defense then calculated the immediate results of this hypothetical attack, using the same data base, methodology, and assumptions as they use for their own studies.*

Given the limitation of 10 ICBMs, the most vulnerable element of the U.S. economy was judged to be the energy supply system. As table 6 indicates, the number of components

*The Office of Technology Assessment wishes to thank the Defense Civil Preparedness Agency for their timely and responsive help in calculations related to this case; the Command and Control Technical Center performed similar calculations regarding a similar U.S. attack on the Soviet Union.

in the U.S. energy system forces the selection of a system subset that is critical, vulnerable to a small attack, and would require a long time to repair or replace.

OTA and the contractor jointly determined that petroleum refining facilities most nearly met these criteria. The United States has about 300 major refineries. Moreover, refineries are relatively vulnerable to damage from nuclear blasts. The key production components are the distillation units, cracking units, cooling towers, power house, and boiler plant. Fractionating towers, the most vulnerable components of the distillation and cracking units, collapse and overturn at relatively low winds and overpressures. Storage tanks can be lifted from their foundations by similar effects, suffering severe damage and loss of contents and raising the probabilities of secondary fires and explosions.

MIRVed missiles are used to maximize damage per missile. The attack uses eight 1-megaton (Mt) warheads on each of 10 SS-18 ICBMs, which is believed to be a reasonable choice given the hypothetical objective of the attack. Like all MIRVed missiles, the SS-18 has limitations of "footprint"—the area within which the warheads from a single missile can be aimed. Thus, the Soviets could strike not any 80 refineries but only 8 targets in each of 10 footprints of roughly 125,000 mi² [32,375,000

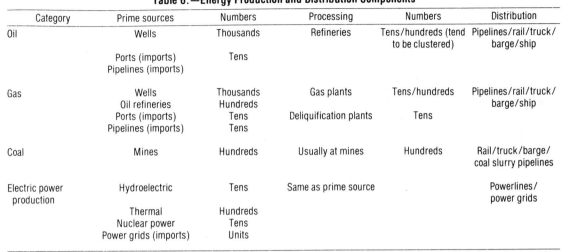

Table 6.—Energy Production and Distribution Components

Category	Prime sources	Numbers	Processing	Numbers	Distribution
Oil	Wells	Thousands	Refineries	Tens/hundreds (tend to be clustered)	Pipelines/rail/truck/barge/ship
	Ports (imports) Pipelines (imports)	Tens			
Gas	Wells Oil refineries Ports (imports) Pipelines (imports)	Thousands Hundreds Tens Tens	Gas plants Deliquification plants	Tens/hundreds Tens	Pipelines/rail/truck/barge/ship
Coal	Mines	Hundreds	Usually at mines	Hundreds	Rail/truck/barge/coal slurry pipelines
Electric power production	Hydroelectric	Tens	Same as prime source		Powerlines/power grids
	Thermal Nuclear power Power grids (imports)	Hundreds Tens Units			

SOURCES: *Vulnerability of Total Petroleum Systems* (Washington, D.C.: Department of the Interior, Office of Oil and Gas), May 1973, prepared for the Defense Civil Preparedness Agency.
National Energy Outlook: 1976 (Washington, D.C.: Federal Energy Administration), February 1976.

hectares]. The SS-18's footprint size, and the tendency of U.S. refineries to be located in clusters near major cities, however, make the SS-18 appropriate. The footprints are shown in figure 13. Table 7 lists U.S. refineries by capacity; and table 8 lists the percentage of U.S. refining capacity destroyed for each footprint.

The attack uses eighty 1-Mt weapons; it strikes the 77 refineries having the largest capacity, and uses the 3 remaining warheads as second weapons on the largest refineries in the appropriate missile footprints. In performing these calculations, each weapon that detonates over a refinery is assumed to destroy its target. This assumption is reasonable in view of the vulnerability of refineries and the fact that a 1-Mt weapon produces 5-psi overpressure out to about 4.3 miles [6.9 km]. Thus, damage to refineries is mainly a function of numbers of weapons, not their yield or accuracy; collateral damage, however, is affected by all three factors. It is also assumed that every warhead detonates over its target. In the real world, some weapons would not explode or would be off course. The Soviets could, however, compensate for failures of launch vehicles by readying more than 10 ICBMs for the attack and programming missiles to replace any failures in the initial 10. Finally, all weap-

ons are assumed detonated at an altitude that would maximize the area receiving an overpressure of at least 5 psi. This overpressure was selected as reasonable to destroy refineries. Consequences of using ground bursts are noted where relevant.

The First Hour: Immediate Effects

The attack succeeds. The 80 weapons destroy 64 percent of U.S. petroleum refining capacity.

The attack causes much collateral (i.e., unintended) damage. Its only goal was to maximize economic recovery time. While it does not seek to kill people, it does not seek to avoid doing so. Because of the high-yield weapons and the proximity of the refineries to large cities, the attack kills over 5 million people if all weapons are air burst. Because no fireball would touch the ground, this attack would produce little fallout. If all weapons were ground burst, 2,883,000 fatalities and 312,000 fallout fatalities are calculated for a total of 3,195,000. Table 8 lists fatalities by footprint.

The Defense Civil Preparedness Agency (DCPA) provided fatality estimates for this attack. DCPA used the following assumptions re-

Figure 13

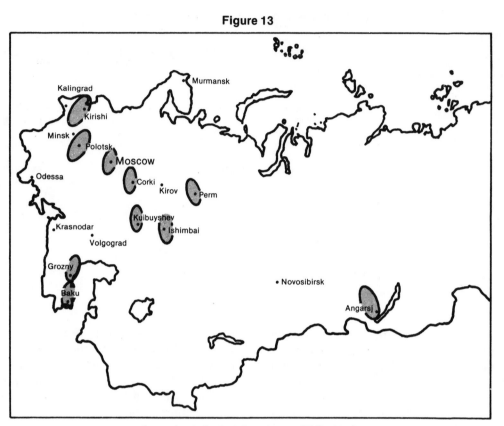

Approximate footprint coverage of U.S. attack

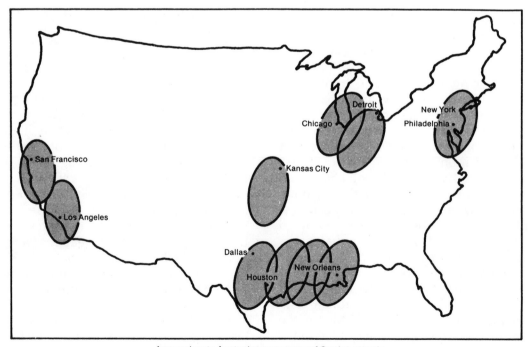

Approximate footprint coverage of Soviet attack

Table 7.—U.S. Refinery Locations and Refining Capacity by Rank Order

Rank order	Location	Percent capacity	Cumulative percent capacity	Rank order	Location	Percent capacity	Cumulative percent capacity
1	Baytown, Tex.	3.6	3.6	34	Avon, Calif.	0.7	47.9
2	Baton Rouge, La.	2.9	6.4	35	Toledo, Ohio	0.7	48.6
3	El Segundo, Calif.	2.3	8.7	36	Corpus Christi, Tex.	0.7	49.3
4	Whiting, Ind.	2.1	10.8	37	Torrence, Calif.	0.7	50.0
5	Port Arthur, Tex.	2.1	12.9	38	Nederland, Tex.	0.7	50.6
6	Richmond, Calif.	2.0	14.9	39	Toledo, Ohio	0.7	51.3
7	Texas City, Tex.	2.0	16.9	40	Port Arthur, Tex.	0.6	51.9
8	Beaumont, Tex.	1.9	18.8	41	Wilmington, Calif.	0.6	52.5
9	Port Arthur, Tex.	1.9	20.7	42	Sugar Creek, Mo.	0.6	53.1
10	Houston, Tex.	1.8	22.5	43	Ferndale, Wash.	0.6	53.7
11	Linden, N.J.	1.6	24.1	44	Sweeny, Tex.	0.6	54.3
12	Deer Park, Tex.	1.6	25.7	45	Borger, Tex.	0.6	54.9
13	Wood River, Ill.	1.5	27.3	46	Paulsboro, N.J.	0.5	55.4
14	Pasagoula, Miss.	1.6	28.9	47	Wood River, Ill.	0.5	55.9
15	Norco, La.	1.3	30.1	48	Benicia, Calif.	0.5	56.5
16	Philadelphia, Pa.	1.2	31.3	49	Wilmington, Calif.	0.5	57.0
17	Garyville, La.	1.1	32.4	50	Martinez, Calif.	0.5	57.5
18	Belle Chasse, La.	1.1	33.5	51	Anacortes, Wash.	0.5	58.0
19	Robinson, Tex.	1.1	34.6	52	Kansas City, Kans.	0.5	58.5
20	Corpus Christi, Tex.	1.0	35.7	53	Tulsa, Okla.	0.5	59.0
21	Philadelphia, Pa.	1.0	36.7	54	Westville, N.J.	0.5	59.5
22	Joliett, Ill.	1.0	37.7	55	West Lake, La.	0.5	60.0
23	Carson, Calif.	1.0	38.7	56	Lawrenceville, Ill.	0.5	60.4
24	Lima, Ohio	0.9	39.6	57	Eldorado, Kans.	0.5	60.9
25	Perth Amboy, N.J.	0.9	40.6	58	Meraux, La.	0.4	61.3
26	Marcus Hook, Pa.	0.9	41.5	59	El Paso, Tex.	0.4	61.7
27	Marcus Hook, Pa.	0.9	42.4	60	Wilmington, Calif.	0.4	62.2
28	Corpus Christi, Tex.	0.9	43.3	61	Virgin Islands/Guam[a]	4.1	66.3
29	Lemont, Tex.	0.8	44.1	62	Puerto Rico[a]	1.6	67.9
30	Convent, La.	0.8	44.9	63	Alaska[a]	0.5	68.4
31	Delaware City, Del.	0.8	45.7	64	Hawaii[a] [b]	0.3	68.7
32	Cattletsburg, Ky.	0.8	46.5	65	Other[c]	31.3	100.0
33	Ponca City, Okla.	0.7	47.2				

[a]Sum of all refineries in the indicated geographic area.
[b]Foreign trade zone only.
[c]Includes summary data from all refineries with capacity less than 75,000 bbl/day. 224 refineries included.
SOURCE: National Petroleum Refiners Association.

Table 8.—Summary of U.S.S.R. Attack on the United States

Footprint number	Geographic area	EMT[a]	Percent national refining capacity	Percent national storage capacity	Air burst prompt fatalities (x 1,000)
1	Texas	8	14.9	NA[b]	472
2	Indiana, Illinois, Ohio	8	8.1	NA	365
3	New Jersey, Pennsylvania, Delaware	8	7.9	NA	845
4	California	8	7.8	NA	1,252
5	Louisiana, Texas, Mississippi	8	7.5	NA	377
6	Texas	8	4.5	NA	377
7	Illinois, Indiana, Michigan	8	3.6	NA	484
8	Louisiana	8	3.6	NA	278
9	Oklahoma, Kansas	8	3.3	NA	365
10	California	8	2.5	NA	357
	Totals	80	63.7	NA	5,031

[a]EMT = Equivalent megatons.
[b]NA = Not applicable.

Photo credit: EXXON Corporation

Baytown refinery, Baytown, Tex.

garding the protective postures of the population in its calculations:

1. Ten percent of the population in large cities (above 50,000) spontaneously evacuated beforehand due to rising tensions and crisis development;
2. Home basements are used as fallout shelters as are such public shelters as subways;
3. People are distributed among fallout shelters of varying protection in proportion to the number of shelter spaces at each level of protection rather than occupying the best spaces first;
4. The remaining people are in buildings that offer the same blast protection as a single-story home (2 to 3 psi); radiation protection factors were commensurate with the type of structures occupied.

These assumptions affect the results for reasons noted in chapter III. Other uncertainties affect the casualties and damage. These include fires, panic, inaccurate reentry vehicles (RVs) detonating away from intended targets, time of day, season, local weather, etc. Such uncertainties were not incorporated into the calculations, but have consequences noted in chapters II and III.

The attack also causes much collateral economic damage. Because many U.S. refineries are located near cities and because the Soviets are assumed to use relatively large weapons, the attack would destroy many buildings and other structures typical of any large city. The attack would also destroy many economic facilities associated with refineries, such as railroads, pipelines, and petroleum storage tanks. While the attack would leave many U.S. ports unscathed, it would damage many that are equipped to handle oil, greatly reducing U.S. petroleum importing capability. Similarly, many petrochemical plants use feedstocks from refineries, so most plants producing complex petrochemicals are located near refineries; indeed, 60 percent of petrochemicals produced in the United States are made in Texas gulf coast plants.[1] Many of these plants

[1] Bill Curry, "Gulf Plants Combed for Carcinogens," *Washington Post,* Feb. 19, 1979, page A3.

would be destroyed by the attack, and many of the rest would be idled for lack of feedstocks. In sum, the attack aimed only at refineries would cause much damage to the entire petroleum industry, and to other assets as well.

All economic damage was not calculated from this attack, because no existing data base would support reasonably accurate calculations. Instead, the issue is approached by using Philadelphia to illustrate the effects of the attack on large cities. Philadelphia contains two major refineries that supply much of the Northeast corridor's refined petroleum. In the attack, each was struck with a 1-Mt weapon. For reference, figure 14 is a map of Philadelphia. Since other major U.S. cities are near targeted refineries, similar damage could be expected for Houston, Los Angeles, and Chicago.

Fatalities and Injuries

The Defense Civil Preparedness Agency (DCPA) provided not only the number of people killed within each of the 2-minute grid cells in the Philadelphia region but also the original number of people within each cell. These results are summarized in the following table for distances of 2 and 5 miles [3 and 8 km] from the detonations:

Deaths From Philadelphia Attack

Distance from detonation	Original population	Number killed	Percent killed
2 mi.	155,000	135,000	87
5 mi.	5,785,000	410,000	52

Detailed examination of the large-scale map also indicates the magnitude of the problems and the resources available to cope with them. These are briefly discussed by category.

Petroleum

Local production, storage, and distribution of petroleum are destroyed. In addition to the two refineries, nearly all of the oil storage tanks are in the immediate target area. Presumably, reserve supplies can be brought to Philadelphia from other areas unless—as is likely—they are also attacked. While early overland shipment by rail or tank truck into north and northeast Philadelphia should be possible, water transport up the Delaware River may not

Figure 14.— Philadelphia and Surrounding Counties

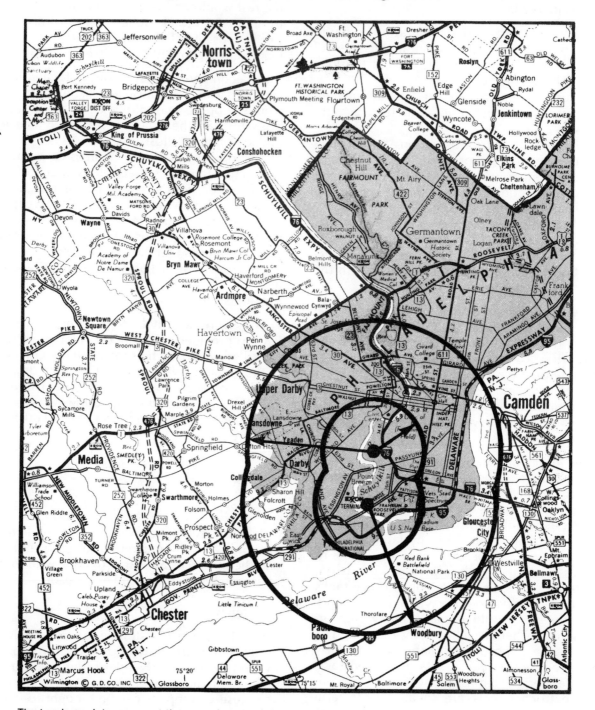

The two large dots represent the ground zeros of the two 1-Mt Soviet weapons. Within 2 miles of these ground zeros, there are approximately 155,000 people of which 135,000 were calculated to have been killed. Within 5 miles, there are 785,000 people of which 410,000 would have died.

be. This busy, narrow channel passes within about 1.3 miles [2.1 km] of one of the targets and could become blocked at least temporarily by a grounded heavily laden iron ore ship (bound upriver for the Fairless Works) or by sunken ships or barges.

Electric Power

There are four major electric powerplants in or near Philadelphia. Table 9 summarizes capacity, average usage (1976), and expected damage to these four installations.

While the usage figures in table 9 are average and do not reflect peak demand, it should be noted that a large percentage of this demand will disappear with destruction of the industrial areas along the Schuylkill River and of a large portion of the downtown business district. Thus, the plant in the Richmond section of Philadelphia, Pa., may be able to handle the emergency load. Assuming early recovery of the Delaware plant, there probably will be adequate emergency electric power for the surviving portion of the distribution system.

Transportation

Air.—The major facilities of the Philadelphia International Airport are located about 1.5 nautical miles [2.8 km] from the nearest burst. These can be assumed to be severely damaged. The runways are 1.5 to 2.5 nautical miles [2.8 to 4.6 km] from the nearest burst and should experience little or no long-term dam-

age. Alternate airfields in the northeast and near Camden, N.J., should be unaffected.

Rail.—The main Conrail lines from Washington to New York and New England pass about a mile from the nearest burst. It can be expected that these will be sufficiently damaged to cause at least short-term interruption. Local rail connections to the port area pass within a few hundred yards of one of the refineries. This service suffers long-term disruption. An important consequence is the loss of rail connections to the massive food distribution center and the produce terminal in the southeast corner of the city.

Road.—Several major northeast-southwest highways are severed at the refineries and at bridge crossings over the Schuylkill River. While this poses serious problems for the immediate area, there are alternate routes through New Jersey and via the western suburbs of the city.

Ship.—Barring the possible blockage of the channel by grounded or sunken ships in the narrow reach near the naval shipyard, ship traffic to and from the port should experience only short-term interruption.

Casualty Handling

Perhaps the most serious immediate and continuing problem is the destruction of many of Philadelphia's hospitals. Hospitals, assuming a typical construction of multistory steel or

Table 9.—Electric Powerplants in Philadelphia

Name	Capacity (kW)	Average usage kW (1976)	Distance from blast	
Schuylkill	249,000 steam + 36,750 internal combustion (I.C.)	111,630	1.3	Electrical equipment destroyed. Plant heavily damaged.
Southwark	356,000 steam + 66,750 I.C.	71,605	2.6	Electrical equipment damaged or destroyed. Plant moderately damaged.
Delaware	250,000 steam + 68,750 I.C.	162,799	4.9	Electrical equipment moderately damaged. Plant intact.
Richmond	275,000 steam + 63,400 I.C.	29,247	6.6	Probably undamaged.
Totals	1,130,000 kW (steam) + 235,650 I.C.	375,281		

SOURCE: *Electrical World: Directory of Electricial Utilities* (New York, N.Y.: McGraw Hill Inc., 1977).

reinforced concrete, would have a 50-percent probability of destruction at about 2.13 miles (1.85 nautical miles [3.4 km]). A detailed 1967 map indicates eight major hospitals within this area; all are destroyed or severely damaged. Another nine hospitals are located from 2 to 3 miles [3 to 4 km] from the refineries. While most of the injured would be in this area, their access to these hospitals would be curtailed by rubble, fire, and so on. Thus, most of the seriously injured would have to be taken to more distant hospitals in north and northeast Philadelphia, which would quickly become overtaxed.

Military

Two important military facilities are located near the intended targets. The Defense Supply Agency complex is located within 0.5 miles [0.8 km] of one of the refineries and is completely destroyed. The U.S. Naval Shipyard is 1.0 to 1.8 miles [1.6 to 2.9 km] from the nearest target and can be expected to suffer severe damage. The large drydocks in this shipyard are within a mile of the refinery.

Other

Several educational, cultural, and historical facilities are in or near the area of heavy destruction. These include Independence Hall, the University of Pennsylvania, Drexel Institute of Technology, Philadelphia Museum of Art, City Hall, the Convention Hall and Civic Center, Veterans Stadium, Kennedy Stadium, and the Spectrum.

Reaction: The First Week

During this period people would be in a state of shock, with their lives disrupted and further drastic changes inevitable. Many would have loved ones killed and homes destroyed. Factories and offices in the target areas would be destroyed, throwing people out of work. People would face many immediate tasks: care of the injured, burial of the dead, search and rescue, and firefighting.

Fires at petroleum refineries, storage tanks, and petrochemical factories would rage for hours or days, adding to the damage caused by blast. Some oil tanks would rupture and the oil would leak onto rivers or harbors, where it would ignite and spread fire. Fires at refineries could not be extinguished because of intense heat, local fallout, an inadequate supply of chemicals to use on petroleum fires, and roads blocked by rubble and evacuees. Petrochemical plants, already damaged by blast, would be further damaged by fire and would leak toxic chemicals. As discussed in chapter II, firestorms or conflagrations might begin, in this case supported by thousands of tons of gasoline. Anyway, the plants would likely be damaged beyond repair. Finally, with fires threatening to burn, poison, or asphyxiate people in shelters, rescue crews would attach top priority to rescuing survivors.

Once it was clear that further attacks were unlikely, the undamaged areas of the country would supply aid. However, the available medical aid would be totally inadequate to treat burns this attack would cause. The radius of third-degree burns (5.2 nautical miles [9.6 km] for a 1-Mt weapon air burst) is far greater than for any other life-threatening injury, and huge fires would cause more burns. But, even in peacetime, the entire United States has facilities to treat only a few thousand burn cases adequately at any one time.

If the attack used ground bursts exclusively, it would cause fewer prompt fatalities (2.9 million instead of 5.0 million for the air burst case), but much fallout. Given the extensive fallout sheltering described above, 312,000 people would die of fallout. Fallout casualties, however, would depend strongly on wind directions: would gulf coast fallout blow toward Atlanta, Miami, Cuba, or Venezuela? Would New Jersey fallout land on New York City on its way out to sea? The problems of shelterees are discussed under "Case 3: A Counterforce Attack Against the United States," in this chapter.

Beyond the physical damage, people would realize that a central assumption of their lives—that nuclear war could not occur—was wrong. Even people beyond target areas would know immediately that secondary effects would irrevocably change their way of life; survivors traveling to undamaged areas would drive this point home. Most would fear further attacks, and would seek protection by evacuating or seeking shelter. While recovery plans could be made and damage assessed, little reconstruction could be done with many people away or in shelters. Thus, the reaction period would not end until most people acted as if they believed the war was over.

Recovery

Once people believed that the war was over, the Nation would face the task of restoring the economy. The human consequences would be severe, but most deaths would have occurred within 30 days of the attack. Economic disruption and the economic recovery process would last much longer.

Restoring an adequate supply of refined petroleum would take years. It is unlikely that any of the attacked refineries could be repaired, although enough infrastructure might survive to make it cost effective to clear and decontaminate the rubble and rebuild on the old sites. The attack would kill many people skilled in building or operating refineries. The attack would also destroy many ports with special facilities for handling large quantities of crude oil and refined petroleum. While intensive use of plant and equipment can substantially increase output for many industries, it can increase a typical refinery's output by only 4 percent. Thus, the attack would leave the United States with about a third of its prewar refining capacity and with little of its prewar oil importing capacity; this situation would persist until new refineries and ports could be built.

The survival of a third of the Nation's refining capacity does not mean that everyone would get a third of the petroleum they did before the war. The Government would surely impose rationing. Critical industries and services would have top priority—military forces, agriculture, railroads, police, firefighting, and so on. Heating oil could be supplied, but at austere levels. Uses of petroleum for which

there were substitutes would receive little or no petroleum. For example, railroads could substitute for airlines, trucks, and buses on intercity routes; mass transit would probably substitute for private automobiles and taxis in local transportation.

The demise of the petroleum industry would shatter the American economy, as the attack intended. A huge number of jobs depend on refined petroleum: manufacture, sales, repair, and insurance of cars, trucks, buses, aircraft, and ships; industries that make materials used in vehicle manufacture, such as steel, glass, rubber, aluminum, and plastics; highway construction; much of the vacation industry; petrochemicals; heating oil; some electric power generation; airlines and some railroads; agriculture; and so on. Thus, many workers would be thrown out of work, and many industries would be forced to close.

The limited direct economic damage, already multiplied by thousands of secondary effects just enumerated, would be multiplied again by tertiary effects. Economic patterns that rest on the petroleum economy would be disrupted. Much of the American way of life is dependent on automobiles, from fast-food restaurants and shopping malls to suburban housing construction and industries located on major highways whose workers commute by car. The many people thrown out of work would have less money to consume things made by others. Service industries of all kinds would be especially hard hit.

These economic changes would lead to social changes that would have further economic consequences. Gasoline rationing would at best severely curtail use of private cars; mass transit would be used to its capacity, which would appear inadequate. Demand for real estate would plummet in some areas, especially suburbs, and skyrocket in others, notably cities, as people moved nearer to work and stores. Such mass movement, even within cities but especially between them, would upset the demographics underlying taxes, schools, and city services. With many people out of work, demand for unemployment compensation would rise at the same time taxes were falling. Vacation patterns would shift; cuts in air and car travel would force people to travel by train, which would lead people to vacation closer to home. The situation following the attack could lead the dollar to tumble, but whether or not that occurred, the curtailment of commercial air travel would prevent most people from traveling abroad. The economic system on which production depends would be radically different. To be sure, most workers and equipment would survive unscathed, and economic recovery would eventually take place.

Production depends, however, not only on the use of physical resources, but also on a wide range of understandings between producers and consumers. These underpinnings would be destroyed by the attack just as surely as if they were targeted. Prices would be uncertain, and various kinds of barter (trading favors as well as goods) would supplement the use of money. Credit and finance could not function normally in the absence of information about the markets for continuing production. Contracts would have uncertain meaning. Many businesses would go bankrupt as patterns of supply and demand changed overnight. Courts would be seriously overburdened with the task of trying to arbitrate among all of these competing claims. Corporations and individuals would be reluctant to make commitments or investments.

Given this disruption, the effort to resume production would require grappling with some basic organizational questions. To which tasks would surviving resources be applied? How would people be put back to work? What mix of goods would they produce? Which industries should be expanded, and which curtailed? Which decisions would Government make, and which would be left to the market?

This organizational task is unprecedented, but in principle it could be performed. Presumably the United States would follow the precedent of the mobilization for World Wars I and II, in which extensive Government planning supplemented private enterprise, and key assets and key people from the private sector were borrowed by the Government for the duration of the emergency. Certain tasks, such as caring for the injured, decontamination, high-priority reconstruction, and serving as an employer of last resort (to say nothing of meeting military requirements), would obviously be handled by the Government. The difficulty would be in planning and facilitating the transformation of the private sector. The combination of unusable factories and service facilities with unemployed workers could easily create a situation analogous to that experienced in the United States between 1929-33.

Long-Term Effects

Postattack society would be permanently and irrevocably changed. People would live in different places, work at different jobs, and travel in different ways. They would buy different things and take different kinds of vacations. The Nation would tend to apply the lessons of the past to future policy by seeking to reduce its vulnerabilities to the last attack. Energy conservation, where not required by regulations, would be encouraged by prices, taxes, and subsidies. Railroads and mass transit would supplant travel by cars and planes; rail and ships would substitute for planes and trucks in hauling freight. Automobile production would drop sharply and would emphasize energy-efficient models; bicycles and motorcycles would be popular. While housing construction would not necessarily end in the suburbs, new homes there would probably be built closer together so that mass transit could serve them. Construction in cities would boom. All houses would be better insulated; more would use solar energy as fuel costs soared.

Farms would be able to obtain adequate supplies of petroleum and its derivatives. Agriculture uses only 4 or 5 percent of the Nation's petroleum, and its products are necessary. While gasoline and petrochemical-based fertilizers and pesticides would be much more expensive, they comprise only a small fraction of farm expenses and would be essential for large-scale efficient agriculture. Moreover much fertilizer is made from natural gas rather than petroleum, so its price would not rise as dramatically as that of gasoline. Petroleum-related cost increases would be passed on to the consumer. The character of agriculture could change, however. In particular, the livestock industry might be sharply curtailed. At every stage, livestock raising, slaughter, and distribution require much more energy than do crops. For example, rapid transportation and extensive refrigeration are required. Meat would become very much more costly in relation to other foods than it is now, and so would become a luxury. If livestock production dropped, a major source of demand for corn, soybeans, and other fodder would decline, possibly slowing price increases for other farm products.

Although refineries and oil importing facilities would be rebuilt, U.S. refining capacity after recovery would probably be less than pre-attack capacity. Increased prices for gasoline and heating oil would shift demand to other sources of energy, raising their prices and encouraging an acceleration of their development.

Patterns of industrial production would shift dramatically because of these changes, forcing massive shifts in demand for skills and resources. Many people and factories would be oriented to the production of things no longer in demand; it would take many years for the economy to adjust to the sudden, massive changes imposed by the attack.

The attack would affect public health. Chapter V discusses the long-term effects of sublethal levels of radiation. Petrochemical plants damaged by the attack would leak car-cinogenous petrochemicals, but numbers of cancer cases from this source, the time of their appearance, and the duration of the threat cannot be predicted. To the extent that contamination or destruction of housing, or economic collapse, force people to live in substandard housing, illness would increase. Not all changes, however, would be for the worse. Some new patterns of living would promote public health. There would be fewer auto, aircraft, and boating accidents. More people would walk or bicycle, increasing exercise. Reduced consumption of meat would reduce dietary fats, heart attacks, and strokes. At some point, Government-imposed controls necessitated by the attack could be lifted because societal changes and market forces (price increases, alternative energy sources, residential patterns, and numbers and efficiency of cars) would achieve the goals of controls without coercion. For example, gasoline rationing would certainly be imposed immediately after the attack, and might be lifted in stages as refining capacity was restored, or subsidies to expand and support mass transit could level off or decline as revenues made it self-supporting.

The Nation's adjustment to all these changes would be painful. The problems would be especially severe because of the speed of their onset. Many people say that the United States would be better off if it was less dependent on cars and petroleum. While changing to new patterns of living via nuclear attack would minimize political problems of deciding to change, it would maximize the difficulties of transition. Problems would appear all at once, while any advantages of new patterns of living would come slowly.

CASE 2: A U.S. ATTACK ON SOVIET OIL REFINERIES

This case investigates what might happen if the United States tried to inflict as much economic damage as possible on the Soviet Union with 10 SNDVs without seeking to maximize or minimize casualties. Petroleum refineries were selected as targets because of their small num-ber and long construction time, and because of the severe economic consequences of doing without refined petroleum.

The Soviet refining industry is at least as vulnerable as its U.S. counterpart, though the vulnerabilities differ slightly. The United States refines more petroleum than does the U.S.S.R., about 17.9 million barrels per day of crude (1978 figures) versus 11.0 million (1980 projection).[2] According to a 1977 source, the U.S.S.R. had 59 refineries, including at least 12 under construction, some of which are very large; the U.S. and its territories have at least 288.[3] All individual refineries in both nations are highly vulnerable to attacks with nuclear weapons. The U.S. attack destroys most of Soviet refining capacity because the U.S.S.R. has few refineries; the Soviet attack destroys most of U.S. refining capacity because U.S. refineries are clustered.

The hypothetical attack targets 24 refineries and 34 petroleum storage sites. Some major refineries are beyond range of Poseidon missiles, so the United States uses 7 Poseidons with a total of sixty-four 40-kiloton (kt) RVs and 3 Minuteman IIIs with a total of nine 170-kt RVs. Because of the dispersal of Soviet refineries and limits of footprint size, each footprint had

fewer refineries than available RVs. The additional RVs were first allocated 2 on 1 against large refineries; remaining RVs were targeted against petroleum storage complexes. As in the U.S. case, every weapon is assumed to detonate over and destroy its target. It is assumed that all weapons are air burst, and the consequences of using ground bursts are noted where appropriate.

Immediate Effects: The First Hour

The attack destroys 73 percent of Soviet refining capacity and 16 percent of Soviet storage capacity, as table 10 shows. Collateral economic damage could not be calculated or collateral damage to a large Soviet city assessed because sufficient unclassified data could not be found.

If all weapons are air burst, the attack kills 1,458,000 people assuming everyone to be in single-story buildings, and 836,000 assuming everyone in multistory buildings; the latter assumption comes closer to reality. If all weapons were ground burst, the attack would kill 1,019,000 people, 722,000 promptly and 297,000 by fallout, assuming the worst case, everyone living in single-story buildings.

The estimated injuries from the attack are substantial under all conditions. Under the single-story assumption on housing, the air-

---

[2]"U.S. Refining Capacity" (Washington, D.C.: National Petroleum Refiners Association, July 28, 1978), p. 1 (U.S. figures), and *International Petroleum Encyclopedia, 1976* (Tulsa, Okla.: Petroleum Publishing Co., 1977), p. 323 (Soviet figures).

[3]*International Petroleum Encyclopedia, 1976*, op. cit., p. 393 (Soviet figures); and "U.S. Refining Capacity," op. cit.; *passim*, (U.S. figures).

Table 10.—Summary of U.S. Attack on U.S.S.R.

Footprint number	Geographic area (approx. center)	EMT[a]	Percent national refining capacity	Percent national storage capacity	Air burst prompt fatalities (x 1,000) SS[b]	MS[c]
1	Moscow	1.20	10.5	2.1	62	41
2	Baku	0.96	9.8	1.5	224	152
3	Ishimbai	1.20	8.7	2.8	25	12
4	Polotsk	0.92	7.5	0.3	52	32
5	Kuibuyshev	1.20	7.4	3.1	127	83
6	Angarsk	0.92	6.9	0.4	130	54
7	Grozny	0.96	6.7	1.6	56	37
8	Kirishi	0.92	6.2	0.3	493	230
9	Gorki	1.20	5.6	1.5	228	153
10	Perm	0.96	3.6	2.1	61	42
	Totals	10.44	72.9	15.7	1,458	836

[a]EMT = Equivalent megatons.
[b]SS = 100 percent of population in single-story buildings.
[c]MS = 100 percent of population in multistory buildings.

burst attack would produce 3.6 million injuries and a surface-burst attack about a million less. If in multistory buildings, the population would suffer 3.8 million injured from an air-burst attack and 2.5 million for the surface burst. (A protection factor of 5 was assumed against fallout from the surface bursts.)

The attack kills fewer Russians than Americans. The differences in fatalities do not mean that the United States is necessarily more vulnerable than the Soviet Union to nuclear attack; rather, the asymmetries occur from the design of the attack. Soviet refineries are farther from cities than are U.S. refineries, and U.S. weapons are smaller, so fewer Russians are within the lethal radii of U.S. weapons. Sensitivity of fatalities and injuries to distance from ground zero is shown in table 11. Had either nation sought to kill people, it would have used different weapons and targeted them differently.

Reaction: The First Week

As in the United States, life for the surviving majority would be totally disrupted. Many would be directly affected by the attack: the injured, those with injured relatives, the home-less, people affected by shortages. Accommodation to a future with a sharply reduced petroleum supply would begin: gasoline and other products might be hoarded, by enterprises if not by individuals. Some less-important industries would probably be closed to save fuel or to allow their workers to shift to the military, agriculture, and essential industry. Until it became clear that the war was over, millions of reservists would be mobilized for military service, placing a heavy demand on the domestic economy to replace them. Because of the mobilization, hours worked and the mix of production would change dramatically and overnight; workers in essential industries might be on 12-hour shifts; other workers not drafted would be pressed into service in essential industries, and quite possibly moved to factories in distant areas. The speed and magnitude of disruption would cause much psychological shock.

How would the Soviet Union cope with the damage? Although a greater percentage of its refining capacity would be destroyed, it would suffer fewer fatalities than would the United States (1.0 million to 1.5 million versus 3.2 million to 5.0 million) and fewer injuries (2.5 million to 3.8 million versus 3.9 million to 4.9 mil-

Table 11.—Approximate Distance (Nautical Miles) of Various Effects From Selected Nuclear Air Bursts (personnel casualties)

	Effect	Weapon yield		
		1 Mt	170 kt	40 kt
Overpressure (crushing)	Lethality—			
	Threshold	0.25	0.15	0.1
	Lung damage—			
	Threshold	2.1	1.1	0.7
	Severe	0.8	0.5	0.3
	Broken eardrums—			
	Threshold	3.5	2.0	1.2
	50%	1.0	0.6	0.4
Translation	Personnel in the open—1%	3.3	1.6	0.9
	Personnel near structures—			
	1%	3.8	1.9	1.0
	50%	2.1	1.0	0.6
Thermal	Third-degree burn—100%	5.2	2.6	1.5
	No burns—100%	8.7	4.8	2.8
	Flashblindness*	10	9	8
	Retinal burn*	25	23	20
Radiation	Lethal dose (1,000 rads)	0.9	0.8	0.7
	No immediate harm (100 rads)	1.2	1.1	1.0

*Daytime safe distance.

lion) because of the lower yield of U.S. weapons and the location of Soviet refineries away from cities. If all weapons were air burst at optimum height of burst, there would be negligible fallout in both countries; if all weapons were ground burst, the Soviet Union would receive far less fallout because of the lower yield of the weapons. Because the Soviets have built many widely dispersed small dispensaries and first aid centers, rather than smaller numbers of modern full-service hospitals concentrated in cities, more of these facilities would survive than in the United States. In addition, many Russians have received first aid training, and people with injuries that could be treated by paramedics, dispensaries, and first aid would probably be better off than their American counterparts; others would be at least as bad off. Those who required treatment at major hospitals would suffer because of the small number of beds in nearby modern hospitals and the inability of the Soviet transportation system to move them elsewhere. Like the United States, the U.S.S.R. could not cope with large numbers (say, over 100) of severe burn cases. There would be many victims of severe burns in both nations who would die for lack of adequate treatment.

The damage, the emergency conditions, and the risk of further attacks would remind everyone of the special horror that the Soviets faced in World War II. The psychological trauma would be exacerbated in the first week by anticipation of crisis economic conditions. The Soviet Government in past crises has proved to be ruthless and efficient in moving people to parts of the country where labor was needed. Such action would be likely in this crisis as well, along with cutbacks in food, consumer goods, housing construction and maintenance, and transportation. Only regimentation would be likely to increase. Life would be grim, and would remain so for years.

Recovery

What course would Soviet recovery take? Economic viability would not be at issue following this attack, and the Government could be expected to remain firmly in control because of the limited scale of this attack. Assuming that there are no further attacks, most of the deaths would occur within 30 days of the attack. While the course of economic recovery cannot be predicted in detail, it is clear that:

- The attack would hurt. The recovery period would be marked by shortage and sacrifice, with particular problems stemming from agricultural shortfalls.

- Nevertheless, the Soviet economy and political system would survive, and would do so with less drastic changes than the United States would probably experience.

- The asymmetries between the two nations in effects for a given attack are greater for this case than for a very large attack.

The political and economic structure of the U.S.S.R. appears designed to cope with drastic emergencies like this attack. While almost all economic assets would be unscathed, resources would need to be shifted rapidly to produce a different mix of outputs. The attack would totally disrupt existing economic plans. The economic planning apparatus and Government control methods in place in the U.S.S.R. would permit the Government to shift plans and resources, but the speed with which such changes could be made is uncertain. To the extent that revisions in the economic plan were not made or were delayed, people and equipment would sit idle or would be producing according to less-efficient priorities, draining scarce resources from higher priority tasks and hindering recovery. Workers would be shifted to different industries as plants closed; some would be forced to move, share apartments with strangers, or work at new jobs (including manual labor in farms or factories).

Some insight into the economic consequences can be obtained by looking at four sectors of the economy—military, agriculture, transportation, and industry. Each of these sectors would have a strong claim on available petroleum, but their total demand would exceed the supply.

The military would have first call on fuel, especially if the war continued. It has adequate stocks to prosecute a war for several weeks. However, unless this attack led to a decisive Soviet victory or to a major relaxation of tensions, the military would need refined petroleum to rebuild its stocks and to carry out normal training.

Soviet agriculture is precarious even in peacetime because of its inefficiency. Agriculture engages about a third of the work force and consumes a third of Soviet gasoline and diesel fuel. (U.S. agriculture, in contrast, uses 2.7 percent of the work force (in 1978) and a small fraction of U.S. refined petroleum.)[4] The Soviet Union imports grain in most years. Nevertheless, the U.S.S.R. has maintained a large cattle industry at considerable expense to provide a consumer good much in demand. Farms use petroleum for tractors and trucks; petroleum and natural gas are feedstocks for fertilizer and pesticides. Agricultural use of petroleum is increasing. One small example is the Soviet use of light aircraft to spread fertilizer; while this task could be done by tractors or by hand, it is much more efficiently done by aircraft.

Cutbacks in petroleum would magnify agricultural inefficiency. Even if the Soviet Union allocated all the petroleum it produced to agriculture, it would not produce enough to sustain agriculture's prewar consumption, and other critical sectors would compete for petroleum. Drawing on inventory would sacrifice later agricultural production for earlier production. Following the attack, the main concern of agriculture would be planting, growing, or harvesting the year's crop; sacrifices and substitutions would be required in other agricultural subsectors to meet this goal with available petroleum. The U.S.S.R. would be likely to divert people from schools, factories, and (depending on the international situation) the military to work the fields, as it does in peacetime, but to a greater extent. The substitution of human labor for mechanical energy would be a poor but perhaps unavoidable trade. The most obvious cutback would be livestock; meat is a luxury, livestock consume much food that could otherwise be used for human consumption, and cattle raising, slaughter, and distribution require much energy. The Soviet Union might slaughter much of its livestock after the attack to free farmers, fields, trucks, and petroleum to produce crops. Russians might have a 3-month orgy of meat followed by two decades without.

Soviet transportation would be pinched. A few top leaders would still have cars; other cars would sit idle for years, monuments to the prewar standard of living. Air transportation would be sharply curtailed, and Soviet supersonic transports would be grounded. Truck transportation would be curtailed, with trucks used almost exclusively for intracity transportation and hauling goods between railroads and loading docks. By elimination, the transportation burden would fall to railroads because of their energy efficiency. Key trunklines are electrified, and might obtain electricity from sources other than petroleum. The Soviets have stored a number of steam locomotives, which would be hauled out, refurbished, and put to use.

The tempo of industrial production would slow. Even as it stands now, the Soviets have barely enough energy and occasional shortages. Electric power would continue, but would probably be cut back 10 to 15 percent,

---

[4]*Statistical Abstract of the United States, 1978* (Washington, D.C.: U.S. Department of Commerce, Bureau of the Census, 1978), lists 91,846,000 employed persons age 16 and over in the United States, of whom 2,469,000 were listed as farmworkers, for January-April 1978 (p. 418). *The Statistical Abstract* does not present the amount of petroleum consumed by American agriculture. Several statistics, however, indicate this number to be a small fraction of total U.S. petroleum consumption. Preliminary 1977 data showed all U.S. prime movers (automotive and nonautomotive) had 26,469,000,000 horsepower, while farms accounted for 328,000,000 horsepower, or 1.2 percent (p. 604). In 1976, industrial consumption of petroleum accounted for 18 percent of total U.S. petroleum consumption (p. 764). And a National Academy of Sciences study found that agriculture accounted for 3.5 percent of total national energy consumption in 1968. *Agricultural Production Efficiency* (Washington, D.C.: National Academy of Sciences, National Research Council. Committee on Agricultural Production Efficiency, 1975), p. 119).

forcing some industries to close and reducing heat and light at other industries and apartments. With transportation cut back, factories would have to wait longer for inputs, lowering productivity.

Some less-essential industries, especially energy- or petroleum-intensive ones, might shut down. Plastics use petroleum derivatives as feedstocks. Aluminum production uses great amounts of energy, though some Soviet aluminum plants, such as at Bratsk in Siberia, use hydroelectric power. Truck production would stop for lack of fuel for existing vehicles, idling the huge Kama River truck plant.

Construction consumes much petroleum, so it would be curtailed except for essential industries, hydroelectric powerplant construction, refining construction, and minimal housing for workers in those occupations.

These changes would disrupt workers' lives. Closing of some plants would idle many workers, forcing them to work in other industries; many could be moved long distances to other plants. Workers would not necessarily be forced to work long hours. While some plants would operate around the clock, others would be closed or cut back to enable the energy they consume to be diverted. At the same time, however, and within limits of substitutability, workers could likewise be diverted from closed to open plants, providing extra labor for factories that remained open extra time.

In sum, the reduction in the standard of living and the amount of disruption would probably be less than in the United States but there might well be more hardship and misery. Russians would have less food, especially protein, than they did before the attack, while American agriculture consumes so little petroleum that its output could probably be maintained, though some variety might be sacrificed. There would be less heat in both nations, but winters are shorter and milder in the United States, and U.S. indoor temperatures in winter could be reduced 5° or 10° F without ill effect. Therefore, heating could probably not be cut as much in the U.S.S.R. as in the United States without jeopardizing health. Cars would be sacrificed at least temporarily in both nations. Soviet industries producing consumer goods would be cut back more sharply than their U.S. counterparts after the attack, and would regain productivity more slowly.

Long-Term Effects

Destroying 73 percent of refining capacity would force the economy onto a crisis footing, curtailing choices and consumer goods, dropping the standard of living from austere to grim, and setting back Soviet economic progress by many years. Recovery might follow the post-World War II pattern, with a slow but steady improvement in the quality of life. But recovery would be slow. The desire to reduce vulnerability to future attacks would undoubtedly divert resources from recovery to such tasks as building some underground refineries. While the United States could possibly recover in a way that would use less petroleum than it did prewar, this course would be difficult for the U.S.S.R. because much of Soviet petroleum goes to necessities. Long-term health and genetic effects would be less than for the United States because of the smaller size of U.S. weapons and the location of Soviet refineries away from people. But the Soviet Government might accept greater radiation exposure for people in order to speed production, increasing such effects.

CASE 3: A COUNTERFORCE ATTACK
AGAINST THE UNITED STATES

The case of a Soviet attack on U.S. strategic forces has received extensive public attention in recent years, since some observers believe it is the least irrational way of waging strategic war. For the purposes of this study, the military success of such an attack (i.e., how many U.S. forces would be destroyed) and the resulting U.S. responses are not important. It is sufficient to assume that such an attack is launched, and to examine the consequences for the civilian population, economy, and society. For this purpose, small variations in the attack design (e.g., whether control centers as well as silos are targeted) are immaterial. While there are many possible variations in the design of a counterforce attack, a question of particular interest is whether the attack would be delivered only against ICBM silos, or whether bomber bases and missile submarine bases would also be attacked. Some of the public discussion of such an attack suggests that an attack on ICBM silos alone could cause much less civilian damage than a full-scale counterforce attack because the silos are more isolated from population centers than are bomber bases. It is certainly true that, holding all the other possible variables constant, an attack that included bomber bases and missile submarine bases would cause more civilian damage than one that did not. Nevertheless, the difference between the ICBM-only attack and a comprehensive counterforce attack was found to be no greater than the difference made by other variables, such as the size of weapons used, the proportion of surface bursts used, and the weather. Both cases are considered in this section; the countersilo attack is a subset of the counterforce attack, and available data is too coarse to support a believable differentiation between the civilian effects of each attack.

Prompt Effects

The blast damage from a counterforce attack is concentrated on military installations. Attacks on submarine bases and bomber bases would cause considerable blast damage to nearby populations and urban structures; attacks on silos would cause relatively little civilian blast damage. Unlike ICBM silos, many bomber bases and fleet ballistic missile submarine (SSBN) support facilities are near cities. (See figure 15.) For example, an attack on Griffiss Air Force Base, near Utica and Rome, N.Y., would place nearly 200,000 people at risk from prompt effects; attacking the SSBN support facility near Charleston, S.C., would place more than 200,000 people at risk; attacking Mather Air Force Base, near Sacramento, Calif., would place more than 600,000 people at risk. The additional attacks would simultaneously reduce the number of people able to provide aid and increase the number of injured or evacuees requiring aid. The attacks would make it harder for people able to provide aid to sustain those needing it.

Countersilo attacks would probably detonate some weapons at or near the Earth's surface to maximize the likelihood of destroying ICBM silos. Surface bursts produce intense fallout, causing most of the damage to the civilian population, economy, and society. The principal civilian impact of adding attacks on bomber and SSBN bases is the large increase in urban destruction.

The Period Before Fallout Deposition

Fallout would begin to reach closer populated areas in a few hours; it would reach many others in a few days. As fallout arrives, radiation levels rise sharply and rapidly. People would therefore have to take any protective actions—shelter or evacuation—before the fallout arrives. This prearrival period would thus be one of intense activity and intense confusion. How would people react? Training could help, but people trained in how to behave under fallout conditions would fare poorly if they could not get to shelters or if shelters were unstocked. To what extent would people

Figure 15.—Counterforce Targets in the United States

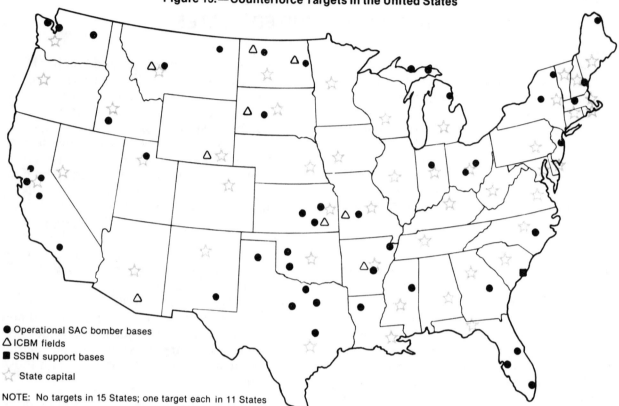

● Operational SAC bomber bases
△ ICBM fields
■ SSBN support bases
☆ State capital

NOTE: No targets in 15 States; one target each in 11 States

panic, seek other family members, or evacuate spontaneously, and what would be the consequences of such actions?

Evacuation would probably be a poor choice, since it would be difficult or impossible to predict which would be the safe areas and which the hot spots, and since a car in a traffic jam would offer poor shelter indeed. The decision on whether or not to evacuate, however, is complicated because evacuation is a reasonable response for people who would be at risk from blast from further attacks even though evacuation is a poor strategy for people at risk from fallout alone.

Shelter would in theory be available to a majority of people, although the best available shelter might not be good enough in areas where the fallout proved to be very intense. However, the practical difficulties of fallout sheltering could be very great. The time to seek shelter could be very limited (and people would not know how long they had), and people would want to get their families together first. A shelter must have a sufficient protection factor. Fallout particles must be kept out of the shelter, which requires a ventilation system more complicated than an open window or door, and if anybody enters a shelter after fallout has fallen there must be some means of decontaminating the new arrival. Water is necessary; heat may be necessary depending on the time of year; sanitation is a problem. Finally, people could not tell how long it was necessary to stay in the shelter without radiation rate meters.

It is obvious that the time of day, the time of the year, and the degree of emergency preparations during the hours or days before the attack would all affect the level of deaths. Whatever the circumstances, the few hours after the attack would see a frantic effort to seek shelter on the part of most of the American population. Then, in densities and locations determined by the attack parameters and the weather, the fallout would descend. Many Americans would be lucky enough to be in areas where the fallout level was low. Many others (between an estimated 2 million and 20 million), would be caught without shelter, or with inadequate shelter, and would die. Still others would suffer from a degree of radiation that would make them sick, or at least lower their life expectency, but would not kill them. The trials of living in fallout shelters would be intensified by the fact that many people would not know which category they and their families were in.

A comprehensive counterforce attack would impose a greater burden than a countersilo attack. Many more people would be injured by prompt effects, and people near bomber and SSBN bases would have only a few minutes warning in which to seek shelter.

Cities in the blast area—those near SSBN or bomber bases—would be heavily damaged. A few cities, such as Charleston, S.C., and Little Rock, Ark., could suffer consequences similar to Detroit in Case 1 (chapter II) or Philadelphia in Case 2 (above in this chapter); most would not. People in blast areas would face hazards as noted in Case 1—injuries from blast, initial nuclear radiation, and thermal radiation, and from such secondary effects as falling buildings and fires. As in other cases, rescue would be difficult, with streets blocked by rubble, water pressure gone, and emergency vehicles destroyed.

People in areas damaged by blast and in the path of fallout would be in greatest peril. Injuries, damage to prospective shelters, damage to transportation, and damage to power and water could make them highly vulnerable. Little Rock, Ark., for example, the site of an ICBM base and a bomber base, would receive both blast damage from a pattern attack (designed to destroy bombers in flight) and intense fallout radiation from the attack on ICBMs.

People in areas neither damaged by blast nor threatened by fallout would believe themselves to be at risk from blast or, at a minimum, from fallout until it was clear that attacks had ended. To these people would fall the burdens of producing necessities and caring for the injured and evacuees. Yet people in these areas, believing themselves to be at risk, would feel compelled to seek shelter or, especially in unattacked cities, to evacuate spontaneously. These actions would reduce the flow of aid to damaged areas. Indeed, the economy would probably shut down until people were certain that the war had ended and until most people could get back to work, probably until the end of the shelter period. Even if some people reported to work, production would be difficult with many absentees. There would be large credit, monetary, contractual, and legal problems. If production stopped even for a week, the loss would be tremendous. This attack would disrupt the economy less than Case 2, however, because most productive resources would remain intact.

Casualty Estimates

In seeking to estimate prompt damage from the attacks, fatalities are the most important component of damage and the most calculable. To estimate fatalities, the critical questions are which areas would be damaged by blast, and to what extent? How much fallout would there be, and where would it be deposited? These questions cannot be answered with great confidence because estimates of deaths from these attacks are highly sensitive to attack parameters and civilian shelter assumptions. However, reference can be made to several recent executive branch studies of counterforce attacks.

OTA drew on several executive branch studies, conducted between 1974 and 1978, of counterforce attacks. These studies differed widely in their results, primarily because of differences in the assumptions they made. OTA felt that it would be more useful to look at the ways in which these assumptions affect the results than to attempt to determine the "correct" assumption for each uncertainty. Consequently, a range of results is presented; it is believed that if OTA had done a new study of this case the results would have fallen somewhere within this range.[5]

The executive branch countersilo studies that OTA drew on indicated that between 2 million and 20 million Americans would die within the first 30 days after an attack on U.S. ICBM silos. This range of results is so wide because of the extent of the uncertainties surrounding fallout. The key uncertainties are:

- **Height of Burst.** — If the fireball touches the ground, it vaporizes some dirt, irradiates it, and draws it up into the mushroom cloud. This material condenses to become fallout. The lower the height of burst, the more of the fireball touches the ground, and the more fallout that is produced. An air burst in which none of the fireball touches the ground creates negligible fallout. Because ICBM silos are very hard, a surface burst offers the greatest probability of destroying the silo with one explosion; it also maximizes fallout. The probability of destroying an ICBM silo is increased if two warheads are targeted against it; opinions differ as to whether the most effective tactic is to use two surface bursts, which doubles the amount of fallout, or one air burst and one surface burst.

- **Weapon Design.** — Some weapons derive a greater portion of their energy from fission (as opposed to fusion) than others; the more fission, the more fallout. The weapon yield affects the amount of fallout; the higher the yield of a given explosion, the greater the fallout.

- **Wind.** — The speed and direction of the wind at various altitudes determines the directions and distance from the explosion at which fallout is deposited, and influences fallout concentration. Winds typically vary with the season; indeed, this variance is so great that it can affect casualties by about a factor of three, as

figure 16 shows. The hourly and daily variation of winds also affects casualties. It is important to bear in mind, when considering possible civil defense measures, that winds could not be accurately predicted even after an attack had taken place, much less in advance.

- **Rain.** — Raindrops collect fallout particles from the radioactive cloud, thereby creating areas of intense fallout where it is raining, and reducing fallout elsewhere.

- **Terrain.** — Hills, buildings, and ground temperature gradients (such as are caused by highways and small lakes) affect the exact pattern of fallout, creating hot spots in some places and relatively uncontaminated spots nearby.

- **Distance.** — Other things remaining constant, fallout decreases with distance from the explosion beyond roughly 50 miles [80 km].

As chapter II explained, radiation from fallout in large doses causes death, in smaller doses causes illness, and in still smaller doses creates a probability of eventual illness or death (hence, lowers life expectancy). As chapter III explained, protection can be obtained when matter is placed between the fallout and people — in general, the more matter (the greater the mass) between a source of radiation and a person, the greater the protection. The degree of protection offered by various materials is described as a protection factor (PF). The adequacy of a given PF depends on the intensity of the fallout. For example, a PF of 20 (typical of a home basement with earth piled over windows and against the walls) would reduce an outdoor radiation level of 60 rem per hour to an indoor level of 3 rem per hour. In this case, a person outdoors for 10 hours would almost certainly be killed by radiation, and a person in the basement shelter would have a good chance of survival. But if the outdoor level is not 60 rems per hour but 600 rems per hour, a PF of 20 is inadequate to save lives.

Calculations of deaths from fallout are made by combining:

- an assumed distribution of fallout, with various intensities at various locations;

---

[5]For example, after the OTA analysis, was completed, a new study was completed showing fatalities from a counterforce attack with the current U.S. civil defense posture to be 8 to 12 million without warning, and 5 to 8 million with warning. See Roger Sullivan et al., "Civil Defense Needs of High-Risk Areas of the United States" (Arlington, Va.: System Planning Corporation, 1979), p. 22.

Figure 16.—Expected Casualties as a Function of Typical Monthly Winds Resulting From an Attack on Selected Military Targets in the United States

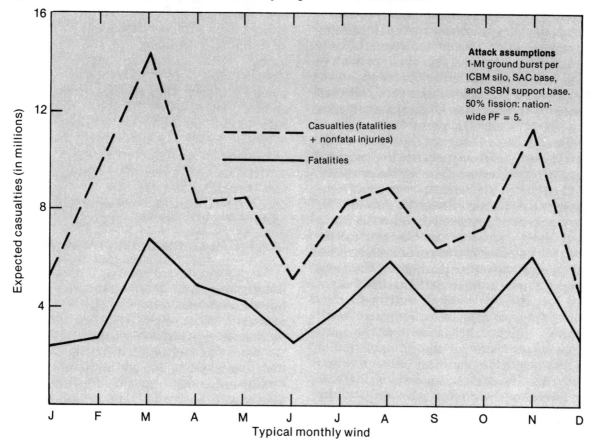

Attack assumptions
1-Mt ground burst per ICBM silo, SAC base, and SSBN support base. 50% fission: nation-wide PF = 5.

- - - Casualties (fatalities + nonfatal injuries)

——— Fatalities

Expected casualties (in millions)

Typical monthly wind

J F M A M J J A S O N D

- an assumed distribution of population within the areas where fallout is assumed to be deposited; and
- an assumed distribution of PFs for the population.

Some computer models use a grid (perhaps 4,000 yards on a side for a fine-grained model, but much larger in other cases) and assume that within each square of the grid the fallout intensity and population density are constant, with PFs mixed. Other calculations use regional or nationwide averages. In general, the calculations show lower numbers of deaths when they assume that the population is widely dispersed, and higher numbers when they take into account concentrations of population. The calculations also show lower numbers of deaths when they assume high PFs; in general, increasing PFs above 40 does not reduce casualties much in the calculations,

but that does not mean that raising a PF above 40 might not save an individual's life in reality. The calculations also show lower numbers of deaths when the winds do not blow fallout into densely populated areas.

The studies mentioned previously made separate calculations for attacks including bomber and missile submarine bases, as well as silos. Assuming that there is no preattack evacuation, calculated deaths range from a low of 2 million to a high of 22 million. The differences result primarily from variations in assumptions regarding fallout protection: the high figure assumes approximately to degree of protection which people receive in their daily peacetime lives (PF of 3), and the low figure assumes that the entire population moves after the attack to fallout shelters with a PF of at least 25. A more reasonable assumption, that the fallout shelters which now exist are utilized by people living near them, produces a calculation of 14 million dead. The same studies also assessed the effects of extensive preattack evacuation (crisis relocation), and found that it reduced the range of predicted deaths. However, the assumptions regarding fallout protection, both for those who are assumed to evacuate and for those who are assumed to remain near home dominate the results. Further detail is in appendix D.

Given the threat U.S. bombers pose to the Soviet Union, a Soviet preemptive counterforce attack on bomber bases would probably seek to destroy the aircraft and supporting facilities rather than cratering the runways. To destroy airborne bombers launched on warning of attack, an attacker might detonate weapons in a spaced pattern over the base. Airbursting weapons rather than ground-bursting them could reduce the threat of fallout but increase casualties from blast and thermal effects; if the weapons were detonated much above the optimum height of burst for maximizing overpressure on the ground, fallout would be negligible and blast damage would be reduced. The attacks against missile submarine bases are much less complex. Ususally a single high-yield weapon with medium-to-good accuracy will destroy docks, piers, cranes, and other facilities—and nearby cities, factories, and people as well.

Accordingly, it is certain that if the only difference between two attacks is that one attacks only ICBM silos and the other attacks bomber and missile submarine bases as well, the latter attack would kill more people. However, the variations in assumptions made about attack design, weather, and fallout protection obscure this. Since these variations reflect genuine uncertainties, it is not possible to determine which set of assumptions and which fatality calculation is most probable. However, some of the extreme assumptions do appear implausible. One Defense Department study notes that its highest fatality figure assumed the use of Soviet weapons larger than those which U.S. intelligence estimates the Soviets possess. Very low fatality estimates assume abnormally low winds, an absence of surface bursts, and /or virtually perfect fallout

protection. On balance, it does not appear possible to sustain greater precision than to say that "studies of hypothetical counterforce attacks show deaths ranging from 1 million to 20 million, depending on the assumptions used." However, the low end of this range (deaths below the 8 to 10 million level) requires quite optimistic assumptions, while the high end of the range is plausible only on the assumption that the attack is not preceded by a crisis period during which civilians are educated about fallout protection.

The data on injuries contained in the executive branch studies are quite limited; for the counterforce attacks, however, the results suggest that injuries would about equal fatalities.

The Contamination Period

For several days or weeks, radioactive contamination would be so intense that people in fallout areas would have to stay in shelters or evacuate. What might be called the "shelter period" begins at each location when fallout starts arriving and ends when people can leave their shelters long enough to do a day's work. The length varies from place to place; many places will receive no fallout, and some hot spots will be hazardous long after surrounding areas are safe. Note, however, that people could go outside for brief periods before an 8-hour day outside a shelter became safe, and could not live in houses with a low protection factor for weeks afterwards. After 2 or 3 months people would ignore the residual radiation, though it would be far higher than is considered "safe" in peacetime.

For the first 10 to 30 days, shelterees would have to remain in shelters almost all the time. Brief excursions outside, for example, to obtain water or food, would substantially reduce the effective protection factor. Life in a shelter would be difficult at best. People would not know if the shelter offered a sufficient PF, or whether further attacks were imminent. The shelter might be dark, as power could be out, and windows would be covered with dirt. Unless the shelter had a good air filtration system, the air would become clammy and smelly, and carbon dioxide concentration would increase. Supplies of food and water might or might not

partly because the United States would have fewer ICBMs available for a second strike, and partly because the Soviets are more likely to take precautionary civil defense measures before a Soviet first strike than before a U.S. first strike. All of these studies consider only fatalities in the 30 days following the attack; they exclude later deaths resulting from relatively less intense radiation or the effects of economic disruption.

For both counterforce and countersilo attacks, with an in-place Soviet population, the fatality estimates are very similar: for the former, from less than 1 to 5 percent of the population; for the latter, from less than 1 to 4 percent. The low end results from using smaller weapons air burst, while the high end results from using larger weapons ground burst. A comprehensive counterforce attack can logically be expected to kill more people than the countersilo attack because the latter is a subset of the former. However, other factors have a greater influnce on numbers of fatalities: A full counterforce attack in which the United States deliberately tried to minimize Soviet fatalities by using small weapons air burst, in which winds were favorable, and in which the Soviets had tactical or strategic warning, would kill far fewer people than a countersilo-only attack in which the United States used one large weapon ground burst against each ICBM silo.

An unpublished Arms Control and Disarmament Agency (ACDA) analysis highlights the importance of sheltering and attack characteristics for fatalities from a U.S. countersilo attack. One estimate is that, with the urban population 90-percent sheltered and the rural population given a PF of 6, Soviet fatalities would range from 3.7 million to 13.5 million, depending on attack parameters. With a degraded shelter posture (urban population 10-percent sheltered and rural population given a PF of 6), fatality estimates for the same set of attacks range from 6.0 million to 27.7 million.

The Shelter Period

If bomber bases (or airfields with long runways that were attacked even though no bombers were present) are attacked, tactical warning could be of great importance to people living nearby. There would be an area near each base (roughly, the area more than 1 mile [2 km] but less than 10 miles [16 km] from a surface burst) in which people who were sheltered at the moment of the blast would have a much greater chance of survival than those who were unsheltered. Soviet civil defense plans envisage that civilians in such high-threat areas would receive some warning, but it cannot be said to what extent this would actually be the case.

Many millions of Soviet citizens live in areas that would receive substantial amounts of fallout from such an attack. Those far enough away from the explosions to be safe from blast damage would have some time (a range from 30 minutes to more than a day) to shelter themselves from fallout, but evacuation from high-fallout areas after the attack would probably not be feasible. The Soviet civil defense program gives attention to blast shelters rather than fallout shelters in urban areas (see chapter III), and while such blast shelters would offer good protection against fallout, some of them may not be habitable for the necessary number of days or weeks for which protection would be required.

The sheltering process would be much more tightly organized than in the United States. The Soviet Government has extensive civil defense plans, and while Americans would expect to try to save themselves under general guidance (informational in character) from the Federal authorities, Soviet citizens would expect the Government to tell them what to do. This introduces a further uncertainty: efficient and timely action by the authorities would be very effective, but it is also possible that Soviet citizens would receive fatal radiation doses while waiting for instructions or following mixed-up instructions. In any event, some hours after the attack would see a situation in which a large number of people in contaminated areas were in fallout shelters, others were receiving dangerous doses of radiation, and those outside the fallout areas were congratulating themselves on their good luck while hoping that no further attacks would take place.

Would Soviet shelterees be better off than their American counterparts? They have several advantages. They are more accustomed to crowding and austerity than are Americans, so would probably suffer less "shelter shock." They would be more accustomed to following Government orders, so to the extent that orders proved correct and were correctly implemented, they would be more evenly distributed among shelters. Training in first aid and civil defense is widespread, which would improve people's ability to survive in shelters. If the U.S. attack used low-yield warheads, fallout would be less widespread and less intense.

Soviet shelterees face some problems that Americans would not. They would be more vulnerable than Americans to an attack in winter. The Soviet economy has less "fat," so other things being equal, Soviet citizens could bring less food and supplies into shelters than could Americans.

Public health is a major uncertainty. To the extent that shelters are well stocked, provided with adequate medications and safe ventilation, have necessary sanitary facilities, are warm and uncrowded, and have some people with first aid knowledge, health would be less of a problem. If Soviet citizens receive less fallout than Americans, they would be less weakened by radiation sickness and more resistant to disease. If conditions were austere but reasonably healthy, public health in shelters would be mainly a matter of isolating ill people and practicing preventive medicine for the others. Doctors would be unnecessary for most such tasks; people trained in first aid, especially if they have some access (by phone or radio) to doctors, could perform most tasks. To be sure, some people would die from being untreated, but the number would be relatively small if preventive care worked. However, isolating the ill would not be easy. It is likely that many people would be moderately ill (from flu, etc.) when they entered their shelter, and radiation would make the others more susceptible to contamination. The Soviet Govern-ment might send medical teams to contaminated areas, especially to shelters containing workers with key skills. The Soviet Army has built tanks and some other military vehicles with protection against fallout, and has trained its soldiers for operations in areas contaminated with fallout. In addition, as in the United States, military helicopters could ferry people and supplies into contaminated areas with limited exposure to crews. Using such resources would obviously improve health of shelterees, but priority military tasks might make these military resources unavailable.

People in hasty shelters, if they could be built, would face worse health problems, despite the legendary ability of Russians to endure hardships. Presumably these shelters would have inadequate supplies, heat, air filtration, sanitary facilities, waterproofing, and so on. Placing people in a cold, damp hole in the ground for 2 weeks with little food and makeshift toilets would make many people sick even in peacetime; how well would such problems be overcome in war?

Soviet civil defense presents a large question mark. Some believe that the Soviets have massive food stockpiles, meticulous plans detailing where each person should go, ample shelter spaces, subways and buildings convertible to shelters, and so on that would be valuable in the shelter period. Others contend that these claims are vastly overstated and confuse speculation about a plan with its existence and the existence of a plan with its operational effectiveness. (See chapter III on civil defense.) If Soviet civil defense works well, it would save many lives; if it doesn't, Soviet shelterees would face conditions at least as hazardous as their American counterparts.

Agricultural losses would, as in the United States, depend on the time of the year when the attack came and on the precise patterns of fallout. In general, Soviet agriculture appears more vulnerable because it borders on inadequacy even in peacetime—even relatively minor damage would hurt, and major crop losses could be catastrophic. On the other hand, for this very reason the Soviets would know how to handle agricultural shortages: surviving production and stockpiles (the extent of Soviet food stockpiles is a matter of controversy, apart from the fact that they are lowest just before each harvest) would probably be used efficiently.

The economy outside the contaminated area would continue to function. There would be more than enough industrial facilities in uncontaminated areas to keep necessary production going. The key task facing Government planners, however, would be using available workers and resources to best advantage. How fast could planners generate new economic plans that were detailed enough for that task? Because the Soviet economy operates closer to the margin than does that of the United States, the Soviets could tolerate less loss of production than could the United States. This would make superproduction the norm, with key factories working all the time. It would lead to suspending production of many consumer goods. It would probably lead the Government to begin decontamination earlier and to take more risks with radiation exposure than would the United States. These actions to increase production would be aided in general by the Government's control of the economy, and in particular by keeping work groups together in shelters and host areas.

Recuperation

As in the United States, economic viability would not be threatened. The key question, which would begin to be answered in the shelter period, is how appropriate Soviet emergency plans are and how rapidly planning mistakes could be corrected. Major shifts, and the inefficiencies that accompany them, would be inevitable. To what extent could planning minimize them? Could a command economy do better under the circumstances than a mixed economy? The Soviet Union's long experience with central planning would mean that the changes would involve details within the existing system rather than changing from one economic system to another.

In the U.S.S.R., as in the United States, the crop loss caused by the attack would depend on season, fallout deposition, which crops were hit by fallout, and so on. Similarly, the amount of food reserves would vary with the season. The immediate goal for agriculture would be to send adequate food supplies to cities. Presumably, the Government would try to meet this goal by tightening controls rather than by giving farmers more capitalistic incentives. For a moderate attack like this one, with little physical damage, controls would probably work.

It is questionable whether adequate labor would be available for agriculture. Depending on the situation, millions of men might be mobilized into the Army. On the other hand the Soviets have well-established procedures for getting military personnel, factory workers, and others to help with harvests; moreover, following a nuclear attack, some workers in nonessential industries would be out of work, and could be sent to farms. The large number of farmers (perhaps 35 to 40 percent of the Soviet work force is in agriculture, compared to 2 or 3 percent in the United States), the fallout contaminating some farmland, and accepting more exposure to radiation would increase the Soviet population's exposure to radiation.

If a year's crop were lost, would there be austerity, short rations, or starvation? How much surplus food is there? In particular, would there be enough to maintain a livestock industry, or would meat be seen as a nonessential consumer good and feed grains diverted for human use?

As in the United States, the attack would create many burdens for the Soviet economy. Military expenditures would probably increase; people injured by the attack would need care, and fewer people would be alive and well to care for them; major changes in the economy would cause inefficiencies; lowered public health standards would increase early production at the expense of later health burdens.

The Soviet Union would not face certain problems that a market economy faces. The legal and financial devices supporting production—money, credit, contracts, and ownership of productive resources—would be far less important than in the United States. Instead, Soviet production would be guided by a central plan. There are reports that contingency planning has been done for postwar recuperation; such contingency plans (or the peacetime plan if there are no applicable contingency plans) would have to be adjusted to take account of the actual availability of surviving workers and economic assets. Without doubt such adjustments would be made, though there would be some waste and inefficiency.

Long-Term Effects

Chapter V discusses the likely long-term health hazards from such an attack.

All things considered, an attack of this nature could be somewhat less damaging than World War II was to the Soviet Union, and Soviet recovery from that conflict was complete. However, it helped that in 1945 the Soviets were victorious and able to draw on resources from Eastern Europe. Much would depend on whether the aftermath of this attack found the Soviet people pleased or appalled at the results of the war and on the relative power and attitudes of the Soviets' neighbors.

CASE 4: A LARGE SOVIET ATTACK ON U.S. MILITARY AND ECONOMIC TARGETS

This case discusses a massive attack that one normally associates with all-out nuclear war. The attack uses thousands of warheads to attack urban-industrial targets, strategic targets, and other military targets. The number of deaths and the damage and destruction inflicted on the U.S. society and economy by the sheer magnitude of such an attack would place in question whether the United States would ever recover its position as an organized, industrial, and powerful country.

OTA favored examining purely retaliatory strikes for both sides, but all of the available executive branch studies involved Soviet preemption and U.S. retaliation. However, the differences between a Soviet first strike and a retaliation do not appear to be appreciably large in terms of damage to the civilian structure. Like the United States, the Soviets have a secure second-strike force in their SLBMs and are assumed to target them generally against the softer urban-industrial targets. Moreover, a U.S. first strike would be unlikely to destroy the bulk of Soviet ICBMs before they could be launched in retaliation.

The effects of a large Soviet attack against the United States would be devastating. The most immediate effects would be the loss of millions of human lives, accompanied by similar incomprehensible levels of injuries, and the physical destruction of a high percentage of U.S. economic and industrial capacity. The full range of effects resulting from several thousand warheads—most having yields of a megaton or greater—impacting on or near U.S. cities can only be discussed in terms of uncertainty and speculation. The executive branch studies that addressed this level of attack report a wide range of fatality levels reflecting various assumptions about the size of the attack, the protective posture of the population, and the proportion of air bursts to ground burst weapons.

The DOD 1977 study estimated that 155 million to 165 million Americans would be killed by this attack if no civil defense measures were taken and all weapons were ground burst. DCPA looked at a similar attack in 1978 where only half the weapons were ground burst; it reduced the fatality estimate to 122 million. ACDA's analysis of a similar case estimated that 105 million to 131 million would die.

If people made use of existing shelters near their homes, the 155 million to 165 million fatality estimate would be reduced to 110 million to 145 million, and the 122 million fatalities to 100 million. The comparable ACDA fatality estimate drops to 76 million to 85 million. Again ACDA gets a lower figure through assuming air bursts for about 60 percent of the incoming weapons. Finally, if urban populations were evacuated from risk areas, the estimated prompt fatality levels would be substantially reduced. The DOD study showed fatalities of 40 million to 55 million, with DCPA showing a very large drop to 20 million from the 100 million level. The primary reason for the 2-to-1 differential is the degree of protection from fallout assumed for the evacuated population.

In summary, U.S. fatality estimates range from a high of 155 million to 165 million to a low of 20 million to 55 million. Fatalities of this magnitude beg the question of injuries to the survivors. None of the analyses attempted to estimate injuries with the same precision used in estimated fatalities. However, DCPA did provide injury estimates ranging from 33 million to 12 million, depending on circumstances. An additional point worth noting is that all of the fatality figures just discussed are for the first 30 days following the attack; they do not account for subsequent deaths among the injured or from economic disruption and deprivation.

The First Few Hours

The devastation caused by a single 1-Mt weapon over Detroit (chapter II), and of two similar weapons denoted near Philadelphia, have been described. In this attack the same destruction would take place in 30 or so other major cities (with populations of a million or greater). Many cities with smaller populations would also be destroyed. The effects on U.S. society would be catastrophic.

The majority of urban deaths will be blast induced, e.g., victims of collapsing buildings, flying debris, being blown into objects, etc. Except for administering to the injured, the next most pressing thing (probably ahead of han-

dling the dead) for most survivors would be to get reliable information about what has occurred, what is taking place, and what is expected. Experience has shown that in a disaster situation, timely and relevant information is critical to avoiding panic, helpful in organizing and directing productive recovery efforts, and therapeutic to the overall psychological and physical well being of those involved. Presumably, the civil preparedness functions would be operating well enough to meet some of this need.

Rescuing and treating the injured will have to be done against near insurmountable odds. Fire and rescue vehicles and equipment not destroyed will find it impossible to move about in any direction. Fires will be raging, water mains will be flooding, powerlines will be down, bridges will be gone, freeway overpasses will be collapsed, and debris will be everywhere. People will be buried under heavy debris and structures, and without proper equipment capable of lifting such loads, the injured cannot be reached and will not survive. The fortunate ones that rescuers can reach will then be faced with the unavailability of treatment facilities. Hospitals and clinics in downtown areas would likely have been destroyed along with most of their stocks of medical supplies. Doctors, nurses, and technicians needed to man makeshift treatment centers are likely to have been among the casualties. The entire area of holocaust will be further numbed by either the real or imagined danger of fallout. People will not know whether they should try to evacuate their damaged city, or attempt to seek shelter from fallout in local areas and hope there will be no new attacks. No doubt some of both would be done.

If this situation were an isolated incident or even part of a small number of destroyed cities in an otherwise healthy United States, outside help would certainly be available. But if 250 U.S. cities are struck and damaged to similar levels, then one must ask, "Who is able to help?" Smaller towns are limited in the amount of assistance they can provide their metropolitan neighbors. It is doubtful that there would be a strong urge to buck the tide of evacuation in order to reach a place where most of the natives are trying to leave. Additionally, the smaller cities and towns would have their own preparedness problems of coping with the anticipated arrival of fallout plus the influx of refugees. In light of these and other considerations, it appears that in an attack of this magnitude, there is likely not to be substantial outside assistance for the targeted areas until prospective helpers are convinced of two things: the attack is over, and fallout intensity has reached safe levels. Neither of these conditions is likely to be met in the first few hours.

The First Few Days

Survivors will continue to be faced with the decision whether to evacuate or seek shelter in place during this interval. The competence and credibility of authority will be under continuous question. Will survivors be told the facts, or what is best for them to know, and who decides? Deaths will have climbed due to untreated injuries, sickness, shock, and poor judgement. Many people will decide to attempt evacuation simply to escape the reality of the environment. For those staying, it likely means the beginning of an extended period of shelter survival. Ideally, shelters must protect from radiation while meeting the minimums of comfort, subsistence, and personal hygiene. Convincing people to remain in shelters until radiation levels are safely low will be difficult, but probably no more so than convincing them that it is safe to leave on the basis of a radiation-rate meter reading. There will be unanswerable questions on long-term effects.

Sheltering the survivors in the populous Boston to Norfolk corridor will present unprecedented problems. Almost one-fifth of the U.S. population lives in this small, 150- by 550-mile [250 by 900 km] area. Aside from the threat of destruction from direct attack, these populations are in the path of fallout from attacks on missile silos and many industrial targets in the Pittsburgh, St. Louis, and Duluth triangle. Depending on the winds at altitude, the fallout from the Midwest will begin arriving 12 to 30 hours after the attack.

At the time when fallout radiation first becomes intense, only a fraction of the surviving urban population will be in adequate fallout shelters. Those that are sheltered will face a variety of problems: making do with existing stocks of food, water, and other necessities or else minimizing exposure while leaving the shelter for supplies; dealing with problems of sanitation, which will not only create health hazards but also exacerbate the social tensions of crowds of frightened people in a small space; dealing with additional people wanting to enter the shelter, who would not only want to share scarce supplies but might bring contamination in with them; dealing with disease, which would be exacerbated not only by the effects of radiation but by psychosomatic factors; and finally judging when it is safe to venture out. Boredom will gradually replace panic, but will be no easier to cope with. Those with inadequate shelters or no shelters at all will die in large numbers, either from lethal doses of radiation or from the combination of other hazards with weakness induced by radiation sickness.

The conditions cited above are generally more applicable to urbanites who are trying to survive. The problems of rural survivors are somewhat different, some being simpler—others more complex. With warning, people living in rural areas could readily fabricate adequate fallout shelters. However, it might be more difficult for a rural shelteree to have current and accurate information regarding fallout intensity and location. The farm family is likely not to have suffered the traumatic exposure to death and destruction, and consequently is probably better prepared psychologically to spend the required time in a shelter. (Possible consequences to livestock and crops are addressed later in this section.)

Outdoor activity in or near major cities that were struck would likely be limited to emergency crews attempting to control fires or continuing to rescue the injured. Crews would wear protective clothing but it would be necessary to severely limit the total work hours of any one crew member, so as not to risk dangerous accumulations of radiation. Areas not threatened by fallout could begin more deliberate fire control and rescue operations. Whether a national facility would survive to identify weapons impact points and predict fallout patterns is doubtful.

The extent of death and destruction to the Nation would still be unknown. For the most part, the agencies responsible for assembling such information would not be functioning. This task would have to wait until the numbing effect of the attack had worn off, and the Government could once again begin to function, however precariously.

The Shelter Period (Up to a Month)

As noted earlier, after the initial shock period, including locating and getting settled in shelters, the problem of sheltering large masses of people will be compounded as the shelter time extends. Survival will remain the key concern. People will experience or witness radiation death and sickness for the first time. Many previously untreated injuries will require medical attention, if permanent damage or death to the individual is to be avoided. Stockpiles of medical, food, and water supplies are sure to become items of utmost concern. Whether some people can safely venture outside the shelter for short periods to forage for uncontaminated supplies will depend on fallout intensity, and the availability of reliable means of measuring it.

This period will continue to be marked by more inactivity than activity. Many areas will have been freed from the fallout threat either by rain, shifting winds, or distance from the detonations. But economic activity will not resume immediately. Workers will remain concerned about their immediate families and may not want to risk leaving them. Information and instruction may not be forthcoming, and if it is, it may be confusing and misleading, and of little use. Uncertainty and frustration will plague the survivors, and even the most minor tasks will require efforts far out of proportion to their difficulty. Many will interpret this as symptomatic of radiation effects and become further confused and depressed. The

overall psychological effects will likely worsen until they become a major national concern, perhaps on the same level with other incapacitating injuries.

Deaths occurring within the first 30 days of an attack are categorized as prompt fatalities. This duration is a computation standard more than it is related to specific death-producing effects, and is the basis for most fatality estimates. However, deaths from burns, injuries, and radiation sickness can be expected to continue far beyond this particular interval.

The Recuperation Period

Whether economic recovery would take place, and if so what form it would take, would depend both on the physical survival of enough people and resources to sustain recovery, and on the question of whether these survivors could adequately organize themselves.

Physical survival of some people is quite probable, and even a population of a few million can sustain a reasonably modern economy under favorable circumstances. The survivors would not be a cross-section of prewar America, since people who had lived in rural areas would be more likely to survive than the inhabitants of cities and suburbs. The surviving population would lack some key industrial and technical skills; on the other hand, rural people and those urban people who would survive are generally hardier than the American average.

While the absolute level of surviving stocks of materials and products would seem low by prewar standards, there would be a much smaller population to use these stocks. Apart from medicines (which tend to have a short shelf life and which are manufactured exclusively in urban areas), there would probably not be any essential commodity of which supplies were desperately short at first. A lack of medicines would accentuate the smallness and hardiness of the surviving population.

Restoring production would be a much more difficult task than finding interim stockpiles. Production in the United States is extremely complex, involving many intermediate stages.

Photo credit: U.S. Air Force

A part of Hiroshima after atomic blast

New patterns of production, which did not rely on facilities that have been destroyed, would have to be established.

It cannot be said whether the productive facilities that physically survived (undamaged or repairable with available supplies and skills) would be adequate to sustain recovery. It seems probable that there would be enough equipment and that scavenging among the ruins could provide adequate "raw materials" where natural resources were no longer accessible with surviving technology.

The most serious problems would be organizational. Industrial society depends on the division of labor, and the division of labor depends on certain governmental functions.

Physical security comes first—a person is reluctant to leave home to go to work without some assurance that the home will not be looted. While some degree of law and order could probably be maintained in localities where a fairly dense population survived, the remaining highways might become quite unsafe, which would reduce trade over substantial distances. The second requirement is some form of payment for work. Barter is notoriously inefficient. Payment by fiat (for example, those who work get Government ration cards) is inefficient as well, and requires a Government stronger than a postwar United States would be likely to inherit. A strong Government might grow up, but most surviving citizens would be reluctant to support a dictatorship by whatever name. The best solution is a viable monetary system, but it would not be easy to establish. Regions or localities might develop their own monies, with "foreign" trade among regions.

The surviving resources might not be used very efficiently. Ideally one would want to conduct a national survey of surviving assets, but the surviving Government would probably not be capable of doing so, especially since people would fear that to acknowlege a surviving stock was to invite its confiscation. To make use of surviving factories, workers would have to live nearby, and they might be unwilling to do so in the absence of minimally adequate housing for their families. Ownership of some assets would be hopelessly confused, which would diminish the incentives for investment or even temporary repairs.

There is a possibility that the country might break up into several regional entities. If these came into conflict with each other there would be further waste and destruction.

In effect, the country would enter a race, with economic viability as the prize. The country would try to restore production to the point where consumption of stocks and the wearing out of surviving goods and tools was matched by new production. If this was achieved before stocks ran out, then viability would be attained. Otherwise, consumption would necessarily sink to the level of new production and in so doing would probably depress production further, creating a downward spiral. At some point this spiral would stop, but by the time it did so the United States might have returned to the economic equivalent of the Middle Ages.

The effect of an all-out attack would be equally devastating to the U.S. social structure. Heavy fatalities in the major urban areas would deprive the country of a high percentage of its top business executives, Government officials, medical specialists, scientists, educators, and performers. There is no measure for estimating the impact of such lasting losses on our society. In addition to the irreplaceable loss of genius and talents, the

destruction of their associated institutions is still another compounding of effects that is overlooked by some recovery estimates. Who could calculate how long to get over the loss of Wall Street, an MIT, a Mayo Clinic, and the Smithsonian?

The American way of life is characterized by material possessions, with private ownership of items representing substantial long-term investments (such as homes, businesses, and automobiles) being the rule rather than exception. Widespread loss of individual assets such as these could have a strong, lasting effect on our social structure. Similarly, the question of whether individual right to ownership of surviving assets would remain unchanged in a postattack environment would arise. For example, the Government might find it necessary to force persons having homes to house families who had lost their homes.

The family group would be particularly hard hit by the effects of general nuclear war. Deaths, severe injuries, forced separation, and loss of contact could place inordinate strains on the family structure.

Finally, major changes should be anticipated in the societal structure, as survivors attempt to adapt to a severe and desponding environment never before experienced. The loss of a hundred million people, mostly in the larger cities, could raise a question on the advisability of rebuilding the cities. (Why reconstruct obvious targets for a nuclear Armageddon of the future?) The surviving population could seek to alter the social and geopolitical structure of the rebuilding nation in hopes of minimizing the effects of any future conflicts.

How well the U.S. political structure might recover from a large-scale nuclear attack depends on a number of uncertainties. First, with warning, national level officials are presumed to evacuate to outlying shelter areas; State and local authorities will take similar precautions, but probably with less success, especially at the lower levels. The confidence and credibility of the system will come under severe strains as relief and recovery programs are implemented. Changes in an already weakened structure are sure to result as many normal practices and routines are set aside to facilitate recovery. Survivors may demand more immediate expressions of their likes, dislikes, and needs. Widespread dissatisfaction could result in a weakening of the Federal process, leading to a new emphasis on local government. An alternative possibility is martial law, which might be controlled in theory but decentralized in practice.

All of this assumes that there would be no significant ecological damage, a possibility discussed in chapter V. Chapter V also discusses long-term health hazards.

CASE 4: A LARGE U.S. ATTACK ON SOVIET MILITARY AND ECONOMIC TARGETS

A U.S. retaliatory attack against the Soviet Union would destroy 70 to 80 percent of its economic worth. The attacking force would consist primarily of U.S. strategic bombers and Poseidon/Polaris SLBMs, since most U.S. land-based ICBMs are assumed lost to a Soviet first strike. Bombers carry gravity bombs and short-range attack missiles having yields of about 1 Mt and 200 kt respectively. Poseidon SLBMs nominally carry up to 10 RVs of 40 kt each.

The attack would strike the full set of Soviet targets—strategic offensive forces, other military targets, economic targets, and cities. Population would in fact be struck, although killing people would not be an attack objective in itself. The objectives would be to cause as much industrial damage as possible and to make economic recovery as difficult as possible. The attacks might not be limited in time. Concentrations of evacuees would probably not be struck, but industries that recovered very quickly after the attack could be.

The immediate effects of the attack would be death and injury to millions of Soviet citizens, plus the destruction of a large percentage of Soviet economic and industrial capacity. As with the all-out Soviet attack, the executive branch studies provided a wide range of casualty estimates. Since the thrust of those analyses was to look at the potential effectiveness of Soviet civil defense, casualties were estimated under various assumptions related to the posture of the population.

If the Soviet population remained in-place, fatality estimates range from a high of 64 million to 100 million (26 to 40 percent of the Soviet population) to a low of 50 million to 80 million (20 to 32 percent). The high-value range is due to the different data bases used by DOD and ACDA and the higher protection levels assumed by ACDA. The low-value range results from the use of day-to-day alert status by the interagency intelligence study as compared to ACDA's use of generated forces, and the types of weapons used against the economic target base in the two studies. With evacuation, the ACDA study estimated that fatalities would be reduced to 23 million to 34 million. It is difficult to judge whether these figures represent a high or low estimate. They could be considered as representing the low side because of the coarseness of Soviet data as used by ACDA. On the other hand, some would say that the evacuation scheme assumed by ACDA was unrealistic, and the results should be considered a high estimate. Nevertheless, Soviet fatalities are lower than the United States for both in-place and evacuated population postures. The lower Soviet fatalities are again primarily due to major differences in the yields of the weapons detonating in each country, and to the greater proportion of Soviet population that lives in rural areas.

As to the cause of fatalities (blast, thermal radiation, and direct nuclear radiation versus fallout radiation), DCPA data suggests that, in large attacks, that is, attacks that include economic or economic and population targets, fatalities are primarily due to prompt effects as opposed to fallout. Prompt effects account for at least 80 percent of the fatalities for all population postures when economic targets or population are included in the attack. ACDA notes a similar result in its study for attacks that include counterforce and other military targets. The reason for this is that in attacks on targets near urban areas, that is, attacks involving economic targets or population, those protected enough to survive the blast effects also have enough protection to survive the fallout. Conversely, those who do not have enough protection against fallout in urban areas near targets will not have enough protection against prompt effects and will already be dead before fallout has an effect.

Estimates of Soviet injuries were generally not included in the analyses. However, one study suggested that injuries might be roughly equal to fatalities under certain attack and exposure assumptions.

The First Few Hours

As chapter III notes, Soviet civil defense can have substantial impact on the full range of effects. Fallout shelters, blast shelters, and industrial hardening can reduce the overall damage from nuclear attack. First aid and civil defense training can ameliorate health problems. Storing supplies in shelters lengthens shelter stay time. Thus, the issue is how well Soviet civil defense would in fact work. Many unknowns—numbers of shelters, amount of food and medicine stockpiles, smaller amounts of surplus resources than the United States—prevent a judgment in detail. It seems safe to assume, however, that Soviet civil defense measures would be at least as effective as U.S. measures and probably better.

Preattack preparations would have a decided influence on damage caused. Since a U.S. retaliatory attack is by definition preceded by a Soviet first strike, it would seem logical that some evacuation would have occurred. However, there are reasons why evacuation might not have taken place. These include the following Soviet concerns: an evacuation could increase the risk of a U.S. attack; the U.S. attack might be so close at hand that an evacuation could increase casualties; a prolonged evacuation might be such an economic disruption that it would be better to wait until

war appeared certain; or war through miscalculation. In any event, a Soviet decision to strike first would allow the Soviets to make preparations—distribute supplies, improve and stock shelters, increase production of essential goods, harvest grain, protect livestock, conduct civil defense training, harden industrial facilities, and so on. These actions would also make Soviet citizens more responsive to civil defense instructions, especially to a warning that an attack was underway. While these actions would be observed by the United States, they would be more ambiguous than an evacuation, so the United States could see them as safeguarding against an attack rather than preparing for one.

The effects of evacuation in reducing casualties could be diluted to some extent by varying U.S. attack strategy. Spreading the attack over a period of time could extend shelter periods, enhance economic disruption, and delay rescue and emergency operations.

The Soviet Union, despite its vast geographical size, is vulnerable to an urban/industrial attack in many of the same ways as the United States. Although there has been extensive publicity on their reported dispersal of industry, indications are that population and industry are becoming more and more concentrated. While some industries may have been moved away from cities, many others have been built near cities. Indeed, some of the industries recently built away from cities are themselves so concentrated that they form new targets of their own. Hedrick Smith describes

> . . . the Kama River Truck Plant as an archetype of the gigantomania of Soviet planners, as a symbol of the Soviet faith that bigger means better and the Soviet determination to have the biggest at any cost.
>
> Kama is the kind of massive crash project that appeals to Russians. . . . It emanates brute strength. In 1971, Soviet construction brigades started from scratch to build the world's largest truck plant in the open, rolling, windswept plains about 600 miles east of Moscow. . . . Kama was not just one factory but six, all huge . . . The production complex, costing in the billions, occupies 23 square miles, an area larger than the entire island of Manhat-

tan. At full capacity, Kama is slated to produce 150,000 heavy trucks and 250,000 diesel engines a year, dwarfing anything in Detroit or the German Ruhr.[6]

The attack could cause "derussification." The U.S.S.R. is a nation of nationalities, of which Great Russians—who dominate politics, industry, and much else—comprise about 48.5 percent of the population. Most Great Russians live in cities, so an attack would reduce their numbers and influence. Derussification could weaken Great Russians' control of the U.S.S.R., with unforeseeable consequences.

Timing makes a critical difference in destruction. An attack at night would have people with their families and more dispersed; they would seek shelter in apartment buildings. An attack during the day would strike people at factories and offices; to the extent they left to find family members, chaos would result as in the United States, but to the extent they sought shelter at work, they would be organized by economic task. Such organization would be useful for postattack recovery.

An attack in winter would expose more people to bitter cold and impede evacuation; an attack in spring or fall, when many roads are made impassable by mud, would hinder evacuation by motor vehicle. An attack near harvest time could result in the loss of an entire year's crop, thus leaving food reserves at a low point. This effect could be magnified if the United States attacked agricultural targets, such as storage silos, dams, and drainage facilities.

Even time of month makes a difference because of the Soviet practice of "storming." The Soviet factory month in practice divides into three periods: "sleeping," the first 10 days; "hot" work, the second 10; and "feverish" work, the third. This division occurs because the economic plan calls for a specified output from each plant by the end of the month, but the inputs needed often arrive only after the 15th or 20th of the month. Thus, perhaps 80

percent of a factory's output is produced in the last 10 or 15 days of the month. (This 80 percent is typically of such reduced quality that Soviet consumers often refuse to buy merchandise made after the 20th of a month.) Hypothetically, an attack around the 15th or 20th of a month would cause the loss of most of a month's production, and would destroy the large inventory in factories of partially completed goods and of inputs that cannot be used until other inputs arrive.

On the other hand, the U.S.S.R. has several strengths. Cities are in general less flammable than U.S. cities, as there are more large apartment buildings and fewer wood frame houses. These buildings would also provide better shelter, especially those that have shelters built in. People would expect to follow instructions and would be less likely to evacuate spontaneously. The Party apparatus would probably survive with a far lower casualty rate than the population at large because it is well distributed and because blast shelters have been constructed for party members. Russians are likely to be less traumatized by shelter conditions, as they are more accustomed to austerity and crowding. The nation is larger, which in theory provides more land area over which people could relocate, but much of the area is mountain, desert, or arctic.

The First Few Days

Actions in this period would greatly affect the number of casualties and the amount of economic damage. Obviously, much damage would have been caused in the first hour. Many people trapped in the rubble could be rescued, would be seriously injured but could survive with medical care or first aid, would be able to seek shelter or evacuate, could prepare hasty fallout shelters, could improve existing shelters, and so on. Some industries would be damaged but not destroyed; if small fires were extinguished, undamaged equipment hardened against blast, exposed equipment protected from rust, and so on, more resources would be available for recovery. Likewise, farms could harvest crops, shelter livestock,

---

[6]Hedrick Smith, *The Russians* (New York: Ballantine Books, 1977), p. 241.

and protect harvested crops in the few days before fallout deposition.

The issue is not what could be done but what would be done. Proper use of time—organization and prioritization to get the most important tasks done with the least wasted effort and resources—would be critical. The Soviet system offers a major advantage in this period. As we noted in the case of a counterforce attack, the Government's role in this crisis would be more clearly defined, and its control over individual action and the economy would be much stronger than that of the U.S. Government in a comparable situation. Its experience with central planning and a command economy would be good preparation for the actions needed—decisions involving large shifts in behavior and resources, obeyed without argument. Its decisions would save some people and industries and condemn others, but delay in order to make better decisions could easily condemn more. Evacuation would have to be ordered in this period, or else would-be evacuees would have to wait until radiation had reached safe levels. For cities damaged only slightly, evacuation would prove difficult but not impossible. With many rail yards and some key bridges out, it would be difficult to get trains to smaller cities. Destruction of petroleum refineries, some petroleum storage capacity (especially that located in rail marshalling yards that were attacked), and some electric power generators, would further impede evacuation by train. Fallout contours would be difficult to predict, so it would be hard to select the best evacuation routes and relocation centers. An attack in winter would add other problems.

Survivors in Soviet cities would face the same severe problems as those in U.S. cities. Many would be injured, trapped in rubble, irradiated with initial nuclear radiation, etc. Many shelters would be destroyed or damaged. Power would be out, so water pressure would be too low for fighting fires. Rubble would impede rescue.

Undamaged areas, especially those not threatened by heavy fallout, would face severe burdens. They would receive many evacuees in the first few days, would send rescue teams and resources to devastated areas, and would strive to produce as much as possible. Evacuees in undamaged areas would be pressed into work in fields and factories, and would be sheltered in public buildings or private homes. The performance of undamaged areas would thus largely determine the nation's ability to prosecute the war and to achieve economic viability. The Government would, however, face a dilemma in how to use resources surviving in undamaged areas: it could maximize current production, leaving workers and resources vulnerable to further attacks, or it could seek to protect workers and resources, thus reducing current production. The specific choices would depend on the likelihood of further attacks, criticality of various products, and so forth, but the dilemma would stand.

An all-out attack would exacerbate the inefficiencies that Soviet industry has in peacetime. The Government would have to decide what it needed to have produced, and whether the factories existed to have them produced. The Government would have far more difficulty correlating inputs and outputs and arranging for their transportation. It would have to assign people to jobs, and arrange to transport, shelter, and care for workers. Many workers would be sick, in shelters, killed, traumatized, or debilitated by radiation sickness. However, the Government would probably be able to control what movement of people did take place. Even in peacetime, the Government has very high control over mobility. People are not in the habit of going anywhere without permission, and everyone's actions must be justified and accounted for. There is little independent travel. The internal passport system strengthens these controls. In wartime, the Government would presumably strengthen its control of transportation. People would have nowhere to go where they could be sure of shelter from fallout unless the Government arranged their transportation and shelter. This control would help the Government maintain economic organization following attack.

The Shelter Period

By all reports, the Soviets are better prepared than Americans to spend extended periods of time in shelters. In their literature well-conceived protective structures are seen that should afford good survivability. Life in shelters and evacuation areas would in some ways be similar to that described in earlier cases. Actions taken before fallout deposition would affect casualties. Public health, number and quality of shelters, and amount of food and medicine stockpiled are uncertainties. Civil defense and first aid training would mitigate deaths, but to an unpredictable extent. People in uncontaminated areas would be best off, followed by those in fallout shelters in contaminated areas, those in secure fallout shelters in blast areas, and those in hasty shelters in contaminated areas.

One public health problem would be especially acute in this case. Antibiotics, which are invaluable in fighting many diseases, are in short supply in the U.S.S.R. even in peacetime. Antibiotics have a short shelf life and cannot be frozen. Large doses of radiation destroy most of the body's antibodies, which fight diseases. Antibiotics are typically used to compensate for the drastic decrease in antibodies in radiation victims, as it takes the body a long time to rebuild its antibodies after large radiation doses. Because of the U.S.S.R.'s limited supply of antibiotics, many people could be expected to die from diseases.

In areas contaminated by fallout but undamaged by blast, shelter life would be less intolerable. Utilities might be working, buildings would be undamaged so would offer better shelter, people would be uninjured, there would be time to prepare and provision shelters, there would be less inclination to evacuate, and there would be less pressure to leave shelters prematurely.

Fallout deposition patterns would become clear in this period, and would largely deter-

mine the damage to agriculture and which industries would need to remain closed. Harvesting crops uncontaminated by fallout would be impeded by fuel shortages, but evacuees would be plentiful and could harvest crops by hand. Similarly, evacuees could work in surviving industries in uncontaminated areas.

The key issue that the Government would face would be successful organization. Production would be far below prewar levels. It would take some time before the Government could take inventory, set priorities, arrange for inputs of workers, resources, and power, and transport the outputs. Most needs in this period would be met from inventory. The Government would thus need to establish strict controls over inventory; it could be necessary to implement severe rationing of food, as was done in Leningrad in World War II.

Problems of organization would be especially critical in light of the intense struggle for resources and the need to use resources as widely as possible. The competition for petroleum, discussed previously in Case 2, would be minimal compared to the competition here. The military, agriculture, industry, transportation, and life support systems would all have urgent claims on resources. Everything would be in short supply; there would be hundreds of bottlenecks instead of one. How would the Government mediate among these claims? There would be far less margin for error than in peacetime, and a decision to use resources for one purpose would almost automatically preclude other courses of action. Viability would be at issue, and deaths would increase because of delays in achieving it.

What sacrifices would the Government demand? Obviously, each critical sector would be called on to make some, and consumer goods would probably be sacrificed completely. Public health would be sacrificed to some extent by starting production in contaminated areas early and by giving people contaminated food rather than nothing.

The Government would probably be able to maintain control. Food rationing, control of transportation and shelters, and internal passports would help the Government restart the economy. Its economic plans would be the only alternative to chaos, and people would expect to obey them and their demands even without controls. Many party members would survive. Contenders for resources would struggle inside the Government, but external threats, the specter of chaos, the urgency of decisions, and the recognized impossibility of getting everything needed would dampen the debate. All sectors would make sacrifices. The military, for example, might be forced to forego fuel-intensive training. In agriculture and industry, manual labor—which would be plentiful—would substitute for machinery. People would use wood for fuel where possible; many would go cold. Coal-burning locomotives would likely be taken from storage. Decisions would be taken quickly and set rigidly. Productivity would decrease before it increased. The standard of living would be far lower, and some would die in this period and the next as a result. The question is—how many?

Recuperation

Production—and with it, standard of living and the number of people production could support—would go down before it went up. Industries would use inventories of supplies for production, then would have to close until supply could be reestablished. Transportation would wind down as petroleum refining was cut off, and petroleum supplies became exhausted or requisitioned by the military. People would be diverted from production by being sick or injured, caring for the sick or injured, or being drafted for military service. What production took place would be far less efficient. Many workers would be debilitated by minor cases of radiation sickness, other illness, malnutrition, psychological shock, and so on. Many would be called on to do tasks for which they lacked the training or the physical strength. Factories would be damaged or could not obtain necessary parts, so industrial processes would have to substitute labor for capital or use shortcuts that would reduce the quality of the product or the efficiency of the process.

If things went well, production would stabilize at a level that made good use of surviving resources, and would recover from there. The Government would increase its control over people and the economy, production of consumer goods would be delayed, many resources would flow to the military, public health would be lower, but sacrifices would pay off. Soviet engineers and plant managers reputedly are skillful at improvising solutions to mechanical problems. Such skills, Government organization and control, and brute force could overcome bottlenecks, use production to expand capacity, and give people austere but adequate food, housing, medical care, and other necessities.

The recovery could go poorly, however. A great many people could require medical care that could not be provided, and would die. The harvest could be lost, and more would die. Starving people would find and eat grain to be planted next year, reducing that crop and causing others to starve. Transportation could collapse, preventing factories from obtaining inputs and making it impossible for their products to be distributed, forcing them to close. Hardening might save key machine tools, but these tools might be buried under tons of rubble or be in intensely radioactive areas, precluding their use. The Government might be unable to conduct a detailed resource inventory that could integrate these tools into the economy, or there might be no way of transporting them to a factory that could use them. A war or threat of war, from NATO, China, or both, might divert surviving industry and materials into producing for the war effort and away from the economy. Which way the economy would go is unpredictable, for there are far too many unknowns. But should economic productivity fall precipitously, for whatever reason, the economy could support fewer people, and more would die. Indeed a failure to achieve viability could cause as many Soviet deaths as the attack itself.

In summary, the effects of a large-scale nuclear attack against Soviet military and urban-industrial targets would remove that nation from a position of power and influence for the remainder of this century. Soviet fatalities, due to asymmetries in weapons yields and population densities, would be lower than those for the United States. However, there is no evidence that the Soviet economy and its supporting industry would be less severely damaged than their U.S. counterparts. Nor is there any evidence that the Soviets face a lower risk of finding themselves unable to rebuild an industrial society at all.

Chapter V
OTHER LONG-TERM EFFECTS

Chapter V.—OTHER LONG-TERM EFFECTS

TABLES

- Therefore, it is not possible to estimate the probability or the probable magnitude of such damage.

With the exception of the discussion of possible damage to the ozone layer, where there has been some advance in knowledge since 1975, these conclusions still hold in 1979.

Moreover, there are at least two other respects in which there are hazards whose magnitude cannot be calculated. It is certain that the radiation derived from a nuclear war would cause mutations in surviving plants and animals; it is possible that some of these muta-

tions might change the ecosystem in unpredictable ways, but this seems unlikely. Furthermore, the possibility cannot be excluded of major changes in human behavior as a result of the unprecedented trauma. Science fiction writers have speculated, for example, that in the aftermath of a nuclear war, the survivors would place the blame on "science" or on "scientists," and through a combination of lynching and book-burning eliminate scientific knowledge altogether. There are cases in history (or rather archeology) of high civilizations that simply stopped functioning (though people survived biologically) after some shattering experience.

FINDINGS

The calculations for long-term radiation hazards, with all their uncertainties, permit an order-of-magnitude conclusion:

- There would be a substantial number of deaths and illness due to radiation among those who were lucky enough to escape a lethal dose during the first weeks after the attack.

- The number of deaths would be very large by peacetime standards, and the hazards

much greater than what is considered tolerable today.
- The number of deaths would be rather small compared to the number of deaths resulting from the immediate effects of the attack—millions compared to tens or hundreds of millions.

In contrast, the incalculable effects of damage to the Earth's ecological system might be on the same order of magnitude as the immediate effects, but it is not known how to calculate or even estimate their likelihood.

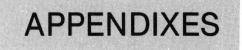

APPENDIXES

APPENDIX A—LETTER OF REQUEST

JOHN SPARKMAN, ALA., CHAIRMAN

FRANK CHURCH, IDAHO
CLAIBORNE PELL, R.I.
GEORGE MC GOVERN, S. DAK.
DICK CLARK, IOWA
JOSEPH R. BIDEN, JR., DEL.
JOHN GLENN, OHIO
RICHARD (DICK) STONE, FLA.
PAUL S. SARBANES, MD.
MURIEL HUMPHREY, MINN.

CLIFFORD P. CASE, N.J.
JACOB K. JAVITS, N.Y.
JAMES B. PEARSON, KANS.
CHARLES H. PERCY, ILL.
ROBERT P. GRIFFIN, MICH.
HOWARD H. BAKER, JR., TENN.

NORVILL JONES, CHIEF OF STAFF
ABNER E. KENDRICK, CHIEF CLERK

United States Senate

COMMITTEE ON FOREIGN RELATIONS

WASHINGTON, D.C. 20510

September 8, 1978

The Honorable Edward M. Kennedy
Chairman, Technology Assessment Board
Office of Technology Assessment
United States Congress
Washington, D.C. 20510

Dear Mr. Chairman:

Several years ago, a study conducted under the auspices of the Office of Technology Assessment at the request of the Committee on Foreign Relations provided guidance which led to substantially improved analyses by the Department of Defense of the effects of limited nuclear war.

The resulting study was released by the Committee and has become an invaluable aid in the study of nuclear conflict. However, the OTA panel, under the chairmanship of Dr. Jerome M. Wiesner, President of the Massachusetts Institute of Technology, which was convened to oversee the study, went on to point out the need for a more thorough and comprehensive study of the effects of nuclear warfare and recommended that such a study be undertaken.

On behalf of the Committee on Foreign Relations, we are writing to request that the Office of Technology Assessment organize and conduct such a study on the effects of nuclear warfare, which would put what have been abstract measures of strategic power into more comprehensible terms. The study should concentrate on the impact which various levels of attack would have on the populations and economies of the United States and the Soviet Union. In the case of larger levels of attack, the study should address impact upon other nations. The earlier Department of Defense analyses concentrated upon short-term effects. In this more comprehensive study, intermediate and long-term, direct and indirect effects should be addressed as well. In the original study, the panel cited in its appendix a list of effects which should be detailed in a comprehensive and systematic way.   The list is attached.

-2-

We believe that this study would be valuable to the Committee, and to the Congress and the general public. It would become a basic reference work in this area of inquiry. We hope that the Office of Technology Assessment will be able to embark upon this project promptly, so that a finished product can be provided the Committee at the outset of the new Congress to assist the Committee in its oversight of strategic arms limitation issues. The earlier effort was conducted with the full support of the executive branch. We stand ready again to seek the assistance of appropriate government agencies in carrying out the necessary supporting work.

Sincerely,

Clifford P. Case
Ranking Member

John Sparkman
Chairman

Attachment

1975 OTA Panel's List of Damage Effects Requiring Examination

1. Damage effects should be detailed in a comprehensive and systematic way. At a minimum, each case examined should include the following information:

    a. Fatalities and injuries resulting from:
    -Direct and indirect blast effects;
    -Indirect effects resulting from fires, disruption of transportation, communications, medical facilities, etc.;
    -Acute radiation deaths from fallout;
    -Cancers, genetic defects, life shortening and other direct effects of radiation exposure resulting from: external exposure, inhalation of radioactive particles, ingestion of material from the food chain or the water supplies;
    -Infections and diseases aggravated by the loss of resistance resulting from exposure to radiation.
    Analysis of exposure should include both people exposed initially and people who have been sent to the area to assist in recovery. There should also be a discussion of world-wide effects with particular attention paid to Canada because of that nation's proximity to many U.S. targets which may be of strategic interest.

    b. The average integrated REM per survivor from all sources (prompt and fallout) should be indicated along with the geographic distribution of these dosages and a discussion of the disabilities resulting from each exposure level.

    c. A detailed analysis should be made of the impact of the attacks on the local areas most heavily affected. The discussion should include a discussion of the feasibility of restoring the area to a viable economy, the land lost to agriculture, manufacturing assets lost, skilled manpower lost, and the impact on local ecologies (permanent altering of watersheds, pollution of streams and rivers with radioactivity, bursting of dams, etc.). The effect of these local losses and problems on the national economy and environment should also be indicated.

    d. An attempt should be made to indicate the magnitude of the effort which would be required to clean up the contaminated area and restore it to its pre-attack condition. It should be possible to draw on the experience which we have had in attempting to restore the Bikini and Eniwetok atolls.

2. An attempt should be made to determine the amount of radioactive material which would be released by U.S. sites damaged by the effects of the enemy attack. Such material might be found in power or research reactors, nuclear material reprocessing facilities, waste disposal areas for radioactive materials, military installations where some nuclear weapons are not in hardened storage areas, weapons carried by aircraft which are on the bases attacked, and possibly on the ICBM's which may be destroyed in their silos. The added fallout from these sources should be included in the assessment of overall radiation exposure.

APPENDIX B—STRATEGIC FORCES ASSUMED

The strategic forces assumed to be available for an early to mid-1980's conflict between the United States and the Soviet Union are derived from open-source estimates of weapons characteristics and force levels. Generally, the forces are assumed to be within SALT II established limits and assume the completion of ongoing intercontinental ballistic missile (ICBM) modernization programs of both superpowers. For the United States this means that yield and accuracy improvements for the MMIII force are carried out. On the Soviet side, it means completing the deployment of their fourth-generation ICBMs, the SS-17, SS-18, and SS-19.

A recent study conducted by the Congressional Budget Office, entitled, "Counterforce Issues for the U.S. Strategic Nuclear Forces," provided table B-1, which shows Soviet forces and their capabilities for the early to mid-1980's.

Western estimates differ as to the exact attributes and capabilities of Soviet strategic systems. As a result some of the assumptions used in the studies drawn on for this report are mutually inconsistent. This would be an impor-

tant factor in an analysis of relative U.S. and Soviet military effectiveness, where the outcomes of a study would be very sensitive to the exact technical data used. In a study of the impacts of nuclear war on civilian population, however, a slight difference in the estimated yield or accuracy of a Soviet weapon will have no corresponding effect on the computation of the consequences of a given attack, relative to the degree of uncertainty that already exists in the prediction of those consequences.

U.S. estimates, on the other hand, are not subject to such great uncertainties. The Congressional Budget Office summary of U.S. forces is shown in table B-2.

It is useful to bear in mind that Soviet ICBM warheads are much higher in yield than their U.S. counterparts. While this has only a marginal impact on relative capabilities to destroy civilian targets on purpose, it means that Soviet attacks on U.S. targets will produce much more collateral damage (i.e. population casualties from attacks on economic targets, or economic and population damage from attacks on military targets) than will U.S. attacks on Soviet targets.

Table B-1.—Estimated Soviet Strategic Nuclear Forces, 1985

Launcher	Number[a]	Warheads per launcher[b]	Total warheads	Yield in megatons[c]	Total megatons	Equivalent megatons
SS-11	330	1	330	1.5	495	432
SS-17	200	4	800	0.6	480	560
SS-18	308	8	2,464	1.5	3,696	3,228
SS-19	500	6	3,000	0.8	2,400	2,580
SS-16	60	1	60	1.0	60	60
Total ICBMs	1,398		6,654		7,131	6,860
SS-N-6. SS-N-8. }	600	1	600	1.0	600	600
SS-N-17. SS-N-18. }	300	3	900	0.2	180	306
Total SLBMs	900		1,500		780	906
Bear	100	1	100	20	2,000	740
Bison	40	1	40	5	200	116
(Backfire)	(250)	(2)	(500)	(0.2)	(100)	(170)
Total bombers	140 (390)		140 (640)		2,200 (2,300)	856 (1,026)
Grand total	2,438 (2,688)		8,294 (8,794)		10,111 (10,211)	8,622 (8,792)

SOURCE: *Counterforce Issues for the U.S. Strategic Nuclear Forces*, Congressional Budget Office, January 1978.

Table B-2.—Estimated U.S. Strategic Nuclear Forces, 1985

Launcher	Number	Warheads per launcher	(Mid-1980's force)			Equivalent megatons
			Total warheads	Yield in megatons	Total megatons	
Minuteman II	450	1	450	1.0	450.0	450
Minuteman III	550	3	1,650	0.17	280.5	512
(with MK-12A)	(550)	(3)	(1,650)	(0.35)	(572.5)	(825)
Titan II	54	1	54	9.0	486.0	232
Total ICBMs.	1,054		2,154		1,216.5 (1,508.5)	1,194 (1,507)
Poseidon	336	10	3,360	0.04	134	403
Poseidon C-4.	160	8	1,280	0.10	128	282
Trident I	240	8	1,920	0.10	192	422
Total SLBMs	736		6,560		454	1,107
B-52 G/H	165	{ 6 SRAM / 4 bombs	990 / 660	0.2 / 1.0	198 / 660	337 / 660
B-52CM	165	20 ALCM	3,300	0.2	660	1,122
FB-111.	60	{ 2 SRAM / 2 bombs	120 / 120	0.2 / 1.0	24 / 120	41 / 120
Total bombers	390		5,190		1,662	2,280
Grand total.	2,180		13,904		3,332.5 (3,629.5)	4,581 (4,894)

SOURCE: *Counterforce Issues for the U.S. Strategic Nuclear Forces*, Congressional Budget Office, January 1978.

Which weapons would be used in our attack cases? In Case 1, Detroit is targeted with a single warhead similar to those deployed on the multiple independently targetable reentry vehicle (MIRVed) SS-18 ICBM or with a large single weapon such as those carried by SS-9 or SS-18 Soviet ICBMs. Leningrad is targeted with yields approximately those of a Minuteman II warhead, a Titan II warhead, and all 10 reentry vehicles (RVs) from a Poseidon submarine-launched ballistic missiles (SLBM). In Case 2, the U.S.S.R. attacks U.S. refinery targets with 10 MIRVed SS-18, warheads, and the United States attacks Soviet targets with a mix of Poseidons and Minuteman III, numbering 73 warheads. In Case 3, each side uses its most accurate MIRVed ICBMs against the other side's silos, and a mix of ICBMs, SLBMs, and bombers against bomber and missile submarine bases.

APPENDIX C—CHARLOTTESVILLE:

A FICTIONAL ACCOUNT BY NAN RANDALL

In an effort to provide a more concrete understanding of the situation which survivors of a nuclear war would face, OTA commissioned the following work of fiction. It presents one among many possibilities, and in particular it does not consider the situation if martial law were imposed or if the social fabric disintegrated into anarchy. It does provide detail which adds a dimension to the more abstract analysis presented in the body of the report.

At first, it seemed like a miracle. No fireball had seared the city, no blast wave had crumbled buildings and buried the inhabitants, no dark mushroom cloud had spread over the sky. Much of the country had been devastated by massive nuclear attack, but the small, gracious city of Charlottesville, Va., had escaped unharmed.

*   *   *

The nuclear attack on the Nation did not come as a complete surprise. For some weeks, there had been a mounting anxiety as the media reported deteriorating relations between the superpowers. The threat of possible nuclear war hung heavy in the world's consciousness. As evidence reached the U.S. President's desk that a sizable number of Americans were deserting the major cities for what they perceived to be safety in the rural areas, he considered ordering a general evacuation. But, with the concurrence of his advisors, he decided that an evacuation call from the Federal Government would be premature, and possibly provocative. There was no hard evidence that the Soviets were evacuating and there was a good chance that the crisis would pass.

Spontaneous evacuation, without official sanction or direction, grew and spread. A week before the attack, Charlottesville had no free hotel or motel rooms. A few evacuees found lodgings with private families, at great expense, but most were forced to camp by their cars in their trailers next to the fast-food chains on Route 29. The governing bodies of Charlottesville and surrounding Albemarle County were rumored to be concerned about the drain on the area resources, without really having any way of turning back newcomers. "If this keeps up," remarked a member of the Albemarle Board of Supervisors, "we're going to be overrun without any war."

A few of the students at the University of Virginia left Charlottesville to join their families. But the majority of the students stayed, believing that they could go home easily if it were necessary.

Refugees came from Washington, 130 miles to the north, and they came from Richmond, 70 miles to the east. A few of the hardier types continued on into the mountains and caverns near Skyline Drive; the majority sought the reassurances of civilization that the small city could provide.

The population of Charlottesville normally stood a little above 40,000, while Albemarle County which surrounds the city like a donut boasted an additional 40,000 to 50,000. With the arrival of the city evacuees, the combined population was well over 120,000.

In the week before the nuclear attack, much of the population familiarized itself with the location of fallout shelters. Little hoarding took place as retailers limited sales of food and other necessities. Transistor radios accompanied both adults and children when they were away from home. However, most of the residents of Charlottesville continued to live as they always had, although they were particularly alert for sirens or bulletin broadcasts on the radio. Many children stayed out of school.

*   *   *

At the sound of the sirens and the emergency radio alerts, most of Charlottesville and Albemarle County hurried to shelter. Fortunately, Charlottesville had a surplus of shelter space for its own population, though the refugees easily took up the slack. Many headed for the University grounds and the basements of the old neoclassical buildings designed by Thomas Jefferson; others headed downtown for the office building parking garages. Carrying a few personal effects, blankets, cans and bottles of food, and transistor radios, they converged in a quiet if unordered mass. For most people, the obvious emotional crises—grief at leaving behind a pet, anxiety at being unable to locate a family member or relative—were suppressed by the overwhelming fear of the impending attack.

Some residents chose not to join the group shelters. Many suburbanites had ample, sturdy basements and food stocks. They preferred not to crowd themselves. In the event, those who had taken the precaution of piling dirt against the windows and doors of their basements found that they provided adequate shelter. Among the rural poor, there was a reluctance to desert the small farms that represented the sum of their life's work. They wondered whether, if they left, they would return to find their means of livelihood gone. Further, many lived far from an adequate public shelter. So they stayed.

*   *   *

Most did not see the attacks on Richmond and on Washington as they huddled in their shelters. But the sky to the east and north of Charlottesville glowed brilliant in the noonday sun. At first no one knew how extensive the damage was.

Communication nationwide was interrupted as the Earth's atmosphere shivered with the assault of the explosions. Each town, city, village, or farm was an island, forced to suffer its selected fate of death or salvation alone. (Some time later it was learned that more than 4,000 megatons (Mt) had destroyed military and industrial targets, killing close to 100 million people in the United States. The U.S. counterattack on the Soviet Union had had a similar, devastating effect. Destruction ranged from the large industrial centers on the coasts and Great Lakes to small farming communities that had the misfortune to be close to the great missile silos and military bases.)

Areas of the country such as the northeast corridor were reduced to a swath of burning rubble from north of Boston to south of Norfolk. Still, there were some sections of the Nation that were spared the direct effects of blast and fire. Inland in Virginia, only the town of Radford, west of Roanoke, received a direct hit. The farming and orchard land of the rural counties were not targets.

Charlottesville, the small but elegant center of learning, culture, and trade in central Virginia, was not hit either. This monument to the mind and manner of Jefferson retained its status as a kind of genteel sanctuary, momentarily immune to the disaster that had leveled the cities of the Nation.

*   *   *

An hour after nothing fell on Charlottesville, rescue squads and police were dispatched to scour the countryside for stragglers to get them to shelters. Because, even if the population was safe from the direct effects of the nuclear warheads, another danger was imminent. Fallout, the deadly cloud of radioactive particles sucked up by the nuclear fireballs, could easily blanket the town of Charlottesville in a matter of hours. And no one could predict how much, and where it would go. Fallout could poison many of those idyllic rural towns and villages that seemed light-years away from the problems of international power and politics. While a few places, such as Roseberg, Ore., would receive no fallout at all, the rest of the Nation would have to constantly monitor to know the level of radiation and where it was located. Fortunately for Charlottesville, the University and the hospitals had sophisticated radiological monitoring equipment, and the training to use it. Many other towns were not so lucky.

Two and one-half hours after the warnings had sounded, the nuclear engineering staff from the University picked up the first fallout. Starting at a moderate level of about 40 rems an hour—a cumulative dose of 450 rems received in a 1-week period would be fatal to one-half of those exposed—the intensity rose to 50 rems before starting the decline to a level of about four-tenths of a rem an hour after 2 weeks. (The total dose in the first 4 days was 2,000 rems, which killed those who refused to believe shelter was necessary, and increased the risk of eventually dying of cancer for those who were properly sheltered.) For the immediate period, it was essential to stay as protected as possible.

For several days, Charlottesville remained immobile, suspended in time. It was unclear just what had happened or would happen. The President had been able to deliver a message of encouragement, which was carried by those emergency radio stations that could broadcast. As the atmosphere had cleared, radio station WCHV was able to transmit sporadically on its backup transmitter and emergency generator in the basement. However, the message from the President posed more questions than it answered—the damage assessment was incomplete. Nevertheless, he said that there was a tentative cease-fire.

In the first days of sheltering, only those with some particular expertise had much to do. Nuclear engineers and technicians from the University were able to monitor radiation in the shelters they occupied, and CB radios broadcast results to other shelters. The doctors were busy attempting to treat physical and psychological ailments—the symptoms of radiation sickness, flu, and acute anxiety being unnervingly similar—while the police and government officials attempted to keep order. The rest waited.

For the time being, the food stocks brought to the shelter were adequate if not appetizing. The only problem was the water supply which, though it kept running because of its gravity system, was contaminated with Iodine 131. Potassium iodide pills, which were available in some shelters, provided protection; elsewhere people drank bottled water, or as little water as possible.

Not all of the shelters had enough food and other necessities. Most shelters had no toilets. The use of trash cans for human waste was an imperfect system, and several days into the shelter period, the atmosphere was often oppressive. As many suffered from diarrhea—the result either of anxiety, flu, or radiation sickness—the lack of toilet facilities was especially difficult.

Shelter life was bearable in the beginning. Communications by CB radio allowed some shelters to communicate with one another, to locate missing family members and friends. A genuine altruism or community spirit of cooperation was present in almost all the shelters—though some of them were fairly primitive. Even those refugees who were crowded into halls and basements with the local residents were welcomed. Parents watched out for one another's children or shared scarce baby food. Most people willingly accepted direction from whomever took charge. Among the majority of the shelter residents, the out-of-town refugees being an exception, there was a sense of relief, a sense that they had been among the lucky ones of this world. They had survived.

Within a few days, the emergency radio was able to broadcast quite regularly. (As the ionosphere does not clear all at once, occasional interruptions were expected.) The station had had no protection from the electromagnetic pulse that can travel down the antenna and shatter the inner workings of electronic equipment during a nuclear explosion. However, by detaching the back-up transmitter at the sound of the warning, the station engineer had protected equipment. Intermittent communications from Emergency Operations Centers got through to Charlottesville officials, though the main communications center at Olney, Md., was silent. Telephone switching facilities were almost entirely out, although the small, independent phone company could expect to be operational fairly quickly. The complex, coast-to-coast trunk lines of Ma Bell might take a year or more to reconnect.

Lifeline of the sheltered community was the CB radio. Rural Virginians had been CB fans long before it became a national craze, and they put their equipment to imaginative use. Prodded by anxious refugees, as well as by local residents who had relatives and friends in other parts of the world, CBers tried to set up a relay system on the lines of an electronic pony express. Though less than perfect, the CB relay was able to bring limited news from outside, most of that news being acutely distressing. From the limited reports, it was clear that there was little left in the coastal cities; those who had abandoned family or friends to come to Charlottesville understood that probably they would never see them again.

The first surge of grief swept over the refugees and those Charlottesville residents who were affected. In time, the sorrow of loss would affect almost everyone. Although they had survived themselves, still they had lost.

* * *

Three days after the attacks, the next large influx of refugees poured into Charlottesville, many of them suffering with the early symptoms of radiation sickness. They had been caught poorly sheltered or too close to the nuclear targets themselves. A few showed the effects of blast and fire, bringing home to Charlottesville the tangible evidence of the war's destruction. Some refugees had driven, while others had hitchhiked or even walked to reach what they hoped was safety and medical help. On the way, many were forced to abandon those who were too weak to continue.

The hospitals were completely overwhelmed. Up to now, the hospitals had managed to treat the ill with some modicum of order. The hospitals themselves were fallout shelters of a kind; patients' beds had been moved to interior corridors for fallout protection; emergency surgery was feasible with the emergency generators, hospital staff slept in the most protected areas. Some borderline

cases in intensive care were released to nature's devices while any elective medical procedures were eliminated. Still, hospitals were able to cope, even with the increasing number of common ailments caused by the shelter crowding.

Suddenly, this changed. Fallout levels were too high for anyone to be out in the open for any length of time, but the people came anyway. The carefully laid plans of the University of Virginia Emergency Room, devised for the possibility of peacetime accidents, were hurriedly modified. No longer was the careful showering and decontaminating of victims possible with the single shower and uncertain water pressure. Instead, patients were stripped of their clothes and issued hospital gowns. With no time for studied decision, doctors segregated the very sick from the moderately sick—the latter to be treated, the former given medication and allowed to die.

Nevertheless, the day came when the hospitals were full. The University Hospital, Martha Jefferson Hospital, the Blue Ridge Sanatorium, and the others were forced to lock their doors to protect those patients they had already accepted.

After being turned away, the sick had no specific destination. Many still clustered around the middle of town near the two major hospitals, taking up residence in the houses abandoned by local residents several days before. With minimal protection from fallout and no medical treatment for other trauma, many died, their bodies left unburied for several weeks.

The combined populations of Charlottesville and Albemarle County rose to 150,000 in the 7 days after the nuclear attack. Slowly, hostility and resentment wedged a gap between residents and refugees who attempted to join the group shelters. The refugees, still in a daze from their experience, believed that they had priority rights after all they had suffered. The local residents viewed the outsiders as a threat to their own survival, particularly as the extent of the war damage was becoming evident.

In fact, the supply of food was not a problem in the short run. Like most other towns and cities, Charlottesville and Albemarle had some 3 weeks worth of food on hand, on home shelves, in supermarkets and wholesale outlets. The Morton Frozen Food plant could be expected to supply a rich diet of convenience foods for a short time, even after the refrigeration was off. The problem was, after the local supplies were exhausted, where could they get more?

Nerves, already frayed by the stresses of the past days, threatened to snap. Older people were irritated by the noise and commotion of children; children resented the lack of freedom. The friction between differing groups became increasingly evident, and vocal. An experiment in communal living was clearly not to the taste of many, and the discomforts, both physical and psychological, had the effect of pushing local residents out of the shelters. (There was some effort to stop them as the radiation levels still posed some hazards; they were urged at least to stay inside most of the time.) Left in the shelters, now, were mostly those out-of-town refugees who had no homes to go to.

Not all the residents of Charlottesville and Albemarle found their homes intact. In some cases they returned to find the house looted or occupied by refugees who were unwilling to give up squatters' rights. Sometimes claims were backed with guns; in a few cases, squatter and owner worked out a modus vivendi of sharing the property.

Some animals had survived, in varying states of health. Unprotected farm animals were dead, while those which had been confined to fairly solid barns with uncontaminated feed had a fair chance of surviving. Many of these farm animals, however, were missing, apparently eaten by hungry refugees and residents. Some pets had remained indoors in good de facto shelters so that, if they had found water, they needed only to be fed to regain health. Worried about the amount of food pets could consume, many families simply put them out to fend for themselves.

For the first week or so after the nuclear attacks, authorities had few options. Simple survival was the priority, the elements of which included food and water distribution, fallout protection, and retention of some civil order. Government was ad hoc, with the leadership of the city and county naturally cooperating, along with the different police forces. As the population left the shelters, however, officials felt that some more formalized system was desirable. After several long meetings—in the basement of the courthouse where the government officials had stayed to avoid fallout—an emergency government, led by the city manager of Charlottesville, was agreed on. The combined city council and the Albemarle County Board of Supervisors also elected the chairman of the board of supervisors as deputy, and the sheriff of the county as chief of public safety to oversee the combined police forces and provide liaison with those military units which were still in the area.

The powers given to the city manager were sweeping in scope, certainly far beyond any powers he had held before, and ran "for the duration of the emergency." While some considered the new form of local government close to martial law, great care was exercised to be sure that the offensive term was not used. In effect, however, Charlottesville and Albemarle were under a highly centralized, almost totalitarian rule.

Whatever it might be called, under the new system, the city manager was able to take over all resources and their allocation. Following to some extent the paper plan that the area had developed, the new government attempted to set out priorities. It was greatly aided by the experts from the University, who volunteered time and expertise to analyzing the needs of the area. (In this respect, Charlottesville was particularly fortunate in having an extensive pool of talent on which to draw.)

However, if Charlottesville was lucky to have reasonably functioning government and a number of experienced planners and managers, and to have suffered comparatively modest disruption from refugees and fallout, the city and county authorities were becoming painfully aware that they were not set up to 'go it alone' without any outside help. Even were the weather suitable for planting, Charlottesville was no longer an agricultural center. There wasn't enough energy to process any food that might be grown. Where would people get clothes and building materials and medicines and spare parts for the cars and buses? The very complexity of American society—its technological marvels and high standard of living—could well prove to be a barrier to the reconstruction of any one part.

*   *   *

During the third week after the attacks, the new rationing system come into force. Individual identification cards were issued to every man, woman and child. Food was distributed at centralized points. Those without I.D. cards were unable to get their ration of flour, powdered milk, and lard—and the processing of cards could take 3 or more days. Some desperate refugees resorted to stealing I.D. cards in order to get food, while an enterprising printer started turning out forgeries within 2 days after the government had first issued cards. Rumors of hoarding and black marketeering abounded. Some of the missing supermarket food turned up in black market centers, accompanied by exhorbitant prices.

Fuel supplies were dropping more rapidly than the government had hoped. Most families were heating their homes with wood, either in fireplaces or in recycled oil drums for stoves. As the winter was waning, the most desperate need was for fuel for driving motors and generators. Even the drinking water was dependent on the emergency generator that ran a single purifying system for the Rivanna Water and Sewer Authority. (Water for other uses could simply be drawn from the gravity-powered reservoir system, bypassing the filtration system entirely.) The hospital and radio stations all ran on small generators. The University could luxuriate in its coal-powered steam heat, but there was no way, save generators or candles and lanterns, to get lights.

No one was exactly certain how much fuel there was in the area. Both jurisdictions had once surveyed, for emergency planning purposes, the fuel storage capacity, and they hoped they could count on having about half of that on hand. Armed guards were assigned to those larger facilities that had not already been raided by the desperate. All private use of cars or tractors was outlawed, and the government threatened to confiscate any moving vehicles.

Electricity was restored, partially, some two weeks after the attack. Workers from the small Bremo Bluff generating plant, about 15 miles away from Charlottesville, succeeded in starting the plant with the coal reserves that were on hand. From then on, limited electricity use was permitted for a few hours hours a day. This was particularly pleasant for those families whose water came from electrically powered well pumps. Well water was issued to children for drinking, as it had escaped the Iodine 131 contamination which was still elevated in the reservoirs.

The radioactivity level continued to drop (after two weeks it was 0.4 rem per hour) and it was "safe" to go outdoors. However, the resulting doses, though too low to cause immediate illness or deaths, posed a long-term health hazard. The authorities, while recognizing that everybody would receive many times the prewar "safe dose," tried to reduce the hazards by urging people to stay inside as much as possible when not picking up food rations at the distribution centers. Life for the residents of Charlottesville revolved around those trips and figuring out ways to make do without the normal supplies and services. Some chanced outings to forage for a greater variety of food, but most were resigned to waiting. There wasn't much else they could do.

*   *   *

Three weeks after the nuclear attack, almost all the Charlottesville and Albemarle County residents had returned to their homes. Those few whose homes had either been occupied by squatters, or been destroyed by fire, easily found some alternate housing with the government's help.

This left the refugees. Though the drop in fallout intensity allowed the refugees to move out of basements and interior halls, they still were forced to live a version of camp life. They spent their endless, empty hours waiting in lines for food, for a chance to use the bathrooms—which at least functioned now—for a chance to talk to authorities. Information from the outside was still sketchy, and for the refugees, this uncertainty added to their already high level of anxiety.

The city manager and the emergency government attempted to solve the refugee housing problem by billeting refugees in private homes. At first they asked for volunteers, but got few. The authorities then announced that any house with fewer than two people per room would be assigned a refugee family. Resistance to this order was strong, and, particularly in the outlying areas where it was hard to check, outright defiance was common. Families would pretend to comply and then simply force the refugees out as soon as the authorities had left. The refugees would struggle back to town, or take up residence in barns or garages.

And still the refugees came to Charlottesville, bringing with them stories of the horrors they had experienced. They camped in schools, in banks, in warehouses. By night the neoclassical architecture of the University was packed with the residents of Arlington and Alexandria. By day, the new downtown mall was awash with a floating mass of men, women, and children, who, with nothing to do, milled around the unopened stores. A retired ambassador was overheard comparing the scene to that of downtown Calcutta.

By now, the emergency government recognized that the need for food was going to be acute. Without power for refrigeration, much food had spoiled; stocks of nonperishable foods were mostly exhausted. As the shortages became clear, the price of food skyrocketed. Many people refused money for food, preferring to barter. Food and fuel were the most valuable commodities, with shoes and coats high on the list as well.

Since shortly after the attack, the city manager had been in contact both with the Federal Government and with the relocated State government in Roanoke. He had repeatedly asked for emergency rations, only to be met with vague promises and explanations about the problems of transportation. He was generally urged to cut rations further and hang on. Help would arrive when it could.

For some time, the relatively few surviving farm animals had been gradually and mysteriously disappearing. The farmers concluded that "those damned city folks" were stealing them for food, although some of the local residents were also making midnight forays on the livestock. Farmers themselves slaughtered animals they had planned to fatten-up for the future. They couldn't spare the feed grain, and they needed food now.

Finally the emergency authorities announced that they would take a percentage of every farmer's livestock to help feed residents and refugees. Farmers were outraged, considering the action simple theft. There were rumors that angry farmers had shot several agents who had tried to confiscate the animals. Though they were offered promissory notes from the city authorities, the farmers thought such payment worthless.

(The radiological experts at the University had been questioned on the advisability of eating the meat of animals with radiation sickness. Many of those beasts which had remained outside during the high fallout period were showing clear signs of illness. The experts decided that the meat would be edible if cooked sufficiently to kill any bacterial invasion—the result of the deterioration of the animal's digestive tract. Strontium 90 would be concentrated in the bones or the milk, not the muscle tissue.)

*   *   *

Although the city government had relatively frequent contact, mostly by radio, with the Federal and State governments, the citizens had to rely on the occasional Presidential message that was broadcast on WCHV. Three weeks after the attacks, the President made a major address to reassure the people. He announced that the cease-fire was still holding and he saw no reason why that would change. He described the damage that the U.S. retaliatory strike had done to the Soviet Union. He also noted that the United States still retained enough nuclear weapons, most of them at sea on submarines, to inflict considerable damage on any nation that attempted to take advantage of the recent past. He did not mention that he suspected that the Soviets also held reserve weapons.

Describing the damage that the country had suffered, the President noted that, even with the loss of over 100 million lives, "We still have reserves, both material and spiritual, unlike any nation on earth." He asked for patience and for prayers.

There had been broadcasts earlier by the Lieutenant Governor of Virginia—the Governor was killed in Richmond—from his shelter in Roanoke. However, as fallout in the Roanoke area was quite high (Radford just to the west had been struck), he was effectively immobilized for some time. The State government appeared less organized than the Federal.

Charlottesville was still on its own. Residents hunted game as the last of the food stocks disappeared, but the fallout had killed most animals that were in the open. Refugees were reduced to stealing. A number of people managed to fill their gas tanks with contraband gasoline and set out to forage in the mountains to the west.

Three and one-half weeks after the attack, an old propeller-driven cargo plane landed at the Charlottesville Airport with a supply of flour, powdered milk, and vegetable oil. The pilot assured the few policemen who guarded the airstrip that more would be on the way by truck as soon as temporary bridges could be built over the major rivers.

The emergency airlift was supposed to supply Charlottesville with food for a week or two.

However, the officials who had calculated the allotment had overlooked the refugees. Charlottesville's population was some three times the normal. (No one was absolutely sure because the refugees moved around a good deal, from camp to camp.)

The first of the deaths from radiation had occured 10 days after the attacks, and the number grew steadily. By now, it was not uncommon to see mass funerals several times a day. The terminally ill were not cared for by the hospitals—there were too many, and there was nothing that could be done for them anyway—so it was up to their families to do what they could. Fortunately there were still ample supplies of morphia, and it was rumored that college students had donated marijuana. The city set aside several locations on the outskirts of town for mass graves.

In addition to those with terminal radiation sickness, there were those with nonfatal cases and those who showed some symptoms. Often it was impossible for doctors to quickly identify those with flu or psychosomatic radiation symptoms. The number of patients crowding the emergency rooms did not slacken off. The refugees, crowded together, passed a variety of common disorders, from colds to diarrhea, back and forth. Several public health experts worried that an outbreak of measles or even polio could come in the late spring. "So far, we have been lucky not to have a major epidemic of typhus or cholera," a doctor observed to his colleagues.

The supply of drugs on hand at the hospitals was dwindling fast. Although penicillin could be manufactured fairly easily in the laboratories at the university, many other drugs were not so simple, even with talent and ingenuity. (The penicillin had to be administered with large veterinary hypodermics as the home-made mix was too coarse for the small disposable hypos that most doctors stocked. There was a considerable shortage of needles.) Other medications were in such short supply that many patients with chronic illnesses such as heart disease, kidney failure, respiratory problems, hypertension, and diabetes died within a few weeks.

* * *

Food riots broke out 4½ weeks after the attacks—precipitated by the first large shipment of grain. Three large tractor-trailers had pulled into the parking lot of the Citizens Commonwealth Building quite unexpectedly, the word of their arrival somehow misplaced between the Agriculture Department dispatchers and the local authorities. The trucks were greeted with cheers until the residents of Charlottesville discovered that they had been shipped raw grain rather than flour. The drivers were taken unawares when empty cans and bottles showered them and one driver jumped in his cab and departed. (The official explanation, delivered some time later, was that processed food was going to those areas where the bulk of the population was sick or injured. It was also assumed that Charlottesville had some livestock reserves.)

With only a fraction of the population knowing what to do with raw grain, a number of angry citizens broke open the sacks and scattered wheat through the parking lot. They in turn were set upon by those who wanted to conserve as much as possible. The local public safety forces waded into the melee with night sticks and tear gas.

Everyone blamed everyone else for the incident, but the fragile glue that had held public order together began to unstick.

From this time on, it was almost impossible for the local authorities, not to mention the State and Federal governments, to convince everyone they were getting a fair share. People in one section of town would watch suspiciously as delivery trucks passed them by and headed somewhere else. Blacks distrusted whites, the poor distrusted the rich and everyone distrusted the refugees as "outsiders."

The refugees were convinced that the local authorities were favoring the residents and tried repeatedly to get State intervention, with little success. Still billeted in dormitories, schools, and motels, the refugee camps were a breeding ground for discontent and even rebellion.

* * *

The presence of the Federal Government was not entirely confined to the occasional delivery of food or radio broadcast. Some time before, the National Guard and the Reserve Unit were moved to North Carolina, partly to give the impression of military readiness, and perhaps to be assigned to dig out cities and start reconstruction. The Government had put out calls for volunteers to help in the reconstruction, but found that most workers, young and old, wanted to stay with their families. A system of national conscription for young men and women with no children was in the planning stage.

The Federal Government attempted to urge refugees back to where they had come from, first to assist in the rebuilding of the damaged cities which were rich in resources, and ultimately to redistribute the population to a more normal pattern. Some refugees were happy to attempt to return, particularly those whose houses were more or less intact. However, those who found their homes destroyed preferred to return to the refugee camps inland. There was nothing to hold them to their former lives. Fearful memories of the past made any time spent in the cities painful.

One day, quite without warning, the city manager was informed that one-half of his fuel stores were to be confiscated by the Federal Government, for the military and for the reconstruction effort. (Earth-moving equipment was gathering on the outskirts of the devastated cities and needed fuel.) After it was clear that there was no way to stop the Government from taking the fuel, the city manager suggested that unmarked tank trucks, well guarded, pick up the stocks at night. He was aware of the effect this action would have on the morale of the population.

Already transportation was difficult for the elderly and those who lived in the rural areas. A sporadic bus service ran from one end of town to the other once a day and an occasional school bus made a sortie out into the suburbs. Bicycles were prized, and sometimes fought over. Those gentlemen farmers whose thoroughbred horses had been protected from fallout could use these animals for transportation, but it was risky to let the animals stand unprotected. Horse thievery had made an anachronistic reappearance.

With even less fuel, the bus service would be cut in half.

*   *   *

By now, barter was clearly established as the preferred means of trade. For a time, the government had paid for commandeered foodstuff and resources with checks and promissory notes, but no one wanted them any more. The local banks had opened for a few days, only to find all their savers lined up to withdraw everything. They closed down. Stores either never opened, or shut down quickly when they were overrun. (Many stores had been looted in the second week after the attack, when the fallout intensity had dropped.) A few people hoarded money, but most thought money worthless.

Workers in the small industries in the Charlottesville area saw no point in turning up for work if all they could get was paper money. They preferred to spend the time hunting for food and fuel. If barter was a highly inefficient way to do business—it's hard to make change for a side of beef—still, it was preferable to using worthless currency.

Psychologically, the population seemed to be in a quiet holding pattern. The refugees, many of them, had survived experiences that would mark them for years. The memories of fire, collapsing buildings, and screaming, trapped people were still vivid, and some would tremble at loud noises. However, the profound grief over what they had lost—family members, possessions, or friends—underlay emotions and made many apathetic and passive. Victims of the nuclear attacks, they appeared willing to be victims afterwards too. Still shunned as outsiders by the resident population, most refugees appeared to accept the exclusion just as the surviving population of Hiroshima and Nagasaki had 30 odd years before.

The effect on the Charlottesville and Albemarle residents was less pronounced. They were disoriented. For each lucky one who had a specific job to do, there were many more who were in effect unemployed. They turned inward to their families or else friends and relatives. Their worries about the future—would there be another attack, would they go back to their old jobs, etc.—made most days rather anxious, unproductive ones. Children particularly reflected a continuous nervousness, picked up from their elders, and had difficulty sleeping at night. Though many parents hoped for a return to normalcy once the schools reopened, others quietly decided not to send their children for fear of a second outbreak of war.

*   *   *

Spring changed a lot of things. A new optimism surfaced as everyone looked forward to planting, to good weather and warmth. The residents of Charlottesville had survived the first hurdle; they felt confident they could survive the next.

At the University, agronomists studied the best crops to plant in the Charlottesville area. No one was certain what effect the nuclear explosions had had on the ozone layer. If indeed the ozone was severely damaged, more ultraviolet rays could reach the crops and perhaps burn them. This effect would be more pronounced on delicate crops such as peas and beans. Instead it was suggested that potatoes and soybeans be encouraged and whatever limited fertilizer became available go to farmers who followed the government guidelines.

The emergency government announced that two-thirds of the former pasture land was to be cultivated. Feed grains were to be used for humans, not livestock. Dairy cattle and chickens were the only exceptions.

The next few months in Charlottesville and Albemarle County had a slow, almost dreamlike quality. Fears of new attacks had abated. It was a time of settling into a new lifestyle, a severely simplified way of being, of making do. Children ate meat, cheese, or eggs rarely, adults practically never. A good pair of shoes was guarded—and worn only on special occasions. (With warmer weather, most children and adults went barefoot, bringing concern to doctors that there would be an increase in parasitic diseases such as hookworm.)

Many people were unable to return to their former jobs. In some cases, their employers never reopened for business, their goods and services being irrelevant in the postattack society. College teachers, for example, had no students to teach; computer programmers had no computers to program.

For some, it was relatively easy to adapt. Electronics experts set up CB and short wave radio repair shops. Cottage industries—sandal and clothing manufacturing from recycled materials, soap and candle making—sprang up in many homes. Some workers were able to acquire new, relevant skills quickly.

Others had to make do with menial jobs—burying the dead, cleaning the streets, assisting carpenters and bricklayers—that took little skill.

And then there were those who could not fit in anywhere. Many found it difficult to adapt to the idleness. Disruption of the 9 to 5 work ethic was a disruption of basic psychological props, of a sense of identity. In the immediate period after the attacks, parents concentrated on protection of their families. Once their families were no longer directly affected, adults were robbed of their traditional roles.

By now, a few of the refugees had melted into the general population. But the vast majority were no further along than in the late winter. The drag on the area resources was significant, and many in the leadership wanted to force them out.

Charlottesville was fortunate in many respects, however. Being located on two easily repairable rail lines—with a major storage yard for cars only two counties away—there was some access to the outside world. Travel was only permitted with a special pass, naturally, and so the younger members of the community resorted to the hallowed art of riding the rods.

Government officials, many of whom had visited Charlottesville and the University frequently in the past, kept in closer contact with the city than with many other locales. Doubtless the area residents benefited with more Federal assistance. As a result, Charlottesville became the unofficial "capital" of the area, economically and politically.

But as autumn approached, a universal depression settled on the residents and refugees. Starvation had been held at bay by the planting—but crop yields were smaller than expected. No one was cold, but the weather was still fine. There seemed to be no appreciable progress towards preattack conditions. Those young men and women who had been conscripted to build housing for the Nation's refugees returned with gloomy reports of the devastation to the Nation's commerce. The east coast was effectively leveled. Where factories were rebuildable, the shortage of materials precluded their operation.

Recognizing that many families would have to make do without heating oil or gas, the Agriculture Extension Service issued pamphlets on how to make your own wood-burning stove. Fortunately for Charlottesville and the surrounding area, trees were plentiful. However, the momentum that had started with the spring planting slowed.

*   *   *

Winter was harder than anyone had expected. There were few additional deaths that could be directly attributed to the nuclear blast effects or the radiation; however, a large percentage of the surviving population was weakened. Lack of medicines, lack of adequate food and reasonable shelter, plus the lingering physical and psychological effects, meant that many were unable to work effectively, even if there were work available. An epidemic of flu raged through the cities of the east where refugees were huddled in camps. Many died, especially children and old people. Although vaccine for this particular, common strain of flu had been developed, the stocks had been destroyed in the attacks.

In the northern sections of the country, food supplies were inadequate and poorly distributed. The average diet—day in, day out—consisted of unleavened bread and potatoes, where there was enough of those. As animal herds, both domestic and wild, had been decimated by fallout and indiscriminate hunting, the only available meat came from dogs, cats, and rats—those animals whose living habits protected them from fallout. Dietary deficiency diseases appeared.

Growing children were the first to notice the lack of replacement clothes—particularly leather shoes. Coats and blankets were highly prized in the cold climates.

Next to food, the most severe shortage was housing. Even with the temporary barracks that had been erected in a cluster around the damaged cities, refugees were crowded two or three to a room. Kitchens were shared by four and five families; bathrooms by as many as 12 people.

Although there was relatively little work to occupy time, and schooling was strictly curtailed, if indeed it existed, there was also very little available recreation. The entertainment industry located in California and New York had been particularly hard hit. Local TV stations could broadcast and rebroadcast those old films and cartoons they had in stock, but little was fed nationwide. In the small towns, public libraries were overwhelmed. In the large cities, the libraries had been destroyed. There were no movie houses to speak of; there were no professional sports. The lack of recreation, perhaps a minor problem, still served to underscore the bleakness of the winter.

In Charlottesville alone, several thousand people died in the first winter after the nuclear attack.

*   *   *

A year almost to the day after the nuclear war between the United States and the Soviet Union, Charlottesville was host to a blue ribbon panel of experts on reconstruction planning. The University had not returned to normal—there were no undergraduate classes as the students had been conscripted for reconstruction work in the cities—but it was a natural meeting place since so many centers of learning had been destroyed.

The questions before the group centered on setting priorities: what were the goals and how could the country reach them?

The U.S. Government still existed, if in a slightly reordered form. The President, now permanently located in the Midwest along with the surviving Members of Congress and the Cabinet, retained the emergency powers he had taken just after the attacks. (Congress had had no choice but to ratify his assumption of these extraordinary powers at the time. However, there was growing resentment that he showed few signs of relinquishing them. Congress was reduced to a kind of advisory body, its Members spending most of their time on helping constituents relocate or obtain aid.)

The State governments had, by and large, re-established themselves, often in new locations. Virginia's government was located in Roanoke, for example, under the Lieutenant Governor. State governments were not as well respected as before; citizens tended to blame them for the mixups in aid distribution. Only the refugees looked to the States for assistance against the local governments, which they distrusted. The residents of an area such as Charlottesville were most loyal to their local government, particularly when that government had a reputation of basic evenhandedness.

Everyone, however, was growing hostile to the imposition of strict governmental controls over their lives—what they could or could not buy, or eat, where they could travel, etc. In certain rural sections, such as Nelson County, south of Charlottesville, farmers had barricaded themselves off, ignored government orders, and occasionally, it was rumored, took potshots at the government agents.

Attempts to conscript the able-bodied to rebuild the damaged areas often failed miserably. Many simply walked off the job and returned to their families. Since there were no adequate records remaining of the prewar population, and no records at all of war deaths, the Government found it an impossible task to track down offenders. (Criminals in medium- and light-security detention facilities had simply evaporated into the population.)

Charlottesville, like the rest of the undamaged parts of the country, still had a huge refugee population that was unwilling or unable to return to former homes. The majority were in camps such as the large facility in the old Lane School, and children were in day care or orphanages, depending on the status of their surviving families. If anything, the refugees were both more apathetic and more rebellious when faced with simple assignments. Lawless bands of teenaged refugees roamed the countryside, hijacking supply trucks and raiding farms and villages. Partly it was simple bravado, partly a way to feed themselves. Most refugees simply sat and waited for the next meal.

Yet even now, the flow of refugees continued. The winter had driven out those who could not find enough to eat or enough shelter. Stories of Vermont families subsisting on maple syrup and wild rabbits might have proven entertaining in the retelling, but those who had survived did not want to repeat the performance.

The medical problems were still acute. Drug supplies were almost exhausted, but the weakened population remained more susceptible to disease. The birth rate had fallen drastically 9 months after the attacks, partly because of the radiation, which produced temporary sterilization—but there had also been a rise in miscarriages, stillbirths, and abnormalities. Infant mortality soared. Experts worried that an unprecedented increase in cancer, particularly in children, could be expected in several years. And there was still the possibility of some devastating epidemic as cholera running unchecked through the population. The Blue Ridge Sanatorium in Charlottesville, which had seen few tuberculosis patients in the last years before the attacks, was making plans to convert back to specializing in the disease. TB was making a comeback.

The Nation's economy was in shambles. The bulk of the oil refining capacity had been knocked out, and only a few facilities were functioning again. The small oil wells around the country that were situated away from target areas produced more oil than the refineries could handle—and it was only a fraction of the need. Coal mining, mostly by the time-honored pick and shovel method as strip mining took heavy equipment, was the only industry that could be called booming. (There was a major migration to the mining areas by the unemployed.) Agriculture, of course, was a major undertaking for much of the population. However, yields from the farms were considerably below what had been hoped for. The lack of pesticides and fertilizer cut heavily into the crops and there was concern about a major insect invasion next summer. Food processing—wheat and corn milling particularly—showed encouraging signs of recovery.

Most major industries, however, were in disarray as a result of lack of energy, lack of raw materials, and lack of managerial expertise. The world economy was staggering from the effect of losing both the United States and the Soviet Union as suppliers and markets. (If the Latin Americans were able to make small fortunes on selling the U.S. refined petroleum, political pressures were building in those countries to raise the prices to double the current rates.)

An efficient system of money still had not been reestablished. The Federal Government paid the military and other Federal employees with dollars and tried to preserve purchasing power through a series of price controls. However, most people were reluctant to accept dollars in exchange for essentials such as food or clothing. As a result, a barter system continued to flourish and the black market, with its highly inflated prices, continued to encourage defiance of the law.

Most experts believed that the experience of post-World War II in Europe and Japan could provide the model for currency reform, including replacement of the dollar, that was necessary to restore an economy based on the division of labor. However, the resolution of two policy issues stood in the way. First, should the market, on one hand, or Government control, on the other, determine the distribution of scarce resources? Second, should the new money go to those with legitimate claims, pensions, promissory notes for goods confiscated during the postattack period etc., or to those who held productive jobs, or even to the entire population even if many were more drag than help to the recovery? Politically, the Government was unable to deny any one of the groups; practically, it was obvious the Government could not satisfy all three.

It was clear that if the economy did not get moving again soon, it might never. Already there were indications that manufacturing was not reestablishing itself with anywhere near the speed the planners had hoped. The amount of shipping, by rail and by truck, was actually down from the mid-summmer high.

"We are in the classic race," remarked one of the participants who had written a major study of postattack recovery some years before. "We have to be able to produce new goods and materials before we exhaust our stored supplies. We can continue to eat the wheat that is in the grain elevators of the Midwest for another year, perhaps. But after that, we have to have the capacity to grow new wheat. When our winter coats wear through, we have to have the capacity to weave the cloth for new ones. When our railroad cars break down, we have to be able to make new ones, or replacement parts. Right now we are a long way from that capacity." Privately, he and a group of conferees agreed that heavy controls on the economy, and ultimately on the population, would be the only way to get things going. Resources, both material and human, were severely limited.

One of the major problems, it was obvious to everyone, was the drag the huge refugee population had on the recovery effort. While numbers of workers were actively engaged in the rebuilding of the cities as well as the factories and services that powered the economy, there were as many more who were unem-

ployed and unemployable for the time being. Their skills were not suited to the priority tasks. Several participants had prepared a statement on what should be done with these nonproductive members of society. "We cannot let this mass of people drain our resources while they do nothing to contribute," it was rumored to say. "If we cannot let them starve outright, we suggest that they be issued only that amount of food which is minimally necessary to sustain life. They should be moved to camps away from the center of activity for reason of public morale." The report was suppressed but several copies were leaked to the press anyway.

The most basic disagreement among the participants in the conference was over the level of reconstruction that might actually be feasible. Optimists cited the phenominal recovery of Japan and West Germany after World War II and insisted that these be the models for the United States in the next 5 to 10 years.

Pessimists, noting the major differences between the post-World War II era and the situation of Japan and Germany, felt these examples were irrelevant, or worse, misleading. "Everyone forgets the amount of aid that came in from outside in the late '40's and early '50's. We don't have the United States, wealth to turn to. Such a goal is unrealistic and unreachable, even with absolute controls on the economy."

The pessimists were divided. Some saw the Nation building itself along the line of some of the Asian nations, which boasted a small technologically advanced segment in the midst of a large agrarian or unskilled worker population, on the model of India or Indonesia. Some thought technology itself would eventually disappear from American society. "If you don't have computers to run, you don't train computer programmers," one expert was overheard to say. "After a while, in a few generations, no one remembers how the machines worked at all. They remember the important things: how to plant crops, how to train draft horses and oxen, how to make a simple pump. We will have survived biologically, but our way of life is going to be unrecognizable. In several generations, the United States is going to resemble a late medieval society."

Because the conferees could not agree on what was a reasonable goal, much less how to get there, the conference report straddled all fences and concluded nothing. Follow-up task forces were appointed and the conferees agreed to meet again in the summer. Perhaps by then they would have a better idea of whether or not they were winning the race.

APPENDIX D—SUMMARY OF REPORT ON
EXECUTIVE BRANCH CALCULATIONS

[Note: The full report, classified SECRET, is available separately to qualified requesters.]

PURPOSE

This appendix summarizes and analyzes studies of the direct effects of nuclear attacks that have been performed by and for various agencies of the executive branch of the U.S. Government in recent years. This review includes those studies whose results are currently viewed by the sponsoring agency as being valid and applicable to the current through mid-1980's time period, with the U.S. and Soviet forces projected under a SALT II agreement.

SCOPE

The estimates of the direct effects of nuclear attacks presented in this paper represent analyses performed by or for the Department of the Defense (DOD), the Arms Control and Disarmament Agency (ACDA), and the intelligence community. Although these analyses describe the direct effects of nuclear attacks in terms of population fatalities and attack damage objectives against military, leadership, and economic target systems, it is recognized that a more meaningful basis for assessing the direct effects of nuclear attacks would be to analyze the effects of such attacks in terms of postwar national survival and recovery. To date, however, analytical capabilities have not permitted such analyses. In fact, the complex issues concerning national recovery should nuclear war occur, or the postwar power and recovery capabilities of the belligerents, have as yet not even been properly formulated for analysis. Until that is accomplished, analyses of the direct effects of nuclear attacks will continue to focus, as have the studies used for this analysis, on one-dimensional first-order direct effects.

Furthermore, all analyses examined in this study assume a "two-shot" nuclear war—the Soviets strike first against all targets included under a particular scenario and the U.S. retaliates against a similar set of Soviet targets. More protracted (and more likely) attack scenarios are not examined. Hence, such factors as the feasibility of sustaining population in a "protected or evacuated" posture over a protracted duration, either in a continuing crisis with no nuclear attacks or one with attacks repeated every few days or so, are not reflected in the damage estimates available from these studies and included in this report.

Five questions provided the focus for the analytical results examined in this study:

1. How many people would be killed by:
   —Prompt effects of nuclear explosions?
   —Fallout radiation?
2. What number of nonfatal but disabling injuries could be expected?
3. What areas would possibly receive damaging levels of overpressure and how many people live or work in those areas?
4. What areas would receive what levels of fallout contamination?
5. What would be the possible extent of fire damage, and what mechanisms would create it?

Answers to these questions, as provided in the various studies used in this analysis, are given in the following section.

SUMMARY OF RESULTS

In viewing the estimated direct effects of nuclear attacks, particularly population casualties, it is important to focus on the *relative* numbers for the various nuclear attack scenarios examined, as opposed to the absolute. The analyses on which these estimates are based do not take into account the many imponderables associated with such a cataclysmic event, the majority of which would cause higher levels of human devastation than are indicated by the analyses of hypothetical attacks. A significant imponderable is the uncertainty of human behavior. Would people really react as planned and as assumed in the computer models? Also, our ability to simulate even the immediate direct effects from thousands of nuclear detonations based on data extrapolations from single bursts is suspect because of its inherent uncertainties. And, finally, the inability to assess the longer term prospects for the immediate survivors, which would depend not only on the availability of subsistence levels of food, medical supplies, etc., but also on how quickly they could adapt

to a radically unfamiliar environment and social structure, further limits the validity of these estimates as a net assessment of the damage to be expected as a result of nuclear war.

Population Damage

Table D-1 summarizes in terms of total national population high- and low-range fatality estimates derived from the various analyses used for this report. In view of the many uncertain factors involved in such estimates, it is not possible to synthesize a "best estimate" range from the results of the studies used for this analyses.

Differences within and between the low and high ranges listed in the table are due primarily to differences in force alert status, weapons laydown, population protection level, population data base, and/or evacuation scheme assumed.

Table D-1.—OTA Attack Cases—Executive Branch Fatality Estimates

Case	OTA attack cases	Population posture	Percent of national fatalities	
			Low range	High range
2	Small attack on U.S.		(not available)	
	Small attack on U.S.S.R.		(not available)	
3	Attack on U.S. ICBMs	In-place	1-3	8-10
	Attack on Soviet ICBMs	In-place	< 1	1-4
	Attack on U.S. CF	In-place	< 1-5	7-11
		Evac.	—	5-7
	Attack on Soviet CF	In-place	1	1-5
		Evac.	1-2	
4	Attack on U.S. CF, OMT, & ECON	In-place	35-50	59-77
		Evac.	10-26	32-43
	Attack on Soviet CF, OMT, & ECON	In-place	20-32	26-40
		Evac.	9-14	
3 (excursion)	Attack on U.S. CF and OMT	In-place	14-23	26-27
		Evac.	—	18-25
	Attack on Soviet CF and OMT	In-place	15-17	22-24
		Evac.	6-9	
4 (excursion)	Attack on U.S. CF, OMT, ECON, and population	In-place	—	60-88
		Evac.	28-40	47-51
	Attack on Soviet CF, OMT, ECON, and population	In-place	—	40-50
		Evac.	22-46	

NOTE: CF = counterforce targets.   OMT = other military targets.   ECON = economic targets.

For Soviet First-Strike Attacks on the United States, Against:

ICBM Targets Only (Case 3). — The 1- to 3-percent spread in the low range results from assuming two 550-kiloton (kt) optimum height-of-burst (OPT HOB) weapons per silo (1-percent national fatalities) versus assuming one 550-kt OPT HOB and one surface burst 550-kt weapon per silo (3-percent national fatalities). The 8- to 10-percent spread in the high range results from assuming one 3-megaton (Mt) OPT HOB and one surface-burst 3-Mt weapon per silo (8 percent) versus assuming two 3-Mt surface bursts per silo (10 percent). The difference between the ranges is due to the difference in the yield of the assumed weapons.

All Counterforce Targets (Case 3). — The less than 1-to 3-percent low range for *in-place U.S. population* fatalities results from the difference in fallout protection levels assumed by DOD and ACDA. The less than 1-percent value assumes an enhanced U.S. in-place fallout protection program that would provide a fallout protection factor (PF) of at least 25 for the entire population. The 3-percent value assumes in-place fallout shelters providing PFs of 10 to 1,000 and that 90 percent of the population would use the shelters. The unprotected portion of the population is assumed to be equally divided between a PF of 3 and 6. The 7- to 11-percent high range also results from differences in fallout protection levels assumed by DOD and ACDA. In this case, the 7-percent value assumes the current U.S. in-place fallout protection program. PFs as low as 5 are assumed for about one-half of the U.S. rural population, and PFs as low as 15 for one-quarter of U.S. urban population. The 11-percent value assumes essentially no U.S. civil defense program and a PF of 3 for the entire U.S. population. The difference between the ranges reflects the differences in the assumed fallout protection levels.

All Counterforce Targets (Case 3). — The 5- to 7-percent high range for *evacuated U.S. population* fatalities reflects ACDA's assumptions concerning the amount of fallout protection available for the combined rural and evacuated urban population. The 5-percent value

assumes 66 percent of the total exurban population would be able to obtain fallout protection of 10 to 40 PF. Those persons not protected were assumed to be equally divided between between a PF of 3 and of 6. The 7-percent value assumes only 33 percent of the total exurban population would be able to obtain fallout protection of 10 to 40 PF. The rest were assumed to be equally divided between a PF of 3 and 6. This range of values is listed as "high" because it results from assuming that no expedient fallout protection upgrading could be achieved by the evacuated population.

Counterforce, Other Military Targets, and Economic Targets (Case 4). — The 35- to 50-percent low range for *in-place U.S. population* fatalities results from assuming day-to-day alert (35-percent fatalities) versus generated forces (50-percent fatalities), and that 90 percent of the U.S. population are sheltered in available civil defense shelters. The 59- to 77-percent high range reflects differences in weapons laydown and population protection level. The 59-percent value assumes a generated forces Soviet attack with about 60 percent of the weapons air burst and that only 66 percent of the U.S. population are sheltered in available civil defense shelters. The 77-percent value also assumed a generated forces attack, but with all weapons ground burst and no civil defense sheltering of the population. The reasons for the differences between the ranges are the differences in assumed population protection levels and weapons laydown.

Counterforce, Other Military Targets, and Economic Targets (Case 4). — The 10- to 26-percent low range for *evacuated U.S. population* fatalities results from differences in assumed weapons laydown. The 10-percent value assumes about half the attacking weapons are air burst. The 26-percent value assumes all weapons are ground burst. Both values in the low range assume expedient upgrading of fallout protection could be achieved by the evacuated population, that is, a fallout PF of at least 25 for the entire U.S. population. The 32- to 43-percent high range reflects ACDA's assumptions as to the fallout protection that could be achieved by the evacuated population. The 32-percent value assumes 66 percent of the total exurban population would be able to obtain fallout protection of 10 to 40 PF. The 43-percent value assumes only 33 percent could obtain such protection. Those persons not protected in each case were assumed to be equally divided between a PF of 3 and of 6. The difference between the ranges can be attributed to: 1) The differences in the levels of fallout protection assumed. The low range assumes expedient upgrading. 2) The less extensive evacuation scheme used by ACDA. The low range (DOD results) assumes 80 percent of all U.S. risk area population is evacuated. The high range (ACDA results) assumes only cities of more than 25,000 population are evacuated. 3) The larger, about 1,000 more equivalent megatons (EMT), attack laydown used by ACDA.

Counterforce and Other Military Targets (Case 3 excursion).

— Within the low range, the spread in values, for *U.S. population in-place,* results from day-to-day alert versus generated forces attacks. Within the high range, the spread reflects day-to-day alert versus generated forces plus low protection levels (no civil defense assumed) versus an assumed in-place civil defense population posture. The difference between ranges is primarily due to the difference in assumed population protection levels.

Counterforce and Other Military Targets (Case 3 excursion).

— The 18- to 25-percent range for *U.S. population evacuated* is based on ACDA analysis and reflects ACDA's assumptions as to the percent of exurban population that would have sheltering available in host areas. The 18 percent corresponds to 66 percent having available shelters and the 25 percent corresponds to 33 percent having available such shelters. This range probably represents high estimates because of the evacuation scheme assumed by ACDA. The 47-percent value assumes degraded protection levels based on DOD's sensitivity analysis, and evacuation of 80 percent of all risk area population. The 51-percent value also reflects degraded protection levels, only 33 percent of the total exurban population are able to obtain protection in rural shelters, and ACDA's less extensive relocation scheme. Once again, the range also

reflects the effect of ground bursting all weapons versus air bursting about half the weapons. The difference between the ranges is due to differences in assumed population protection levels.

Counterforce, Other Military Targets, Economic, and Population (Case 4 excursion).

— In this case the 60- to 80-percent fatality range for U.S. population in-place reflects the impact of the protection levels assumed. The 60-percent value corresponds to the high protection levels used by DCPA. The 88-percent value corresponds to the more modest levels assumed by OSD analysts. This range is listed as "high" because of the severity (all ground bursts and all but 10- to 15-percent of Soviet weapons) of the attack used.

Counterforce, Other Military Targets, Economic, and Population (Case 4 excursion).

— The 28- to 40- percent low range for *U.S. population evacuated* reflects the differences between DOD's and ACDA's assumptions concerning levels of fallout protection, evacuation scheme, and weapons laydown. The 28-percent value assumes expedient upgraded protection levels as specified by DCPA and evacuation of 80 percent of all risk area population. The 40-percent value reflects ACDA's less extensive evacuation scheme (only cities with population greater than 25,000 are evacuated) and no expedient upgrading of protection levels. In addition, the 28-percent value results from an attack with all weapons ground burst and the 40- percent value assumes about half the values are air burst. The 47- to 51-percent high range also results from differences in fallout protection, evacuation scheme, and weapons laydown. In this case the 47-percent value assumes degraded protection levels based on DOD's sensitivity analysis, and evacuation of 80 percent of all risk area population. The 51-percent value also reflects degraded protection levels, only 33 percent of the total exurban population are able to obtain protection in rural shelters, and ACDA's less-extensive relocation scheme. Once again, the range also reflects the effect of ground bursting all weapons versus air bursting about half the weapons. The difference between the ranges is due to differences in assumed population protection levels.

For U.S. Retaliatory Attacks on the U.S.S.R., Against:

ICBM Targets Only (Case 3).—The low, less than 1-percent, value assumes one OPT HOB weapon per silo. In this case fatalities are less than 1 percent for attacks using only 40-kt, only 200-kt, or only 1-Mt weapons. The high range of 1 to 4 percent results from assuming one ground-burst weapon per silo. In this case the 1-percent value assumes only 200-kt weapons and the 4-percent value assumes only 1-Mt weapons are used. The differences between the range reflects the effect of OPT HOB weapons versus ground bursting all weapons.

All Counterforce Targets (Case 3).—The less than 1-percent low value for *in-place Soviet population* assumes relatively good fallout protection for the entire Soviet population and, in the case of ACDA's analysis, a U.S. attack based on a preplanned laydown using in part U.S. ICBMs that do not survive the Soviet first strike. The high range reflects differences in weapons laydown, population protection levels, and data bases used by ACDA and DOD. The less than 1-percent value reflects ACDA's preplanned attack laydown, relatively good fallout protection assumptions, and use of a coarser Soviet population data base. The 5-percent value reflects DOD's attack laydown, which does not attrite U.S. weapons due to a Soviet first strike, lower fallout protection assumptions, and use of a finer Soviet population data base. The difference between the ranges results from all these differences in assumptions.

All Counterforce Targets (Case 3).—The less than 1- to 2-percent variation results from differences in population protection levels assumed by ACDA for *evacuated Soviet population.* The less than 1-percent value assumes 66 percent of the exurban population use available sheltering. Those not using such sheltering are assigned protection levels of 3 and 6 in equal shares. It is difficult to judge whether this represents a low or high range. On one hand the range could be considered on the low

side because of the coarseness of the Soviet data base used by ACDA. Conversely, the evacuation scheme assumed by ACDA would suggest that it be considered a high range.

Counterforce, Other Military Targets, and Economic Targets (Case 4).—The 20- to 32-percent low range for *in-place Soviet population* fatalities results from differences in force alert status and weapons laydown assumed. The 20-percent value reflects day-to-day alert forces and an attack using only 40-kt air-burst weapons against economic targets. The 32-percent value reflects generated forces and an attack using a mixture of weapons against economic targets. The 26- to 40-percent high range reflects differences between ACDA and DOD assumptions. The 26-percent value from ACDA analysis assumes relatively good population protection levels and a lower amount of EMT used against economic targets than assumed in the DOD analysis. The 40-percent value from DOD analysis reflects lower population protection levels, a finer population data base, and a larger attack against economic targets than used in the ACDA analysis. The difference in assumptions made by DOD, ACDA, and the interagency intelligence group.

Counterforce, Other Military Targets, and Economic Targets (Case 4).—The 9- to 14-percent range reflects the difference in population protection levels used by ACDA for *evacuated Soviet population.* The 9-percent value assumes 66 percent use available shelters. The 14 percent assumes only 33 percent use available shelters. It is difficult to judge whether this reflects a low or high range. The coarseness of the Soviet data base used by ACDA would suggest it be treated as a low range. Conversely, the ACDA evacuation scheme would suggest it be considered a high range.

Counterforce and Other Military Targets (Case 3 excursion).—The differences within both ranges for *Soviet population in-place* reflects the variation in protection levels assumed by ACDA. The difference between the ranges is due to the alert status of U.S. forces used.

Counterforce and Other Military Targets (Case 3 excursion).—The 6- to 9-percent range reflects the variation in protection levels assumed by ACDA for *evacuated Soviet population,* 66 percent use available shelters versus 33 percent. As in the previous cases, with Soviet population evacuated, it is difficult to judge if this is a low or high range of fatalities.

Counterforce, Other Military Targets, Economic, and Population (Case 4 excursion). — Fatality estimates range from 40 to 50 percent for *Soviet population in-place* based on DOD analysis. The variation is primarily due to differences in assumed population protection levels. Given the rather low protection levels assumed by DOD, the range probably represents the high level of Soviet fatalities.

Counterforce, Other Military Targets, Economic, and Population (Case 4 excursion). — Fatality estimates range from 22 to 26 percent for *Soviet population evacuated* based on ACDA analysis. The variation reflects differences in assumed population protection levels; 66 percent use available shelters versus 33 percent. Once again it is difficult to judge whether this is a high or low range. The coarse data base used by ACDA suggests their estimates are low, but the evacuation scheme suggests they might be high.

In examining the fatality ranges listed in table D-1 it should be noted that the differences between U.S. and Soviet fatality levels for comparable attacks and population postures can be primarily attributed to:

- The nature of the nuclear attacks assumed in the various studies; that is, the assumption that the Soviets attack first and the United States retaliates in the various attack scenarios examined.

- The higher yields of Soviet weapons, which result in significantly higher levels of nuclear yield detonating in the United States than the U.S.S.R. for comparable attack cases.

Although the data on nonfatal injuries available from the studies used in this analysis are quite limited, the results suggest that:

- For attacks against ICBMs or counterforce target sets, nonfatal injuries would about equal fatalities.
- For attacks that include economic targets, but not population per se, nonfatal injuries would vary from about 20 to 40 percent of total casualties.
- For attacks including population, nonfatal injuries vary from about 8 to 25 percent of total casualties.

Military and Economic Damage

Unlike population damage levels, which (except for excursions to Case 4) result only collaterally from attacks on other target sets, damage levels against military and economic target sets are input objectives used in structuring the attack laydowns examined in the various analyses on which this report is based. Damage levels attained against these target systems in the studies examined in this analysis were:

For Soviet First-Strike Attacks Against the United States:

Counterforce Targets (Percent Total Damaged). — ICBMs (42 to 90 percent), SAC bomber bases (90 to 99 percent), and submarine support facilities (90 to 99 percent).

Other Military Targets (Percent Installations Damaged). — Major military leadership facilities (90 to 95 percent), State capitals (95 percent), DCPA and FPA emergency operating centers (95 percent), and other military installations (77 to 90 percent).

Economic Targets. — 70- to 90-percent damage of the national manufacturing value of the economic targets attacked.

For U.S. Retaliatory Attacks Against the U.S.S.R.:

Counterforce Targets (Percent Total Damaged). — Bomber bases (70 to 90 percent).

Other Military Targets (Percent Installations Damaged). — Major military leadership facilities (70 to 90 percent), major political leadership facilities (70 to 90 percent), and other military installations (20 to 50 percent).

Economic Targets. — 70- to 90-percent damage of the national manufacturing value added plus capital replacement cost of the economic targets attacked.

As in the case of population fatalities, the differences between U.S. and Soviet damage levels against strategic forces, other military targets, and economic targets can be attributed to the assumption that the Soviets strike first and to the larger yields of Soviet weapons.

APPENDIX E—SUGGESTIONS FOR

FURTHER READING

Physical Effects of Nuclear Warfare

Ayers, R. N., "Environmental Effects of Nuclear Weapons" (3 vols.), Hudson Inst., HI-518, December 1965.

Batten, E. S., "The Effects of Nuclear War on the Weather and Climate," RAND Corp., RM-4989, November 1966.

Bennett, B., "Fatality Uncertainties in Limited Nuclear War," RAND, R-2218-AF, November 1977.

Defense Civil Preparedness Agency, U.S. Department of Defense, "DCPA Attack Environment Manual," Publication CPG 2-1A, 9 vols., June 1973 (vol. 4 revised June 1977).

Drell, S. and von Hippel, "Limited Nuclear War," *Scientific American,* November 1976.

Glasstone and Dolen, eds: *Effects of Nuclear Weapons,* 3rd ed., U.S. Department of Defense and Department of Energy, Washington, D.C., 1977.

Green, J., "Response to DCPA Questions on Fallout," Defense Civil Preparedness Agency, Washington, D.C., November 1973.

Mark, J. C., "Global Consequences of Nuclear Weaponry," *Annual Review of Nuclear Science,* 1976, 26:51-87.

National Academy of Sciences, "Effects of Multiple Nuclear Explosions Worldwide," Washington, D.C., 1975.

U.S. Arms Control & Disarmament Agency, "The Effects of Nuclear War," Washington, D.C., April 1979.

U.S. Congress, Senate, Committee on Foreign Relations, Subcommittee on Arms Control, International Organizations, and Security Agreements, Hearings: Effects of Limited Nuclear Warfare, 94th Cong., 1st sess. (1975). 61 p.

U.S. Congress, Senate, Committee on Foreign Relations, Subcommittee on Arms Control, International Organizations, and Security Agreements, Comm. Print: "Analyses of Effects of Limited Nuclear Warfare," 94th Cong., 1st sess (1975). Contains, among other things, the Sept. 11, 1974, Briefing on Counterforce Attacks by Secretary of Defense, James R. Schlesinger, and the report of the Office of Technology Assessment Ad Hoc Panel on Nuclear Effects.

Economic Impact of Nuclear War (General) and Economic Recovery From Nuclear War

Goen, R., et al., "Analysis of National Entity Survival," Stanford Research Institute, November 1967.

Goen, R., et al., "Critical Factors Affecting National Survival," Stanford Research Institute, 1965.

Goen, R., et al., "Potential Vulnerabilities Affecting National Survival," Stanford Research Institute, 1970.

Hanunian, N., "Dimensions of Survival: Postattack Survival Disparities and National Viability," RAND Corp., RM-5140, November 1966.

Hirshleiter, J., "Economic Recovery," RAND, P-3160, August 1965.

Katz, A., "Economic and Social Consequences of Nuclear Attacks on the United States," U.S. Senate, Committee on Banking, Housing, and Urban Affairs, 96th Cong., 1st sess. (March 1979).

Laurius, R., and F. Dresch, "National Entity Survival: Measure and Countermeasure," Stanford Research Institute, 1971.

Lee, H., et al., "Industrial Production and Damage Repair Following Nuclear Attack," Stanford Research Institute, March 1968.

Pettis, Dzirbals, Krahenbuhl, "Economic Recovery Following Nuclear Disaster: A Selected, Annotated Bibliography," RAND Corp., R-2143, December 1977.

Sobin, B., "Post Attack Recovery," Research Analysis Corp., RAC-P-51, June 1970.

Winter, S. G., Jr., "Economic Recovery From the Effects of Thermonuclear War," RAND, P-2416, August 1961.

Winter, S. G., Jr., "Economic Viability After Nuclear War: The Limits of Feasible Production," RAND, RM-3436, September 1963.

Economic Impacts of Nuclear War (Specific), Including Agricultural Impacts

Brown, S., "Agricultural Vulnerability to Nuclear War," Stanford Research Institute, February 1973.

Jones, T. K., "Industrial Survival and Recovery After Nuclear Attack: A Report to the Joint Committee on Defense Production, U.S. Congress," The Boeing Co., Seattle, Wash., 1976.

Killion, et al., "Effects of Fallout Radiation on Crop Production," Comparative Animal Research Laboratory, July 1975.

Leavitt, J., "Analysis and Identification of Nationally Essential Industries, Vol. I: Theoretical Approach," Institute for Defense Analyses, P-972, March 1974.

Stanford Research Institute, "U.S. Agriculture: Potential Vulnerabilities," January 1969.

Stanford Research Institute, "Agricultural Vulnerability in the National Entity Survival Context," July 1970.

Stephens, M. M., "Vulnerability of Total Petroleum Systems," Office of Oil and Gas, Department of the Interior, May 1973.

Administrative, Social, Psychological, etc., Factors Relating to Postattack Issues

Allmitt, B., "A Study of Consensus on Social and Psychological Factors Related to Recovery From Nuclear Attack," Human Sciences Research, Inc., May 1971.

Brown, W. M., "Emergency Mobilization for Postattack Reorganization," Hudson Institute, HI-874/2, May 1968.

Brown, W. M., "On Reorganizing After Nuclear Attack," RAND, P-3764, January 1968.

Dresch, F., "Information Needs for Post-Attack Recovery Management," Stanford Research Institute, April 1968.

Ellis, Dresche, "Industrial Factors in Total Vulnerability," Stanford Research Institute, April 1968.

Hirshleiter, J., "Disaster and Recovery: A Historical Survey," RAND, RM-3079, April 1963.

Iklé, F. C., *The Social Impact of Bomb Destruction,* Norman, Okla., University of Oklahoma Press, 1958.

Janis, I., *Air War and Emotional Stress,* New York: McGraw Hill, 1951.

Vestermark, S., (ed.), "Vulnerabilities of Social Structure," Human Sciences Research, Inc., December 1966.

Winter, S. G., Jr., "The Federal Role in Post Attack Economic Organization," P-3737, RAND, November 1967.

Civil Defense

Aspin, Les, "The Mineshaft Gap Revisited," Congressional Record, Jan. 15, 1979, pp. E26-35.

Egorov, P.T., et al., *Civil Defense,* Springfield, Va.: National Technical Information Service, 1973. A translation of *Grazhdanskaya Oborna,* 2nd ed., Moscow, 1970.

Gouré, L., *War Survival in Soviet Strategy,* Washington, D.C.: Advanced International Studies Institute, 1976.

Gouré, L., *Soviet Civil Defense in the Seventies,* Washington, D.C.: Advanced International Studies Institite, 1975.

Kaplan, F. M., "The Soviet Civil Defense Myth: Parts I & II," *Bulletin of the Atomic Scientists,* March and April 1978.

Kincaid, W., "Repeating History: the Civil Defense Debate Renewed," *International Security,* winter 1978.

Oak Ridge National Laboratory, Civil Defense (Grazhdanskaya Oborna) (translation), December 1973.

Sullivan, R., et al., "Candidate U.S. Civil Defense Programs," System Planning Corp., March 1978.

Sullivan, R., et al., "Civil Defense Needs of High-Risk Areas of the United States," System Planning Corporation, SPC 409, 1979.

U.S. Arms Control and Disarmament Agency, "An Analysis of Civil Defense in Nuclear War," Washington, D.C., December 1978.

U.S. C.I.A., "Soviet Civil Defense," Director of Central Intelligence, NI78-10003, July 1978.

U. S. Congress, Senate, Committee on Banking, Housing, and Urban Affairs, (Hearings on Civil Defense), Jan. 8, 1979.

[This glossary is excerpted from the larger one in *The Effects of Nuclear Weapons,* 3rd ed., compiled and edited by Samuel Glasstone and Philip J. Dolan, prepared and published by the U.S. Department of Defense and the U.S. Department of Energy, Washington, D.C., 1977.]

Alpha Particle: A particle emitted spontaneously from the nuclei of some radioactive elements. It is identical with a helium nucleus, having a mass of four units and an electric charge of two positive units.

Cloud Column: The visible column of weapon debris (and possibly dust and water droplets) extending upward from the point of burst of a nuclear (or atomic) weapon.

Crater: The pit, depression, or cavity formed in the surface of the Earth by a surface or underground explosion. Crater formation can occur by vaporization of the surface material, by the scouring effect of air blast, by throwout of disturbed material, or by subsidence. In general, the major mechanism changes from one to the next with increasing depth of burst. The apparent crater is the depression which is seen after the burst; it is smaller than the true crater (i.e., the cavity actually formed by the explosion), because it is covered with a layer of loose earth, rock, etc.

Dynamic Pressure: The air pressure that results from the mass air flow (or wind) behind the shock front of a blast wave. It is equal to the product of half the density of the air through which the blast wave passes and the square of the particle (or wind) velocity behind the shock front as it impinges on the object or structure.

Electromagnetic Pulse: A sharp pulse of radio frequency (long wavelength) electromagnetic radiation produced when an explosion occurs in an unsymmetrical environment, especially at or near the Earth's surface or at high altitudes. The intense electric and magnetic fields can damage unprotected electrical and electronic equipment over a large area.

Fallout: The process or phenomenon of the descent to the Earth's surface of particles contaminated with radioactive material from the radioactive cloud. The term is also applied in a collective sense to the contaminated particulate matter itself. The early (or local) fallout is defined, somewhat arbitrarily, as those particles which reach the Earth within 24 hours after a nuclear explosion. The delayed (or worldwide) fallout consists of the smaller particles that ascend into the upper troposphere and into the stratosphere and are carried by winds to all parts of the Earth. The delayed fallout is brought to Earth, mainly by rain and snow, over extended periods ranging from months to years.

Fire Storm: Stationary mass fire, generally in built-up urban areas, causing strong, inrushing winds from all sides; the winds keep the fires from spreading while adding fresh oxygen to increase their intensity.

Fission Products: A general term for the complex mixture of substances produced as a result of nuclear fission. A distinction should be made between these and the direct fission products or fission fragments that are formed by the actual splitting of the heavy-element nuclei. Something like 80 different fission fragments result from roughly 40 different modes of fission of a given nuclear species (e.g., uranium-235 or plutonium-239). The fission fragments, being radioactive, immediately begin to decay, forming additional (daughter) products, with the result that the complex mixture of fission products so formed contains over 300 different isotopes of 36 elements.

Gamma Rays (or Radiations): Electromagnetic radiations of high photon energy originating in atomic nuclei and accompanying many nuclear reactions (e.g., fission, radioactivity, and neutron capture). Physically, gamma rays are identical with X-rays of high energy, the only essential difference being that X-rays do not originate from atomic nuclei but are produced in other ways (e.g., by slowing down (fast) electrons of high energy).

Height of Burst (HOB): The height above the Earth's surface at which a bomb is detonated in the air. The optimum height of burst for a particular target (or area) is that at which it is estimated a weapon of a specified energy yield will produce a certain desired effect over the maximum possible area.

Kiloton Energy: Defined strictly as 10^{12} calories (or 4.2×10^{19} ergs). This is approximately the amount of energy that would be released by the explosion of 1 kiloton (kt) (1,000 tons) of TNT.

Megaton Energy: Defined strictly as 10^{15} calories (or 4.2×10^{22} ergs). This is approximately the amount of energy that would be released by the explosion of 1,000 kt (1 million tons) of TNT.

Neutron: A neutral particle (i.e., with no electrical charge) of approximately unit mass, present in all atomic nuclei, except those of ordinary (light) hydrogen. Neutrons are required to initiate the fission process, and large numbers of neutrons are produced by both fission and fusion reactions in nuclear (or atomic) explosions.

Nuclear Radiation: Particulate and electromagnetic radiation emitted from atomic nuclei in various nuclear processes. The important nuclear radiations, from the weapons standpoint, are alpha and beta particles, gamma rays, and neutrons. All nuclear radiations are ionizing radiations, but the reverse is not true. X-rays, for example, are included among ionizing radiations, but they are not nuclear radiations since they do not originate from atomic nuclei.

Nuclear Weapon (or Bomb): A general name given to any weapon in which the explosion results from the energy released by reactions involving atomic nuclei, either fission or fusion or both. Thus, the A- (or atomic) bomb and the H- (or hydrogen) bomb are both nuclear weapons. It would be equally true to call them atomic weapons, since it is the energy of atomic nuclei that is involved in each case. However, it has become more-or-less customary, although it is not strictly accurate, to refer to weapons in which all the energy results from fission as A-bombs or atomic bombs. In order to make a distinction, those weapons in which part, at least, of the energy results from thermonuclear (fusion) reactions of the isotopes of hydrogen have been called H-bombs or hydrogen bombs.

Overpressure: The transient pressure, usually expressed in pounds per square inch, exceeding the ambient pressure, manifested in the shock (or blast) wave from an explosion. The variation of the overpressure with time depends on the energy yield of the explosion, the distance from the point of burst, and the medium in which the weapon is detonated. The peak overpressure is the maximum value of the overpressure at a given location and is generally experienced at the instant the shock (or blast) wave reaches that location.

Rad: A unit of absorbed dose of radiation; it represents the absorption of 100 ergs of nuclear (or ionizing) radiation per gram of absorbing material, such as body tissue.

Rem: A unit of biological dose of radiation; the name is derived from the initial letters of the term "roentgen equivalent man (or mammal)." The number of rems of radiation is equal to the number of rads absorbed multiplied by the relative biological effectiveness of the given radiation (for a specified effect). The rem is also the unit of dose equivalent, which is equal to the product of the number of rads absorbed and the "quality factor" of the radiation.

Roentgen: A unit of exposure to gamma (or X) radiation. It is defined precisely as the quantity of gamma (or X) rays that will produce electrons (in ion pairs) with a total charge of 2.58×10^{-4} coulomb in 1 kilogram of dry air. An exposure of 1 roentgen results in the deposition of about 94 ergs of energy in 1 gram of soft body tissue. Hence, an exposure of 1 roentgen is approximately equivalent to an absorbed dose of 1 rad in soft tissue. See *Rad*.

Thermal Radiation: Electromagnetic radiation emitted (in two pulses from an air burst) from the fireball as a consequence of its very high temperature; it consists essentially of ultraviolet, visible, and infrared radiations. In the early stages (first pulse of an air burst), when the temperature of the fireball is extremely high, the ultraviolet radiation predominates; in the second pulse, the temperatures are lower and most of the thermal radiation lies in the visible and infrared regions of the spectrum. For high-altitude bursts (above 100,000 feet [30,480 meters]), the thermal radiation is emitted as a single pulse, which is of short duration below about 270,000 feet [82,296 meters] but increases at greater burst heights.

Case 2: Small Attacks on U.S. and Soviet Energy Production and Distribution Systems

OTA Study on the Effects of Nuclear War

February 27, 1979

TABLE OF CONTENTS

CHAPTER I - INTRODUCTION

CHAPTER II - APPROACH AND METHODOLOGY

CHAPTER III - ANALYSIS

i

I. INTRODUCTION

A. PURPOSE

The purpose of this report is to provide a basic understanding and overview of the likely effects resulting from a limited nuclear attack conducted against either the US or Soviet Union energy production and distribution systems.

The analysis upon which this report is based was conducted as a portion of a larger analytic effort. The overall study, being directed by the Office of Technology Assessment (OTA), US Congress, considers five major nuclear attack categories. These range in size from an attack upon a single city through an attack of the magnitude associated with a first strike by a fully generated force directed against a wide range of military and urban/industrial targets.[1]

B. SUMMARY

1. General

The analysis upon which this report is based consists of three main parts. These are: (1) identification and selection of a target set, (2) calculations of direct damage resulting from a limited nuclear attack upon this target set, and (3) calculation of collateral damage which resulted from the limited attack. The first subject is addressed in detail in Chapter II of this report and the latter two subjects are discussed in detail in Chapter III. In this section of the report a brief summary of each of these three phases is presented.

2. Target Selection

This task sought to provide a basic understanding of the effects of a limited nuclear strike directed at each nation's energy production and distribution system in a manner intended to maximize recovery time. In order to establish a specific target, the general category of energy related targets was examined to find a particular set of targets which

---

[1](U) "OTA Study on the Effects of Nuclear War: Attack Cases," unpublished paper, U.S. Congress, Office of Technology Assessment, December 22, 1978.

1

fit the criteria of: (1) existing in a reasonable number, (2) relatively vulnerable to nuclear effects, (3) no easy substitute is available, and (4) which are of high value to the national economy. Petroleum refineries fit the general criteria, and inasmuch as they tend to be somewhat clustered geographically, petroleum refineries were selected as the prime target. In the case of the United States there were about 300 operating refineries in 1978. It is estimated that the Soviet Union will have about 60 operating refineries in the 1980s. Refineries are, by their characteristics and nature, vulnerable to the blast effects of nuclear weapons, particularly since they are usually surrounded by large amounts of crude and refined product storage. Consequently, a high degree of fire damage would be likely in the aftermath of a nuclear attack. After selecting petroleum refineries as the prime target, the weapon selection process described in Chapter II (see Sections C and D), was conducted. The resulting attack plan is summarized in Table 1 below. It should be noted that in the case of the US attack on the Soviet Union, both refining and storage facilities were targeted. This was done because it was not possible to attack all of the Soviet refineries because of the geographic distribution of the refineries and the footprint limitations of the US missiles. Since there were additional independently targetable warheads available on these missiles, these warheads were allocated to petroleum storage sites within the footprint of the US missiles. Missile footprint constraints are discussed in Chapter II, Sections C and D.

TABLE 1

SUMMARY DESCRIPTION OF ATTACK

Attacking Nation	Strategic Nuclear Delivery Vehicles			Refineries		Storage Sites	
	Name	Missiles/ MIRVs	Yield/ MIRV (MT)	Attacked	Number of MIRVs[a] Allocated	Attacked	Number of MIRVs Allocated
US	POSEIDON	7/64	0.04	21	35	29	29
	MM III	3/ 9	0.17	3	4	5	5
	TOTALS	10/73	--	24	39	34	34
USSR	SS-18/2	10/80	1.0	77	80	--	--

[a] 2 on 1 assignment of MIRVs for larger refineries

2

3.   Damage Assessment

The probable results of the limited attack, outlined in Table 1 above, are described in detail in Chapter III of this report. In that chapter the types of damage described fall into two general categories: direct and collateral. Direct damage, in this analysis, is damage incurred by the target set. Collateral damage is defined as all other damage that would result from a nuclear attack. Such damage may be measured in a number of ways, however, the most generally recognized method of assessing collateral damage is in terms of population fatalities resulting from a nuclear attack. Table 2, below is a summary of the results of the analysis for both an airburst and surface burst attack. The airburst is the most destructive in terms of collateral damage. It must be recognized that the attack objective was destruction of petroleum refineries. Hence, the airburst collateral damage has been calculated assuming a height of burst which was optimized for destruction of petroleum refineries (or in some cases petroleum storage tanks) and not the optimum height of burst for destruction of cities. Therefore, collateral damage was not maximized in the attack.

TABLE 2

SUMMARY OF RESULTS

Result	US	USSR
Refining Capacity Destroyed (Percent of National Capacity)	64	73
Storage Capacity Destroyed (Percent of National Capacity)	--	16
Airburst Prompt Fatalities	5,031,000	1,458,000[a] 836,000[b]
Surface Burst:		
Prompt Fatalities	2,883,000	722,000[a]
Fallout Fatalities	312,000	297,000[a]
Total Fatalities	3,195,000	1,019,000[a]

[a] Assuming 100% single story buildings

[b] Assuming 100% multi-story buildings

3

C.   OBSERVATIONS

This analysis addresses a limited nuclear attack basically directed at the US and USSR petroleum refineries. There are asymmetries between the target sets and strategic nuclear delivery vehicles (SNDVs). The effect of these asymmetries were mitigated by the vulnerability of petroleum refineries in the case of direct damage calculations. On the other hand, the same asymmetries led to significant differences in collateral damage calculations. The results are described below:

- **Refineries, Size and Number**   There are a large number of US petroleum refineries. With a few exceptions, each one of these refineries contributes only a small portion of the total US refining capacity. The Soviet Union has a smaller number of very large refineries and a few smaller refineries. As a result of this asymmetry, destruction of 77 US refineries would reduce US national refining capacity by approximately 64 percent. On the other hand, much of the Soviet refining capacity is concentrated in a number of large refineries and destruction of 24 refineries would reduce Soviet national refining capacity by approximately 73 percent.

- **Refineries, Location**   In the United States petroleum refineries tend to be grouped and clustered in certain geographic areas. In the Soviet Union, while there is also some grouping, the smaller number of refineries is more widely distributed. This distribution makes it infeasible to target the same number of refineries in each nation with the same number of SNDVs.

- **Collateral Damage**   The prime criterion used for weapon selection was number of independently targetable warheads. As a result 80 Soviet 1 MT MIRVs (80 EMT) from 10 SS-18 ICBMs were allocated to the target set. For the US attack sixty-four 40 KT and nine 170 Kt MIRVs (a total of 10.44 EMT) were allocated to the target set. This asymmetry coupled with asymmetries in population distribution with respect to refineries resulted in the differences in calculated collateral damage. Approximately 5 million prompt fatalities in the United States and no more than approximately 1.5 million prompt fatalities in the Soviet Union result in the case of an airburst attack.

- **Collateral Damage Calculations**   The calculation methods used by CCTC and DCPA were similar in most respects. There were two primary differences in assumptions: DCPA disregarded weapon accuracy and DCPA and CCTC assumed dissimilar sheltering conditions. This first difference turns out to be minor because of the large yield of the Soviet weapons. The latter assumption can cause large differences in results. For instance, assuming a single story distribution instead of a multi-story distribution results in an 80% increase in Soviet fatalities (i.e., 836,000 versus 1,458,000 fatalities).

5

II. APPROACH AND METHODOLOGY

A.   PROBLEM DESCRIPTION

The general attack description provided by the Office of Technology Assessment is as follows:[2]

> Small attacks on the US and the Soviet energy production and distribution systems. Each attack should use 10 SNDVs,[3] choosing SNDVs from the Soviet arsenal that appear appropriate to attack US targets, and vice versa. Targeting should be a plausible approximation of the way in which such a limited attack might be carried out if it were desired to maximize recovery time.

Given sufficient time and resources, the targeting selection process would probably be conducted as is outlined below:

- Identify and locate individual targets in both nations' energy production and distribution systems.

- Establish the vulnerability of each of these targets to nuclear weapons effects.

- Estimate the amount of recovery time for each target in a post attack environment.

- Considering the characteristics of the SNDVs available to each nation, each target's vulnerability to nuclear weapons effects, and estimated recovery time, plan an attack so as to maximize recovery time.

Having completed the four-step target selection process which is described above, the remainder of the analytic effort would be reduced to a calculation of the direct and collateral nuclear weapons effects including any possible synergistic effects.

---

[2] "OTA Study on the Effects of Nuclear War: Attack Cases," unpublished paper, U.S. Congress, Office of Technology Assessment, 22 December 1978.

[3] SNDVs- Strategic Nuclear Delivery Vehicles. The definitions of acronyms, abbreviations, technical terms, and phrases associated with strategic nuclear weapons and nuclear weapons effects used in this report are taken from: "SALT Lexicon," revised edition, U.S. Arms Control and·Disarmament Agency, Washington, D.C. undated; or The Effects of Nuclear Weapons, 3d ed, U.S. Department of Defense and US Department of Energy, 1977, Samuel Glasstone and Philip J. Dolan, eds.

6

The magnitude of the methodology described above is far beyond the scope of this effort, and would require the use of large, complex computer models. As a result, it was necessary, to make one major simplifying assumption concerning the target set selection. Petroleum refineries, a key component of both nations' energy production systems, were selected as the primary targets. The rationale behind this selection process is described in Section B (SELECTION OF THE TARGET SET) below. Having taken this step, it was determined that the complexity of the weapon selection process was also somewhat reduced. The weapon selection process is described below in Section C (WEAPON SELECTION).

B. SELECTION OF THE TARGET SET

1. Criteria

It was assumed that the National Command Authority (NCA) limited each attack to ten (10) SNDVs. In such a case, the targeting planner would then select a combination of nuclear delivery systems and targets which would result in a significant disruption of the enemy's energy production and distribution systems. The prime criterion established for attack planning purposes was to select targets that would maximize recovery time. The petroleum industry, and particularly petroleum refineries, was selected as an exemplar target subset which met the established criteria. The rationale for this a priori selection is detailed in paragraph 3 (Selection of the Petroleum Refining and Storage Subset), below. However, as a prelude to that paragraph, an overview of the composition of the energy production and distribution systems is provided in general terms below.

2. Target Set Description

Both the US and USSR maintain large complex energy systems which are widely dispersed through each nation. Although in both cases there tends to be some concentration of components near large cities, the primary energy production sources tend to be independent components. In an effort of this magnitude, it is not reasonable to expect that a complete description can be provided. However, inasmuch as some basic understanding of energy production and distribution is necessary to the understanding of the rationale behind the a priori target subset selection described in paragraph 3 (Selection of Petroleum Refining and Storage Subset), this paragraph describes the major components of each of the primary energy sources. There are four major sources of energy available

7

to the user, these are: (1) oil, (2) natural gas, (3) coal, and (4) electric power. A large portion of US and Soviet electric power production is based upon the use of oil, gas, and coal. However, within the general categories, the key components of the system which are necessary to provide power to the user are the source, processing facility, and distribution network. Table 3 below, a matrix display of the key components of the energy system, provides an indication of the numbers and locations of individual components. In one case, distribution, the numbers and locations are not listed. This is because the distribution systems for oil, gas, and coal either consist of a multitude of easily replaceable elements, such as trucks, or are relatively invulnerable to nuclear attack and easily repaired, such as pipelines which are normally below ground and can be readily replaced if damaged. Distribution of electric power in the United States, and in most of the Soviet Union, is accomplished through widespread and interconnected networks. Damage to powerlines can be readily by-passed and except for some switching and distribution points, most of the network can be fairly easily rebuilt. Hence, energy distribution systems were not considered as targets for the limited nuclear attack because of the foregoing, that is, their widespread locations and multitude of individual aim points.

The problem of target subset selection considering the limited number of individual warheads available to the targeteer, was then partially solved by constructing Table 3 and determining which of the key components of the nation's energy production systems could be significantly affected by a limited nuclear attack. This process is described below in paragraph 3 (Selection of Petroleum Refining and Storage Subset).

3. Selection of the Petroleum Refining and Storage Subset

The candidate target sets in Table 3 were limited to a smaller group which had few individual aim points, were not readily replaceable, or for which an alternate source did not exist. The candidates which fit into this reduced group were the processing set of the prime fossil fuels: (1) coal mines, (2) oil refineries, and (3) gas processing and gas deliquification plants. It should be noted that most of both nations' electric power production is derived from fossil fuels and hence any reduction in fossil fuel availability would probably also affect electric power production.

8

TABLE 3

ENERGY PRODUCTION AND DISTRIBUTION COMPONENTS

CATEGORY	PRIME SOURCES	NUMBERS	PROCESSING	NUMBERS	DISTRIBUTION
OIL	Wells Ports (Imports) Pipe Lines (Imports)	Thousands Tens	Refineries	Tens/Hundreds (tend to be clustered)	Pipe Lines/ Rail/Truck/ Barge/Ship
GAS	Wells Oil Refineries Ports (Imports) Pipe Lines (Imports)	Thousands Hundreds Tens Tens	Gas Plants Deliquification Plants	Tens/Hundreds Tens	Pipe Lines/ Rail/Truck/ Barge/Ship
COAL	Mines	Hundreds	Usually at Mines	Hundreds	Rail/Truck/ Barge/Coal Slurry Pipe Lines
ELECTRIC POWER PRODUCTION	Hydro Electric Thermal Nuclear Power Power Grids (Imports)	Tens Hundreds Tens Units	Same as Prime Source		Power Lines/ Power Grids

SOURCES: Vulnerability of Total Petroleum Systems: (Washington, D.C., Department of the Interior, Office of Oil and Gas), May 1973, prepared for the Defense Civil Preparedness Agency.

National Energy Outlook: 1976, (Washington, D.C., Federal Energy Administration), February 1976.

9

Consider a targeting schema which includes targets from each of the individual candidate groups. The advantage of such a targeting schema is that it reduces the problem introduced by weapon footprint (see Section C. WEAPON SELECTION, below), because of the availability of a number of targets in any general locality. However, while the total grouping of fossil fuel production facilities comprises a large set of diverse individual targets, selection of one particular type of target for a limited nuclear attack could serve to compound a nation's recovery problem provided these targets represent a substantial portion of a nation's energy supply. Such an attack would cause a nation wide fuel shortage, a nationwide demand for materials and equipment necessary for one type of facility, and a nationwide demand for the engineering design and construction experience required to build the type of facility destroyed. Additionally, if the attack were concentrated on one industry, personnel casualties would occur which would result in a shortage of trained operational and managerial personnel necessary to operate that type of facility which, in turn, would prevent their relocation to unattacked facilities in attempts to increase production. The limited size of the attack further dictates a concentration against a single system. The objective is to destroy the most important units of this key component. To satisfy the criterion of maximizing recovery time, the specific targets selected must have no practical substitute and not be readily replaceable. Petroleum refineries generally satisfy these conditions, as is noted below:

- Both the United States and Soviet Union are heavily dependent upon petroleum as an energy source. For example, it has been estimated that by 1980, between 45 and 54 percent of the United States energy demand will be satisfied by petroleum products.[4] For the Soviet Union, about 36 percent of that nation's 1980 energy demand will be met by the same source.[5]

- The transportation sector is heavily dependent upon petroleum products. A serious shortage of petroleum products would, by itself, cause serious disruption to the transportation sector, thereby hampering recovery efforts. The dependence of the transportation sector upon petroleum products is illustrated

---

[4] *Project Interdependence: US and World Energy Outlook Through 1990*, (Washington, D.C., U.S. Congress, Congressional Research Service, November 1977), p. 40 and pp. 45-62.

[5] John P. Hardt, Ronda A. Bresnick, and David Levine, "Soviet Oil and Gas in the Global Perspective," <u>Project Interdependence</u>, p. 808.

10

by the fact that in 1974, of the 18 quadrillion Btu's consumed in this economic sector, 96% were supplied from petroleum products.[6] This represents a projection consumption in the 1980 time frame of about one-half of the nation's energy demand.[7]

- A substantial portion of national electrical production is derived from petroleum products. For example, 22% of the US energy demand by electric utilities was supplied by approximately 13.4 quadrillion Btu's of petroleum products.[8] Projections show that the development of nuclear power and other changes in the electric production sector will decrease this demand to between 10 to 16% by the mid-1980s; however, this is still a substantial use of petroleum products.[9]

- Another substantial amount of petroleum is used for industrial fuel and power. For example, in 1974, about 4.4 quadrillion Btu's (representing approximately 21% of use in this sector) were supplied by petroleum products.[10]

- Another 1.4 quadrillion Btu's of petroleum and petrochemical products (i.e., liquid refinery gas, still gas, napthas, lubricants, waxes, etc.) were used as raw materials and feedstock in 1974.[11]

- While not directly translatable into equivalent figures, it should be kept in mind that the military is a large consumer of petroleum products. Almost all military vehicles (i.e., tanks, armored vehicles, self-propelled howitzers, aircraft, and all but a few ships) require refined petroleum products for fuel. Any serious degradation of petroleum supplies would thereby seriously impare the capability of military units.

---

[6] National Energy Outlook, p. C-2.

[7] Ibid, pp. 15-18.

[8] Ibid, p. C-2.

[9] "Exploratory Study of the Energy Crisis", (Falls Church, Va: Lulejian & Associates, Inc., 1973), pp. G-3 through G-24.

[10] National Energy Outlook, p. C-2.

[11] Ibid.

11

Many of these peacetime uses of petroleum products referred to could be curtailed in a post attack environment. However, in a petroleum-short environment any reduction in demand for petroleum products (e.g., curtailment of non-essential travel, replacement of petroleum-based non-essential materials with substitutes, reduction or elimination of petroleum as a fuel to non-essential industries, etc.) would probably be outweighed by the increased demand of those industries devoted to recovery. While some uses of petroleum, such as residential heating, electric power production, etc. could be reduced by a combination of stringent conservation measures and by shifting these users to alternative fuel sources, this would be a slow and torturous process, especially in a post-nuclear attack environment where all sectors are competing for the same resources. An example of how slow this process might be is best illustrated by considering the short term surge capacity of coal supply. It requires about "4 to 7 years to open a large new mine and the 'surge' capacity of the industry (to increase production rapidly) is limited."[12] This may not be the most serious constraint; however, when one considers that even in peacetime, it requires at least five years to build a coal-fired electric power plant.[13]

Thus, as has been briefly noted above, petroleum is an essential ingredient to our national economy and industry. It is not readily replaceable and we can presume that it must be similarly important to the Soviet Union. Therefore, petroleum refineries can meet the established attack criteria if the refining capacities of both nations can be significantly disrupted with the limited number of SNDVs available to the targeting planner.

4. Description of the Target Set

There are about 300 major oil refineries in the United States and about one-fifth that number in the Soviet Union. Since one of the requirements is to attack the refining capacity in a manner which maximizes damage, individual targets are ranked in order of their capacity. Such a ranking method is used in Tables 4A and 4B below; however, because of differences in data sources, definition of units and other data inconsistencies, it was

---

[12] National Energy Outlook, p. 169.

[13] Ibid, p. 174.

12

TABLE 4B
US REFINERY LOCATIONS AND REFINING
CAPACITY BY RANK ORDER

Rank Order	Location	Percent Capacity	Cumulative Percent Capacity	Location	Rank Order	Percent Capacity	Cumulative Percent Capacity
1	Raytown TX	3.6	3.6	Avon CA	34	0.7	47.9
2	Baton Rouge LA	2.9	6.4	Toledo OH	35	0.7	48.6
3	El Segundo CA	2.3	8.7	Corpus Christi TX	36	0.7	49.3
4	Whiting IN	2.1	10.8	Torrence CA	37	0.7	50.0
5	Port Arthur TX	2.1	12.9	Nederland TX	38	0.7	50.6
6	Richmond CA	2.0	14.9	Toledo OH	39	0.7	51.3
7	Texas City TX	2.0	16.9	Port Arthur	40	0.6	51.9
8	Beaumont TX	1.9	18.8	Wilmington CA	41	0.6	52.5
9	Port Arthur TX	1.9	20.7	Sugar Creek MO	42	0.6	53.1
10	Houston TX	1.8	22.5	Ferndale WA	43	0.6	53.7
11	Linden NJ	1.6	24.1	Sweeny TX	44	0.6	54.3
12	Deer Park TX	1.6	25.7	Borger TX	45	0.6	54.9
13	Wood River IL	1.5	27.3	Paulsboro NJ	46	0.5	55.4
14	Pasagoula MS	1.6	28.9	Wood River IL	47	0.5	55.9
15	Norco LA	1.3	30.1	Benicia CA	48	0.5	56.5
16	Philadelphia PA	1.2	31.3	Wilmington CA	49	0.5	57.0
17	Garyville LA	1.1	32.4	Martinez CA	50	0.5	57.5
18	Belle Chasse LA	1.1	33.5	Anacortes WA	51	0.5	58.0
19	Robinson TX	1.1	34.6	Kansas City KA	52	0.5	58.5
20	Corpus Christi TX	1.0	35.7	Tulsa OK	53	0.5	59.0
21	Philadelphia PA	1.0	36.7	Westville NJ	54	0.5	59.5
22	Jollett IL	1.0	37.7	West Lake LA	55	0.5	60.0
23	Carson CA	1.0	38.7	Lawrenceville IL	56	0.5	60.4
24	Lima OH	0.9	39.6	Eldorado KA	57	0.5	60.9
25	Perth Amboy NJ	0.9	40.6	Meraux LA	58	0.4	61.3
26	Marcus Hook PA	0.9	41.5	El Paso TX	59	0.4	61.7
27	Marcus Hook PA	0.9	42.4	Wilmington CA	60	0.4	62.2
28	Corpus Christi TX	0.9	43.3	Virgin Islands/Guam[a]	61	4.1	66.3
29	Lemont TX	0.8	44.1	Puerto Rico[a]	62	1.6	67.9
30	Convent LA	0.8	44.9	Alaska[a]	63	0.5	68.4
31	Delaware City DE	0.8	45.7	Hawaii[a][b]	64	0.3	68.7
32	Cattlettsburg KY	0.8	46.5	Other[c]	65	31.3	100.0
33	Ponca City OK	0.7	47.2				

Source: National Petroleum Refiners Association

Note: a. Sum of all refineries in the indicated geographic area.

b. Foreign trade zone only.

c. Includes summary data from all refineries with capacity less than 75,000 BBL/DAY. 224 refineries included.

necessary to convert refining capacity to some common unit. In Tables 4A and 4B, this common unit is percent of gross national refining capacity. Secondly, in the case of the Soviet data (Table 4A) the listing includes all new plants known to be planned or under construction which will account for an estimated 1,960,000 barrels of crude per day (BBL/day), an increase of approximately 22 percent of the reported 1976 Soviet refining capacity. Finally, there are inconsistencies in the Soviet data. It may be noted on Table 4A that the last entry "other" represents 43.7 percent of Soviet capacity. This is not a single refinery but represents a total of 15 refineries, and this entry was made by the data source for the reasons stated below:[14]

> This plant-by-plant listing made available for the first time falls short of official reports of 45 refineries with a total capacity of 9,100,000 BBL/day. The difference of 15 refineries with a capacity roughly estimated at 4,830,000 BBL/day is listed to reconcile this survey total which is also available this year for the first time in recent history.

The US data represents individual locations for refineries with a capacity of 75,000 BBL of crude oil per day and larger. Excluded from the listing are individual refineries in Alaska, Puerto Rico, the Virgin Islands, Guam, and Hawaii. These excluded refineries, which are included in summary form near the end of the list, account for about 6.5 percent of the total US refining capacity of 17.8 million barrels of crude oil per day.[15] The last entry on Table 4B represents 224 US refineries each with a capacity of less than 75,000 BBL of crude per day.

---

[14] International Petroleum Encyclopedia, 1976.

[15] "US Refining Capacity," (Washington, D.C.: National Petroleum Refiners Association, July 28, 1978), p-1.

14

C. WEAPON SELECTION

The target subset selection process, as shown above, was largely dictated by the number of elements in the subset, the importance of the element to the energy system, the replaceability of the element, and the amount of recovery time required. After considering these factors, the petroleum refineries were selected as the target set. The next stage of the targeting process is to determine if it is possible to substantially reduce the refining capacity. This analysis is necessary in order to obtain some information about the vulnerability of petroleum refineries to nuclear weapon effects considering the characteristics of the strategic nuclear weapons which will be available to both nations to attack the refineries.

In a typical refinery similar elements are usually grouped together for the purpose of efficiency. The key elements that significantly impact upon production capacity are the basic crude distillation units, the cracking units, the cooling towers, the power house and boiler plant. Fractionating towers are the primary vulnerable components of the crude distillation and cracking units. The severe winds from a nuclear air burst can overturn and destroy these units, and also serves as the destruction mechanism for cooling towers. This grouping of key components is illustrated on Figure 1, a schematic of a typical small to medium size Soviet refinery. While some US refineries tend to occupy larger areas (typically about 20 to 40 thousand square feet) the key production elements are usually grouped for the same purpose. Blast (i.e., overpressure) and fragmentation are the primary damage mechanisms against the power plant and boilers.[16] According to Glasstone,[17] the chief cause of damage to petroleum storage tanks, large numbers of which are located at or near any refinery, appears to be lifting of the tank from its foundation. Severe damage in the case of storage tanks is determined when loss of contents occurs with possible secondary effects, such as the development of fires. Thus,

---

[16] "First Quarters Technical Report: ARPA-Long Range Research & Development Program System Study (U)," (LaJolla, California, Science Applications, Inc.) 1973, SECRET/RESTRICTED DATA.

[17] The Effects of Nuclear Weapons, pp. 227-8.

15

FIGURE 1

Typical small to medium size Soviet Refinery

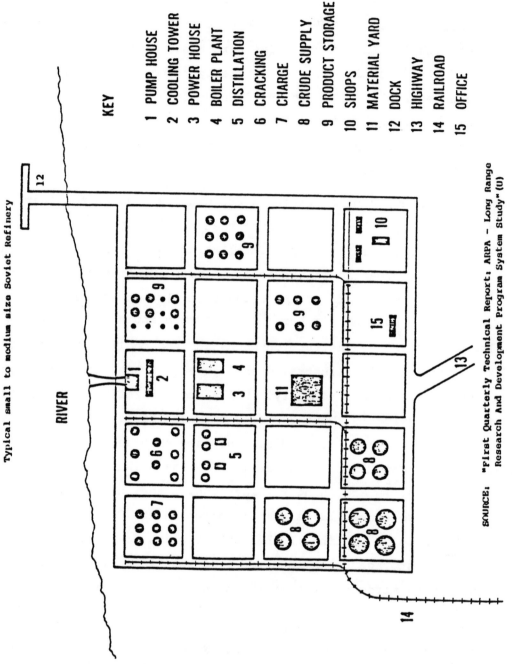

KEY

1 PUMP HOUSE
2 COOLING TOWER
3 POWER HOUSE
4 BOILER PLANT
5 DISTILLATION
6 CRACKING
7 CHARGE
8 CRUDE SUPPLY
9 PRODUCT STORAGE
10 SHOPS
11 MATERIAL YARD
12 DOCK
13 HIGHWAY
14 RAILROAD
15 OFFICE

RIVER

SOURCE: "First Quarterly Technical Report; ARPA – Long Range
Research And Development Program System Study" (U)

16

refineries and their associated tank farms are relatively soft targets, and for all practical purposes, one may assume that an arriving nuclear warhead from a strategic weapon will severely damage or destroy a refinery. A more detailed discussion of nuclear weapon effects on petroleum refineries and tank farms is proved in Section III of this report. However, because of the number of targets (petroleum refineries) and their relative vulnerability to nuclear effects, the total number of individually targetable warheads becomes a more important consideration than either yield or accuracy when considering modern strategic weapons. To illustrate this--keeping in mind the basic premise that for each nuclear weapon which arrives, a refinery is essentially destroyed--Figures 2 and 3 may be examined. Figure 2 illustrates the cumulative percentage of refining capacity for the largest 100 US refineries. Figure 3 illustrates the same information for all Soviet refineries. In this figure, however, the 15 "other" refineries which were previously treated as a group have now been treated as 15 individual entries each with a capacity of approximately 322,000 barrels of crude per day.

An inspection of Figures 2 and 3 indicates that a total of 59 nuclear weapons may be used to target 100% of the Soviet refining capacity and that the same number of nuclear weapons delivered against the largest US refineries will cover only 65% of our refining capacity. The targeting problem at this point is reduced to one of selecting the strategic nuclear weapons with the largest number of individually targetable warheds. Table 5 lists the primary characteristics of strategic nuclear delivery vehicles for both forces in 1980. An evaluation of Table 5 indicates that with the criteria previously established, the US POSEIDON or TRIDENT I missile and the USSR SS-18/2 missile must be used. However, the final US choice did not include TRIDENT I missiles since these systems may not be available in the early 1980s.

There is one other problem associated with missile targeting which has not yet been discussed. A missile with Multiple Independently Targetable Reentry Vehicles (MIRVs) has a "footprint" or area over which it is capable of delivering independent warheads. The size of this footprint is a function of the amount of fuel available for the missile to maneuver and missile range capability. While unclassified footprint data are not available, it has been assumed that an ICBM has a larger footprint than the shorter range SLBMs.

17

FIGURE 2

CUMULATIVE US REFINING CAPACITY

1978

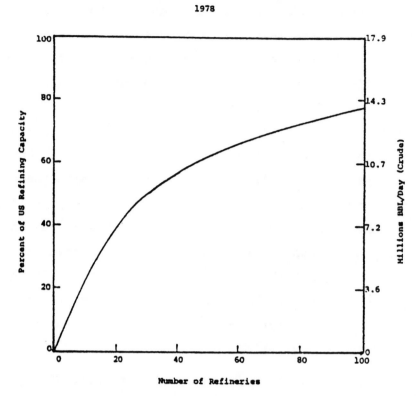

Source: National Petroleum Refiners Association

FIGURE 3

CUMULATIVE USSR REFINING CAPACITY

1980 PROJECTION

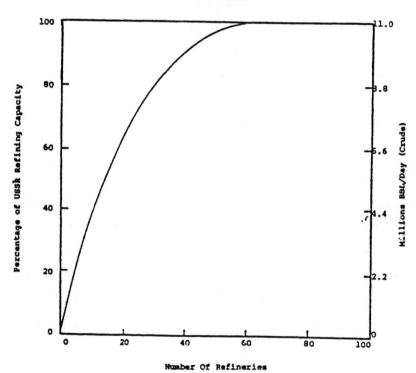

Source: International Petroleum Encyclopedia 1976

Table 5.

US AND USSR STRATEGIC WEAPONS SYSTEMS
-1980-

US				USSR			
SYSTEM	YIELD/ WARHEAD (MT)	MIRVs	TOTAL NUMBER OF SNDVs	SYSTEM	YIELD/ WARHEAD (MT)	MIRVs	TOTAL NUMBER OF SNDVs
ICBM				ICBM			
TITAN II	9	1	54	SS-11	1.0	1	500
MM II	1.0	1	450	SS-16	1.0	1	60
MM III	.17	3	550	SS-17	0.2	4	212
				SS-18/1	18.0	1	154
				SS-18/2	1.0	8	154
				SS-19	0.2	6	300
SLBM				SLBM			
POLARIS	0.6	1	96	SS-N-6	1.0	1	544
POSEIDON	0.04	10	464	SS-N-8	1.0	1	476
TRIDENT I	0.1	10	32				
B-52							
SRAM	0.2	a	a				
BOMBS	2.0	a	a				

SOURCES: A. A. Tinajero, Projected Strategic Offensive Weapons Inventories of the U.S. and U.S.S.R.: An Unclassified Estimate, Washington, D.C.: Library of Congress Congressional Research Service, 77-59F, 24 March 1977.

Les Aspin, "Civil Defense" Congressional Record (reprint) Vol 125 No. 1, Jan 15, 1979, p-5.

a. Combinations of up to 20 SRAMs and 4 bombs on 316 aircraft.

19

For the purposes of this study it was assumed that an SLBM had a footprint in the shape of an elipse with a major axis of 200 miles down range and a minor axis of 100 miles cross range. ICBMs were assumed to have a footprint with 500 and 300 mile limits. In Section D below, a more detailed discussion is provided on the effects of target footprint upon weapon targeting.

D.   ATTACK DESCRIPTION

The general attack plan was laid out, from the foregoing considerations. When the geographic distribution of Soviet refineries was considered, it was noted that there were three high value isolated targets some of which are located beyond POSEIDON missile range. It was decided that these targets would be attacked with MINUTEMAN III missiles. The remaining refineries, subject to footprint restrictions, were attacked with POSEIDON missiles. The final US attack plan then called for the use of seven POSEIDON and three MINUTEMAN III missiles for a total of ten independent footprints. There were in each footprint, less refineries than the number of available independently targetable warheads. These additional warheads were first allocated in a 2-on-1 fashion on large refineries and then any extra warheads were targeted against Soviet petroleum storage complexes. The final targeting plan attacked twenty-four refineries and thirty-four storage sites. Because the refineries targeted include most of the large Soviet refineries, approximately 72 percent of Soviet refining capacity was targeted in the planned attack. For the Soviet attack on the United States, the limitations imposed by the weapon footprint was less of a problem due to two factors. First, only the SS-18/2 ICBM was considered and therefore a larger footprint was available. Second, there are many more refineries in the United States, and these refineries tend to be clustered in certain geographic areas. For the 80 independently targetable warheads available on 10 SS-18/2 missiles it was possible to allocate weapons against 77 individual refineries which account for 67% of the overall US refining capacity. The three remaining warheads were used in a 2-on-1 attack on the largest refinery in their respective footprints.

Figures 4 and 5 below represent the approximate footprint coverage of the planned attack. Figure 4 represents the US attack on Soviet petroleum refineries and petroleum storage sites, and Figure 5 represents the same

20

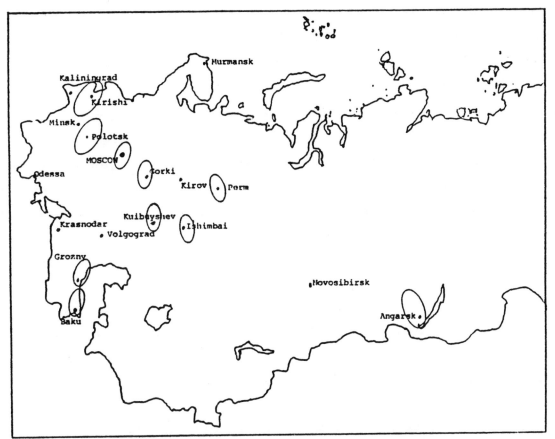

Figure 4 - Approximate Footprint Coverage of US Attack

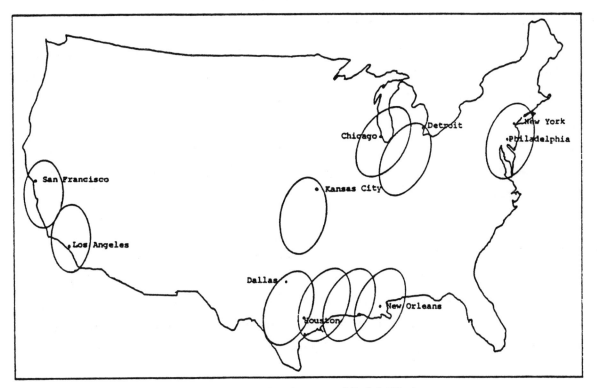

Figure 5 - Approximate Footprint Coverage of Soviet Attack

21

information for the Soviet attack on US refineries. The location of several large cities are shown on these charts for orientation purposes only.

E.   METHODOLOGY

Thus far in Chapter II the discussion of target and weapon selection·has been addressed in general terms. If the analysis were restricted to an evaluation of the direct results of a nuclear attack (i.e., calculation of refinery capacity destroyed) the general method used would have provided sufficient data to complete the analysis. However, this was not the case in that it was necessary to provide an estimation of the collateral damage which would result from such an attack. These estimations were to be obtained from three sources. Estimates of collateral damage resulting from the Soviet attack were obtained from the Defense Civil Preparedness Agency (DCPA). Estimates of collateral damage resulting from the US attack were provided by the Department of Defense Command and Control Technical Center (CCTC) and some additional collateral damage calculations resulting from the US attack on the Soviet Union were obtained from calculations performed by a private research firm. In order to perform the calculations, the three computer models required a precise definition of the weapon characteristics and aim points. The general process used to precisely locate the targets is described below.

In the case of Soviet targets, the aim point (i.e., DGZ-desired ground zero) was obtained from classified sources and these locations were provided to CCTC along with weapon characteristics. Using these data, CCTC then provided the independent private research firm with a demographic data base for use in the independent calculations. In addition, CCTC also provided raw collateral damage calculation data which have been integrated into the results presented in Chapter III of this report.

Location of US refineries presented more of a challenge. Fortunately, the data obtained from the National Petroleum Refiners Association provided the location of the city or town in which the refinery was located. Using these data, cross referenced with location data by county or parish, it was then possible to identify the petroleum refinery on maps published by the U.S. Geological Survey, Washington, D.C. These topographic maps which exist for the

22

entire United States, present a well defined representation of streets, major buildings and installations. Topographic features for 7.5 minutes of Longitude and 7.5 minutes of Latitude are of such detail that individual refineries may be identified by their characteristics in those few cases where the map annotation does not specify "oil refinery."

23

III. ANALYSIS

A. OVERALL

1. Introduction

The preceding chapter of this report contained a description of the general approach used to establish attack parameters and the general analytical methodology used to calculate both direct and collateral damage. This chapter, presents a more detailed description of differences in the computer models, a detailed discussion of both direct and collateral damage, and a discussion of the limitations and uncertainties resulting from those assumptions, analytical methods, and data used in this report.

2. Computer Models

Three computer models were used during the analysis to calculate collateral damage. A general description of these models and differences among them is provided below.

a. Collateral damage in terms of fatalities and injuries was provided by The Defense Civil Preparedness Agency (DCPA) for the Soviet attack on US refineries. DCPA's data base for US casuality calculations consists of three separate bases: (1) 1975 census data, (2) a survey of the numbers and types of shelters available (updated yearly by DCPA) and, (3) average monthly wind direction and speed at five levels of altitude across the US (obtained from Global Weather control). Since DCPA is only concerned with megaton class weapons with accuracies (i.e., CEP's) of a few hundred feet, two simplifying assumptions have been made (1) accuracy is disregarded and, (2) a computation of effects every two minutes of latitude and longitude is sufficient. In practice this last assumption entails dividing the country up into grids which are two minutes by two minutes in latitude and longitude and assuming that the overpressure, dynamic pressure, radiation, and fallout calculated at the center of a grid cell applies to the entire population within the particular cell.

24

The population is distributed in the shelters (subways, basements, steel framed buildings, etc.) within the grid cells as desired. In this particular case the following assumptions were made as to sheltering:

- Ten percent of the population near military installations and in large cities (normal population greater than 50,000) are evacuated before hand due to rising international tensions.

- Those people having home basements were told to take shelter in them. Three-fourths of these basements were assumed to be available in addition to public shelters (subways, etc.) for public use. It was assumed that shelters were occupied in proportion to the numbers available with no attempt made to occupy the best shelter first.

- The remaining people were assumed to be in buildings which offer about the same protection from blast as a single story home.

- Radiation protection factors were compenserate with the type of structures occupied.[18]

For prompt effects (overpressure and initial radiation), DCPA developed a set of mathematical functions which relate the initial radiation or peak overpressure to the probability that a person is injured or killed (within a structure type). Since overpressure, for example, at the center of the grid cell is assumed to apply to all the people within the cell, this probability is interpreted as the fraction of the population injured or killed within the cell.

For fallout effects, DCPA uses its wind data in conjunction with a fallout model developed by the Office of the Director of Defense Research and Engineering, Weapons Systems Evaluation Group (WSEG) to calculate the fallout radiation levels with time for vast areas of the US. These radiation levels are then used to calculate casualties in a manner similar to the initial radiation casualty calculation above. The only additional assumption here is that survivors try to leave areas which are very high in fallout radiation (presumably warned by civil defense mechanisms after the attack).

---

[18]A radiation protection factor (PF) is the ratio of the exterior radiation level to the interior radiation level. Thus, if the particular structure has a PF of 10, then the radiation level inside the structure is one-tenth of that outside.

Thus for each grid cell, the initial and fallout radiation levels and the peak overpressure level are first calculated. These levels are then used to calculate the fraction of the population killed and injured in each of the main shelter conditions within the grid cell. These are simply summed for each grid cell and then across all the cells to give the total number of people killed and injured.

b.   Collateral damage in terms of fatalities and casualties was provided by the Department of Defense Command and Control Technical Center (CCTC) for the US attack on Soviet refineries and petroleum storage. CCTC's data base for USSR casualty calculations consists of two data bases: (1) the 1979 Target Data Inventory (which contains the location and sizes of population centers and the type of housing associated with the centers) and (2) the average monthly wind direction and speed at five levels of altitudes across the USSR (obtained from Global Weather control).

For purposes of illustration, CCTC was tasked to provide calculations for several shelter distributions. People were assumed to be in wither wood framed houses or multi-story buildings. Then, within these two main cases, calculations were performed for protection factors of 2, 5, 10, and 50.

The method used in calculating prompt and fallout fatalities and casualties was the physical vulnerability system.[19] This system takes into account weapon accuracy, the response of people to different levels of blast and radiation, the actual distribution of people with respect to the weapon aimpoint, and population responses to fallout radiation levels over time.[20] The fallout model employed was the same one used by DCPA - i.e., the

---

[19]"The Physical Vulnerability Handbook - Nuclear Weapons (U), Defense Intelligence Agency, AP-550-1-2-69-INT, (CONFIDENTIAL).

[20]"Description of Mathematics for the Single Integrated Damage Analysis Capability (SIDAC)," National Military Command System Support Center, Technical Memorandum TM15-23, 1 July 1973.

WSEG model. Thus, the only real differences between the methodologies used
by DCPA and CCTC are that:

- DCPA used a coarser population grid than CCTC.
- DCPA assumed a probability of kill or injury based on a single calculation at the center of its grid cells while CCTC uses an average probability of damage.
- DCPA disregards weapon accuracy.[21]

     c. An existing private contractor's model was adapted for use as
an analytical tool during the study. This model was used to calculate
collateral damage in terms of prompt fatalities for the US attack on Soviet
refineries and storage sites. The demographic data base for this model was
provided by CCTC. The only difference between the CCTC calculations and the
contractor's was that an assumption was made in regard to the size of
population centers.[22] The assumption made was that if the center's population
was 100,000 or less than the diameter of the center was 1.2 n.m. However, if
the center had a population of over 100,000, then the diameter was assumed to
be 2.0 n.m. In comparing the results from the contractor model and CCTC's,
an overall difference of less than 2 percent was found to exist. The advantage to
the contractor's model over that of CCTC's was that any sheltering distribution
of people between single story residences, multi story buildings, basements,
and underground shelters could be made. The contractor's model was not adapted
to fallout calculations due to time constraints.

B. EFFECTS

1. General

     The general description of a nuclear blast, given below, is based
upon the details and sequence of events that would occur in conjunction with
a one megaton weapon detonated at an altitude of 7,000 feet. This chronology
is to provide the reader with a fuller understanding of the effects of a nulcear

---

[21] It should be noted that CCTC made computer calculations in addition to the
ones noted above which also disregard weapon accuracy. While fatalities
and casualties at individual points differed between the two runs, overall
results were within 3% of each other.

[22] A city or urban area is usually described in terms of small population
centers (circles) ranging in size from 1.0 n.m. to 4 n.m. in diameter.

blast upon a populated area. While the effects of a 40 KT or 170 KT airburst are very similar, there is obviously a variance in magnitude.

Like most physical phenomena, the effects of a nuclear explosion are influenced by its environment. Both meteorological and surface conditions (as well as weapon construction) may significantly alter the effects from similar weapons. The effects that various physical conditions may produce will not be addressed; rather, a typical case will be presented.

Through means of a chemical explosion, the fissionable elements of a nuclear warhead are brought together. With large yield weapons, such as the one being described, the uncontrolled fission reaction resulting from this critical mass triggers a second thermonuclear reaction (fusion) from heavy water (tritium) elements incorporated in the weapon's construction. The net effect is the almost instantaneous release of the same amount of energy as would be released in the detonation of 1,000,000 tons of TNT.

2. Thermal Effects

Less than a millionth of a second after the detonation, the temperature at the burst point has jumped to several tens of millions of degrees. Since, at this time, the vast amount of energy is contained in a small volume (the immediate vicinity of the original warhead), the air pressure will also elevate to over a million times that of normal atmospheric conditions. The spread of this pressure signals the beginning of the blast wave. The crushing pressures and violent winds associated with blast waves cause much of the destruction resulting from a nuclear explosion. This process is described in more detail later.

The high temperature causes large amounts of energy to be radiated. Initially, this radiation is mainly in the form of X-rays which are absorbed within a few feet by the surrounding air. It may be noted, that these events have occurred in a time span which is measured in millionths or thousandths of a second, while events which are covered later in this description, occur over a period of time ranging from a few seconds to a few hours. At this early point in the explosion, temperature and pressure gradients cover a wide range in a matter of a few feet or even inches near the central point of the explosion.

It is not unreasonable, at this point, to visualize the explosion as a glowing glass sphere with temperatures and pressures at its center similar to those at the center of the sun, while at the surface conditions are near normal. As this glowing sphere influences its surrounding environment, the sphere expands to dissipate its energy. There is a sharp transition between the inside and the outside of the sphere. As the X-rays are absorbed by the air, the air is heated to the point where visible, ultraviolet, and infrared light are radiated. The result is an extremely hot, luminous mass of air which is commonly called the fireball

Approximately one percent of the total thermal radiation will be emitted within the first one-tenth of a second; this is the first thermal pulse. There is also a longer, larger second pulse which will yield the remaining 99 percent of the energy as heat and light. The primary threats to people during the first thermal pulse are flash blindness and retinal burns. This first pulse occurs so rapidly that the human eyelid blink reflex is non-functional. Flash blindness is a temporary condition similar to the dazzle associated with photo flashbulbs, only of a much longer duration. Retinal burns are permanent eye injuries which occur because concentration of the fireball light on the retina raises the temperature to the point where this non-regenerative tissue is destroyed. Because of the construction of the human eye, flash blindness and retinal burns can occur at great distances from the blast. Given the altitude of the particular explosion being examined, the safe distance on a clear day is approximately 10 miles for flash blindness and 25 miles for retinal burns. At night these safe distances are approximately 45 and 55 miles, respectively.

As the second thermal pulse begins, the fireball is almost 500 feet in diameter and expanding rapidly. Within ten seconds, the fireball will reach its maximum width of about a mile. During this period the fireball is a swirling toroid of hot luminous air. An updraft exists, which in low air-bursts is of sufficient strength to suck small particles of dirt into the fire-ball. These will become radioactive and fall out of the atmosphere later.

During the growth of the fireball, it is also rising because its hot gases are lighter than those of the surrounding cooler air. The net effect of the updraft, growth of the fireball, and its rise in the case of a weapon

29

detonated on or near the ground is the well known radioactive mushroom cloud. This will not occur in the case being considered since the height of burst is sufficient to preclude any significant amounts of debris being sucked up into the fireball. Thus, any significant amounts of fallout are also precluded. After approximately a minute, the luminous cloud that was the fireball has cooled to such an extent that it no longer emits visible light and has risen to almost six miles in altitude.

As previously stated, the second thermal pulse which starts about one-tenth of a second after detonation is of longer duration and contains more thermal radiation than the first pulse. For that reason, this second pulse is more dangerous in terms of personnel injuries and property damage. There are two main threats associated with this second thermal pulse: flashburns and fire. The rapidity at which the thermal flux is delivered is the key to understanding its effects on people and their surroundings. Within ten seconds of the blast, more than one-third of the one megaton weapon's energy will have been delivered as light and heat. Like most biological systems, man is unable to adapt to a violently changing physical environment. Thus, the amount of energy delivered in a few seconds by a nuclear explosion would not be as damaging to people if it were delivered over several minutes. In the short concentrated delivery of thermal radiation in a nuclear explosion, the thin outer layer of many materials which are not normally thought of as being very combustible (i.e., wood siding, trees, heavy fabric, plastics, etc.) will char but will not sustain a fire. This statement should not be construed as minimizing the power of thermal radiation. The potential for third degree burns and fire at distances which are relatively safe from blast and initial radiation effects of a nuclear weapon is very high.[23] At a distance of five miles, the thermal flux will cause a third degree burn on any exposed human tissue. (A third degree burn is the complete destruction and charring of tissue.) The danger from burns is not fully dissipated until a distance of about 8.5 miles from ground zero. It is interesting to note that at this range, blast damage effects include little more than broken windows.

While primary fires will occur (e.g., fires resulting from the instantaneous ignition of combustible materials such as draperies, debris, etc.), these are not normally considered to be a major cause of fire damage.[24]

_____

[23]"The Impact of Fires Produced by Tactical Nuclear Weapons," (LaJolla, California, Science Applications, Inc., December 1976), p. 15.

[24] Ibid., p. 6-8.

What is of major concern are the secondary forces which are sure to occur from the breaking of gas mains, electric power lines, etc. Also of primary consideration in the destruction of a refinery is the vast amount of uncontained fuel which is sure to ignite. Many conflagrations and possibly firestorms would undoubtedly result. While other radiations (gamma rays, neutrons, beta particles and alpha particles) account for another one-sixth of the weapon's total energy, in this case these effects would extend little beyond ground zero. Therefore, initial radiation was not germaine to this discussion or the analysis.

Tables 6 and 7 below summarize the extent of some of the effects which have been described above.

Table 6

Population Burns

Range (n.m.)	Percent of Exposed Population Burned and Extent of Burns	
5.2<	100%	3rd Degree
5.5	50%	3rd Degree and 50% 2nd Degree
6.2	50%	2nd Degree and 50% 1st Degree
7.8	50%	1st Degree and 50% No Burns
8.6>	100%	No Burns

SOURCE: The Effects of Nuclear Weapons, p. 564-65

Table 7

Ignition Ranges of Various Materials

Range (n.m.)	Material
4.0	Drapery (light)
4.6	Drapery (dark)
3.2	Cotton Clothing (light)
3.8	Cotton Clothing (dark)
6.0	Newspaper
3.6	Roll Roofing
4.7	Plywood (flaming)
3.8	Sand (exploding, popping

SOURCE: The Effects of Nuclear Weapons, p. 287-89

31

3.   Blast Effects

About one-half of the energy released by a nuclear detonation is concentrated in a blast or shock wave, which is described below.

Shortly after the fireball is formed, a spherical high pressure air wave moves rapidly outward from the fireball. This blast wave may also be thought of as a rapdily expanding bubble, as in the analogy used for the fireball. There are entreme physical differences between the inside and out-side of the bubble. Initially, this difference is several million pounds per square inch (psi). After approximately ten seconds, when the fireball has expanded to its maximum size of one mile, the blast wave will have travelled almost three miles along the ground in all directions at a speed in excess of the speed of sound. At this point (three miles from ground zero), the difference between the pressure in front of the shock wave and the pressure just behind the shock wave will be about seven psi. The general variation of pressure as a function of time is represented in Figure 6 below.   Once the shock wave strikes the ground, the blast wave as a whole is no longer spherical.

Figure 6

Pressure Variation Over Time

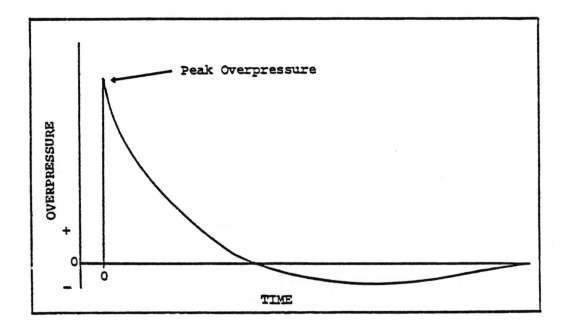

32

The wave is reflected from the earth's surface and merges with the remaining portion of the incoming shock wave in what is known as the "Mach Effect." For the one MT weapon being addressed, this effect will occur about one mile from the point directly under the blast (ground zero). As the blast wave passes a fixed point (see Figure 6), the pressure jumps from the normal ambient pressure of about 14.7 psi to a maximum "peak overpressure," the magnitude of which is a function of the nuclear weapon yield, height if burst, and distance from ground zero. All objects undergo compression during this portion of the blast effect which will last about three seconds at three miles from ground zero. The initial overpressure decreases rapidly from its maximum and, in fact, will decrease to below ambient pressure for a short period of time after the blast wave passes.

The other phenomenon characteristic of the blast wave beside compression is strong winds (normally called dynamic pressure) which can reach velocities of several thousand miles per hour close to ground zero. At a distance of three miles from the one megaton airburst these winds will exceed 200 miles per hour for a short interval. The drag forces resulting from these high velocity winds are one of the major causes of building destruction. The process works something like this: a structure is subjected to a huge crushing force, first on the side toward the blast and shortly thereafter on all sides as the blast wave passes, with little chance for an equalization of pressure. At the same time, the structure is subjected to winds that can be far beyond normal hurricane strength. A building covered with sheet steel can be crushed like a tin can and then blown away. At overpressures of 2 to 5 psi, a two-story wood frame home can be completely destroyed. The first floor is crushed, the main frame is splintered, and the already heavily damaged second story will crash through the first floor. For overpressures of 5 psi and higher, a wood frame home becomes a jumble of splintered wood which has been blown away from its foundation. Steel framed and reinforced concrete buildings, such as office buildings and highrise apartments, are severely damaged at overpressures ranging from 2 to 10 psi depending upon their method of construction. In any event, between the range of 4 to 10 psi, exterior walls can be expected to crack and fail. The accompanying high winds will cause most of the materials of the upper floors to be ejected out the side of the building.

33

Fractured interior and exterior walls, furniture, and people would be thrown hundreds of feet, leaving the bare steel frame of such buildings in the wake of the blast. At overpressures of 10 psi, 2.2 miles from ground zero, the dynamic pressure is sufficient to topple the steel frame while the material is being ejected.

Thus far, the effects of the blast on structures has been discussed. However, it is obvious that any damage to buildings in a populated area will be accompanied by fatalities and injuries to people. Those people unfortunate enough to be inside a building which collapses (six miles or less from this blast) are likely to be crushed or at the minimum, severely injured. Those outside may be crushed or severely injured by flying debris. At distances up to 6.5 to 7 miles, broken bones and damage to internal organs from flying debris will be the primary damage mechanisms. As far as nine to ten miles, flying glass will cause serious injuries. Closer to the blast, the effects are significantly more damaging. People will be picked up by the high winds and thrown against stationary objects. This effect (called translation) results in broken bones and ruptured internal organs. At a distance of 3.5 miles rrom ground zero, an average sized person will attain a velocity of 12 to 14 miles per hour, prior to impact. At such a speed, severe injury (i.e., skull fracture, punctured lung, ruptured spleen, etc.) can be expected as a result of sudden deceleration. A large percentage of the population at this distance will incur fatal injuries. Approximately one mile closer to ground zero (i.e., 2.5 miles from ground zero) the mortality rate will be about 50 percent.

Overpressure alone will directly affect humans. Severe and fatal lung damage will occur within a mile of the blast. Lung hemmorage or edema (swelling due to fluid accumulation) can result in suffocation in a matter of minutes. If lung damage is severe, air bubbles can enter the blood stream, and when they reach the brain or heart, the resulting air embolic obstruction will cause death in short course. Also associated with severe lung hemmorage is fibrin emboli (related to the body's blood clotting mechanism) which will cause damage to the brain and other critical organs.

Some of the other effects on the human body are eardrum damage (up to 3.4 miles from ground zero), suffocation caused by inhalation of airborne dust, and blackouts from minor head injuries and temporary circulation disruption.

34

Inside of a building, the blast wave is somewhat attenuated depending upon building placement and aperture geometry. At lower pressures, where the structure does not fail, fatalities are unlikely.

It may be noted that the most significant blast effects occur within the range of extreme thermal flux (e.g., 100% third degree burns inside of 5.2 miles). Because the duration of the second thermal pulse is only ten seconds, people can take some cover during this period and avoid most of the effects. However, the blast wave, unlike the thermal pulse, will "bend" around corners and go into buildings. In short, there are few hiding places. It must be remembered that when the second thermal pulse has ended (after ten seconds), the blast wave has traveled about 2.5 miles. It will continue to cause death, destruction, and injuries for about four times that distance 50 seconds after the explosion. So that while the blast effects appear to be less destructive to the population, it is actually the primary cause of casualties and destruction. Personnel casualty and structural damage radii are summarized in Tables 8 and 9.

4. Details of Effects on a Selected Urban/Industrial Area

a. Soviet Attacks on Refineries Near Philadelphia

The Soviet attack on US refineries includes two large refineries in southwest Philadelphia. They are lcoated at 2.2 and 3.7 nautical miles (n.m.) from the center of the city. Since the Soviet weapons have a yield of one megaton, these weapons can be expected to produce severe damage to the city, including a large number of fatalities and injuries. Figure 7, a map of the Philadelphia area, illustrates both the ground zeros of the two weapons attacking these two refineries and two and five mile radius circles around these two points. The effects of these attacks on Philadelphia serve as general indicators for the effects of attacks on similarly located refineries (e.g., Los Angeles-Long Beach, Leningrad, and Moscow), subject, of course, to significant differences in relative locations and weapon yields.

35

TABLE 8

APPROXIMATE DISTANCE (NAUTICAL MILES) OF VARIOUS EFFECTS
FROM SELECTED NUCLEAR AIR BURSTS

PERSONNEL CASUALTIES

	EFFECT	Weapon Yield		
		1 MT	170 KT	40 KT
Blast	Lethality - Threshold	0.25	<0.25	<0.25
	Lung Damage - Threshold	2.1	1.1	0.7
	Severe	0.8	0.5	0.3
	Broken Eardrums - Threshold	3.5	2.0	1.2
	50%	1.0	0.6	0.4
Translation	Personnel in the Open - 1%	3.3	1.6	0.9
	Personnel Near Structures - 1%	3.8	1.9	1.0
	50%	2.1	1.0	0.6
Thermal	Third Degree Burn - 100%	5.2	2.6	1.5
	No Burns - 100%	8.7	4.8	2.8
	Flashblindness*	10	9	8
	Retinal Burn*	25	23	20
Radiation	Lethal Dose (1000 rads)	0.9	0.8	0.7
	No Harm (100 rads)	1.2	1.1	1.0

* Daytime Safe Distance

TABLE 9

APPROXIMATE DISTANCE (NAUTICAL MILES) FOR 50% PROBABILITY
OF DESTRUCTION FROM NUCLEAR AIR BURSTS

	STRUCTURE TYPE	Weapon Yield		
		1 MT	170 KT	40 KT
Building Types	• Wood Frame	4.5	2.5	1.5
	• Masonry Load Bearing Walls, 1 or 2 Story	2.8	1.6	0.9
	• Steel Framed, 2 to 10 Stories	1.9	0.8	0.3
	• Reinforced Concrete Framed, 2 to 10 Stories	1.8	0.9	0.5
Electric Power Plants	• Electrical Equipment (8 months recovery)	2.6	1.4	0.8
	• Power Plant (1 year recovery)	1.2	0.5	0.2
Railroads	• Control and Switching	3.5	1.8	1.1
	• Roundhouses	2.6	1.3	0.7
Refinery Type Targets		2.0	1.0	0.6

Figure 7

PHILADELPHIA & SURROUNDING COUNTIES

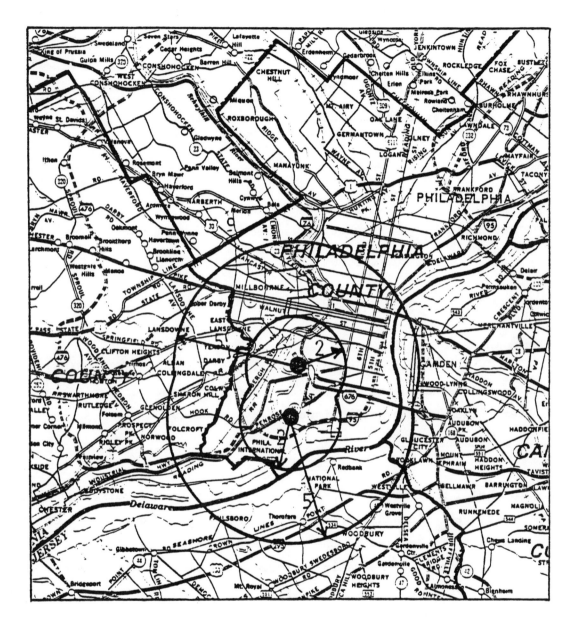

The two large dots represent the ground zeros of the two one megaton Soviet weapons. Within 2 miles of these ground zeros, there are approximately 155,000 people of which 135,000 were calculated to have been killed. Within five miles, there are 785,000 people of which 410,000 would have died.

37

Fatalities and Injuries

DCPA provided not only the number of people killed within each of the two minute grid cells in the Philadelphia region but also the original number of people within each cell. These results are summarized in Table 10A for distances of two and five miles from the detonations.

TABLE 10A

Estimated Fatalities with Distance in the Attack on Philadelphia

Distance from Detonation	Original Population	Number Killed	Percent Killed
2	155,000	135,000	87
5	785,000	410,000	52

Detailed examination of the large scale map also provides some indications of the magnitude of the problems and the resources available to cope with them. These are briefly discussed by category.

Petroleum

Local production, storage and distribution of petroleum will be essentially destroyed. In addition to the two refineries, nearly all of the oil storage capacity is located in the immediate area of the attacks. The nearest available source is the refinery storage complex at Marcus Hook, which is also attacked. Presumably, reserve supplies can be brought from elsewhere; however, the other area will be faced with the same problem. While early overland shipment by rail or tank truck into north and northeast Philadelphia should be possible, water transport up the Delaware River may not be. This busy channel passes within about 1.3 miles of one of the targets and could become, at least temporarily, blocked by sunken ships, barges, etc. For example, grounding of a heavily laden iron ore ship (bound upriver for the Fairless Works) in this narrow portion of the channel could pose serious problems.

38

<u>Electric Power</u>

There are four major electric power plants in or near Philadelphia. Table 10B below summarizes capacity, average usage (1976) and expected damage to these four installations.

TABLE 10B

Electric Power Plants in Philadelphia

Name	Capacity (KW)	Average Usage, Kilowatt Hours (1976)	Distance From Blast	Status
Schuylkill	249,00 steam + 36,750 internal combustion (I.C.)	977,880,000 = 111,630 KW	1.3	Electrical equipment destroyed. Plant heavily damaged.
Southwark	356,000 steam + 66,750 I.C.	627,262,000 = 71,605 KW	2.6	Electrical equipment damaged or destroyed. Plant moderately damaged.
Delaware	250,000 steam +68,750 I.C.	1,426,119,000 = 162,799 KW	4.9	Electrical equipment moderately damaged. Plant intact.
Richmond	275,000 steam +63,400 I.C.	256,206,000 = 29,247 KW	6.6	Probably undamaged.
TOTALS	1,130,000 KW (Steam) +235,650 (I.C.)	375,281 KW		

SOURCE: <u>Electrical World: Directory of Electrical Utilities</u>, (New York, N.Y.: McGraw Hill Inc., 1977).

While the usage figures in Table 10B are average and do not reflect peak demand, it should be noted that a large percentage of this demand will disappear with destruction of the industrial areas along the Schuylkill River and of a large portion of the downtown business district. Thus, the plant at Richmond may be able to handle the emergency load. Assuming early recovery of the Delaware plant, there probably will be adequate emergency electric power for the surviving portion of the distribution system.

39

Transportation

Air. The major facilities of the Philadelphia International Airport are located about 1.5 n.m. from the nearest burst. These can be assumed to be severely damaged. The runways are 1.5 to 2.5 n.m. from the nearest burst and should experience little or no long term damage. There are alternate airfields in the northeast and near Camden, New Jersey which should be unaffected.

Rail. The main Penn Central lines from Washington to New York and New England pass within about a mile of the nearest burst. It can be expected that these will be sufficiently damaged to cause at least short term interruption. Local rail connections to the port area pass within a few hundred yards of one of the refineries. This service will suffer long term disruption. An important consequence is the loss of rail connections to the massive food distribution center and the produce terminal in the southeast corner of the city.

Road. Several major northeast-southwest highways will be severed at the refineries and at bridge crossings over the Schuylkill River. While this poses serious problems for the immediate area, there are alternate routes through New Jersey and via the western suburbs of the city.

Ship. Barring the potential blockage of the channel by grounded or sunken ships in the narrow reach near the naval shipyard, ship traffic to and from the port should experience only short term interruption.

Casualty Handling

Perhaps the most serious immediate (and continuing) problem would be the location of a large percentage of the total medical facilities of the city within the area of the heaviest expected damage. Assuming a typical hospital construction is multistory, steel or reinforced concrete, the radius at which there is a 50% probability of destruction to hospitals is about 1.85 n.m. The detailed geological survey map indicates that there are eight major hospitals within this area. Any of these which are not destroyed will be severely damaged. Considering problems of access, they will be essentially useless.

Another nine hospitals are located from two to three miles from the refineries. This is the area of the most intense need for casualty handling. Again, however, rubble, fires, etc. will pose serious access problems. Thus,

40

it can be expected that most of the seriously injured will have to be taken to more distant hospitals in the north and northeast areas. It can be assumed that these facilities will be quickly overtaxed as will the means to transport the injured.

Military

There are two important military facilities located near the intended targets. The Defense Supply Agency complex is located within 0.5 miles of one of the refineries and will be completely destroyed. The U.S. Naval Shipyard is 1.0 to 1.8 miles from the nearest target and can be expected to suffer severe damage. The large drydocks in this shipyard are within a mile of the refinery.

Other

With respect to long term recovery problems, there are several educational, cultural and historical facilities located in or near the area of potential heavy destruction. These include:

> University of Pennsylvania
> Drexel Institute of Technology
> Philadelphia Museum of Art
> Independence Hall
> The City Hall
> Convention Hall and the Civic Center
> Veterans Stadium, Kennedy Stadiu, and
>   the Spectrum

Summary

A Soviet attack with two 1 MT air bursts on the two refineries in southwest Philadelphia will create nearly a half million prompt fatalities and over a half million injuries out of a total affected population of about two million. As one might expect, a large percentage of these casualties will be concentrated in the central, western and southern portions of the city, including a large portion of the business district.

41

Even without considering the problems of secondary fires,[25] rubble blocking main arteries, and massive evacuation efforts, the problems of transporting and treating over a half million injured will be insurmountable. Massive casualty evacuation to other areas will be required. Life support for the uninjured survivors will also require resources from other areas (petroleum, food, water, temporary shelter, etc.).

The long term recovery problem for the most severely damaged area in the heart of the city is beyond calculation.

  b. Summary of US Attacks on Refineries Near Moscow

The US attack on Soviet refineries includes two targets near Moscow attacked by POSEIDON RVs (40 KT).

The radii of some effects for both 40 and 170 KT yields (POSEIDON and MM III, respectively) are shown to the side of Figure 8, which is a map of Moscow.

As the Moscow map indicates, the collateral effects of the US attacks on the refineries near the city of Moscow can be expected to be much less than those in Philadelphia.

---

[25] While not examined, there is the possibility of a fire storm developing, particularly over the center city area. The following quote is of interest:

"The most fearsome and probably misunderstood feature of urban conflagrations is the 'fire storm.' A fire storm occurs when many small fires combine in a single massive flame with temperatures ranging from 1000° to 2000° F, a heat capable of causing the spontaneous combustion of all organic material. Unaffected by normal wind currents, the fire storm produces a powerful column of thermal updrafts that act as a huge chimney to draw winds into the fire from all directions at velocities over 50 mph. Fire storms develop only over areas of highly combustible materials; in urban areas this means 20 to 30 percent of the structures must be multiple-storied, covered buildings. Open buildings, yards, roads, and extensive park areas reduce the chances of fire storms developing. Single story buildings usually cannot support a fire storm--in terms of combustible materials--unless they are densely concentrated, as in Tokyo."

The Great International Disaster Book, James Cornell, Charles Scribner Sons/ N.Y., 1976.

42

Figure 8

RANGE OF EFFECTS IN RELATION TO MOSCOW

MOSCOW

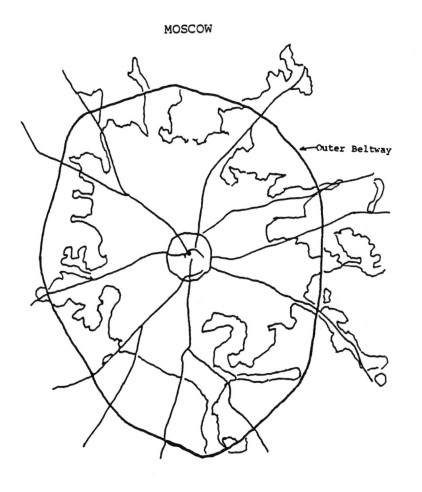

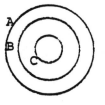

40 KT

170 KT

```
0           5          10
Nautical Miles
```

50 Percent Probability of Severe Damage to Buildings

    A - Wood Frame

    B - Masonry (1-2 stories)

    C - Steel or Reinforced
        Concrete (1-10 stories)

43

5. Target Set Effects

The major production equipment at most refineries are centrally located for reasons of efficiency in the refining process. Because of this method of construction and layout it may be assumed that detonation of a nuclear weapon will effectively eliminate the refining capacity at that location. The severely damaged area at the refineries will initially extend from 60 percent to 100 percent of the facility depending upon weapon yield and refinery size. In addition, it must be considered that the processing of any flammable liquid invokes potential dangers should any petroleum vapors or gases enter the atmosphere. There are over two hundred sources of fire in an average refinery, so uncontained gases which would result from a nuclear explosion would have little trouble finding an ignition source if the thermal pulse did not by itself start a major fire.[26]

Secondary fire damage would greatly compound the initial destruction caused by the nuclear explosion. One must consider that in the post attack environment whatever fire-fighting capability remains will probably be devoted to damage control in any nearby populated areas. The magnitude of a refinery fire is difficult to imagine. For example, during the course of this analysis, a fire occurred at one of the selected US refineries in a small portion of its associated storage facilities. Under near ideal peacetime conditions, it required half a day to bring the fire under control and a large portion of the near by population center was evacuated as a safety precaution. Hence, it may be assumed that a refinery's total capacity will be destroyed by the nuclear blast and resulting fires. It has been estimated that "a seriously damaged plant cannot be rebuilt in any satisfactory time related to a nuclear war".[27]

Figure 11 illustrates the percentage of refining capacity that will be destroyed in both the US and USSR as a function of the number of refineries attacked. The shaded area is an indication of uncertainty which is attributed to weapon reliability. The upper boundaries represent the results for 100 percent reliable arriving weapons and the lower bound representing 85 percent weapon reliability.

---

[26] *Vulnerability of Total Petroleum Systems*, p. 52.

[27] Ibid.

44

Figure 11

COMPARISON OF DIRECT DAMAGE TO

US & USSR REFINING CAPACITY

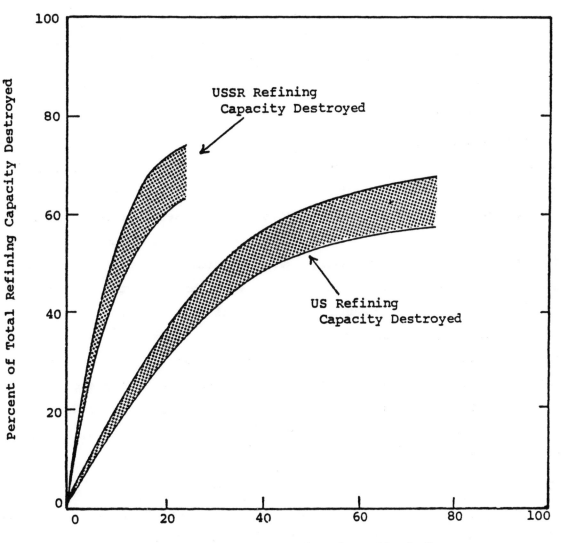

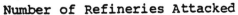
Number of Refineries Attacked

45

Not illustrated on Figure 11 is the damage expected to be incurred at Soviet petroleum storage facilities. This is calculated to be approximately 15 to 16 percent of the total Soviet national storage capacity.

6. Collateral Damage

In addition to direct damage which results from the attacks, there would also be a great amount of damage to the surrounding areas. As noted in the case of Philadelphia, which was discussed previously, some of this damage would occur at military installations, some at other industrial areas, and some in populated urban areas. In this analysis the measure of collateral damage which is examined in detail is that which is associated with the population; however, industrial damage is discussed in general terms as a background.

Even though it has been noted that many US refineries are located in or near population centers, these sections of the populated areas are generally in the form of an industrial area or industrial park. As a result of such industrial colocation, which may be presumed to occur to a lesser degree in the Soviet Union, the collateral damage effects of a nuclear attack would thus include significant damage to both nations' industry. The measurement of the amount and type of industrial damage is well beyond the scope of this effort. It would require the accumulation of large amounts of industrial data in a form not known to exist for US industry today and utilization of large classified data bases and computer models for Soviet data. In general, one may theorize that much of this accompanying collateral damage would occur to facilities that are associated with the petroleum industry. Such facilities include petroleum storage tanks, harbor and port facilities, railroads, pipeline terminals, and in some cases, the headquarters of petroleum corporations.

The prime criterion used in target and weapon selection was destruction of petroleum refining capacity. As a result, the number of independently targetable warheads was maximized, subject to weapon footprint constraint. For these conditions, the weapon assumed to be used by the Soviets was the SS-18/2, an ICBM with eight independently targetable warheads of 1 MT each. US weapons used were seven POSEIDON SLBMs with eight or ten independently targetable warheads of 40 KT each and three MM III ICBMs with three independently targetable warheads of 170 KT each. This resulted in a gross yield of 80 MT for Soviet weapons and 4.09 MT for US weapons. However, gross yield is not a satisfactory measure of blast effects against urban-industrial targets. This measure (gross yield) does not consider the fact that a weapon's destructive power does not grow linearly with increases in yield. For the same target, a 1 MT weapon is not 25 times as destructive as a 40 KT weapon.

Accordingly, in order to estimate the destructive capability of weapons, a measure called equivalent megatons (EMT) is used. In this measure, the yield is taken to some fractional power. This accounts for the fact that the blast is spherical in nature and a significant portion of the weapon effects are directed harmlessly upward into the atmosphere rather than along or onto the ground. Using the commonly accepted fractional power of 0.67, the Soviet weapon yield is 80 EMT and the US weapon yield is 10.44 EMT. If all other factors were equal, one would expect that collateral damage in the two nations would fall in the ratio of 80 to 10.44. However, all other parameters are not equal, as is described below.

In addition to the disparity in EMT, population distribution with respect to petroleum refineries must be considered in the anlysis of collateral damage. As previously noted, many US refineries are located in or near densely populated area (e.g., Los Angeles, Philadelphia, and the suburbs of Chicago). This is not generally true of Soviet refineries which, like many important Soviet industries, are located away from densely populated areas. Additionally, with a few exceptions, Soviet populated areas tend to be smaller and less densely populated than US population centers. The coupling of these factors: EMT differences, refinery locations, and population distribution, all contribute to a lower magnitude of collateral damage in the Soviet Union than in the United States.

Tables 11 and 12 below are a summary of the collateral damage (in terms of prompt fatalities) which would result from a US attack on the Soviet refineries and a USSR attack on US refineries respectively. Two cases are given. With respect to an airburst case, which results in the largest amount of collateral damage, it is expected that between 836 thousand and 1.4 million prompt fatalities would occur in the Soviet Union and about five million prompt fatalities would occur in the United States. These data, for the airburst only case, are also shown on Figures 12 and 13 by footprint. In the case of the surface

47

TABLE 11

SUMMARY OF US ATTACK ON USSR

Footprint Number	Geographic Area (Approx Center)	EMT	% National Refining Capacity	% National Storage Capacity	Airburst Prompt Fatalities (x 1000)	
					SS	MS
1	Moscow	1.20	10.5	2.1	62	41
2	Baku	0.96	9.8	1.5	224	152
3	Ishimbal	1.20	8.7	2.8	25	12
4	Polotsk	0.92	7.5	0.3	52	32
5	Kulbuyshev	1.20	7.4	3.1	127	83
6	Angarsk	0.92	6.9	0.4	130	54
7	Grozny	0.96	6.7	1.6	56	37
8	Kirishi	0.92	6.2	0.3	493	230
9	Gorki	1.20	5.6	1.5	228	153
10	Perm	0.96	3.6	2.1	61	42
	TOTAL	10.44	72.9	15.7	1,458	836

Legend: EMT – Equivalent Megatons.
SS – 100% of population in single story buildings.
MS – 100% of population in multi–story buildings.

48

TABLE 12

SUMMARY OF USSR ATTACK ON US

Footprint Number	Geographic Area	EMT	Percent National Refining Capacity	Percent National Storage Capacity	Airburst Prompt Fatalities (X 1000)
1	TX	8	14.9	NA	472
2	IN, IL, OH	8·	8.1	NA	365
3	NJ, PA, DE	8	7.9	NA	845
4	CA	8	7.8	NA	1252
5	LA, TX, MS	8	7.5	NA	377
6	TX	8	4.5	NA	377
7	IL, IN, MI	8	3.6	NA	484
8	LA	8	3.6	NA	278
9	OK, KA	8	3.3	NA	365
10	CA	8	2.5	NA	357
TOTALS		80	63.7	NA	5031

Legend: EMT – Equivalent Megatons
NA – Not Applicable

49

burst, it is expected that from prompt and fallout effects, between approximately one million and 800 thousand Soviet fatalities[28] and approximately three million US fatalities would occur. Fallout contours for the US and the USSR are shown in Figures 14 and 15 respectively.

C. UNCERTAINTIES AND LIMITATIONS

The data and results which have been presented in this report are subject to many limitations and uncertainties as a result of the data, methods, and assumptions that were used. The following is a series of brief statements which address the more important aspects of these limitations and uncertainties and their causes.

- <u>Weather Data and Local Weather</u>. March winds and clear weather were used as the meteorological conditions for both the DCPA and CCTC computer models. The presence of large amounts of moisture (rain or snow) in the atmosphere may affect the blast wave in the low over-pressure region. According to Glasstone:[29]

  > Meteorological conditions...can sometimes either enlarge or contract the area over which light structural damage would normally be expected. For example, window breakage and noise have been experienced hundreds of miles from the burst point. Such phenomena...are caused by the bending back to the earth of the blast wave by the atmosphere.

  A heavy rain in a region where a nuclear explosion occurs may have the effect of preventing or putting out many small fires and thus reducing the possibility of a major conflagration occurring. However, on the other hand, if the airborne debris encounters a region of percipitation, a large amount of radioactivity may be brought to the earth with the rain or snow. The distribution of fallout will then be less regular than those predicted and local "hot spots" of heavy contamination may occur.[30]

---

[28] Average March winds were assumed, and an average protection factor of 5 was assumed for the Soviet Union. The two figures for the Soviet Union represent 100% single-story occupany and 100% multi-story occupany, respectively.

[29] <u>The Effects of Nuclear Weapons</u>, p. 93.

[30] Ibid, p. 416.

Figure 12

USSR ATTACK ON US PETROLEUM REFINERIES

Air and Surface Burst

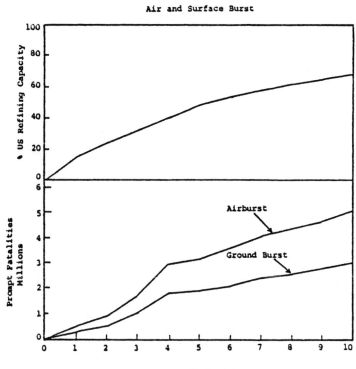

Footprint

Figure 13

US ATTACK ON USSR PETROLEUM

REFINERIES AND PETROLEUM STORAGE

Airburst

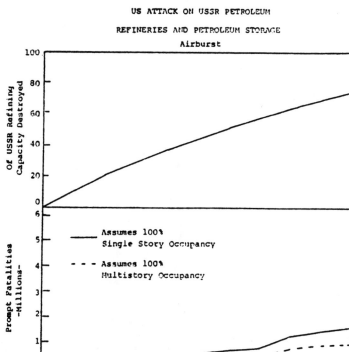

Footprint

51

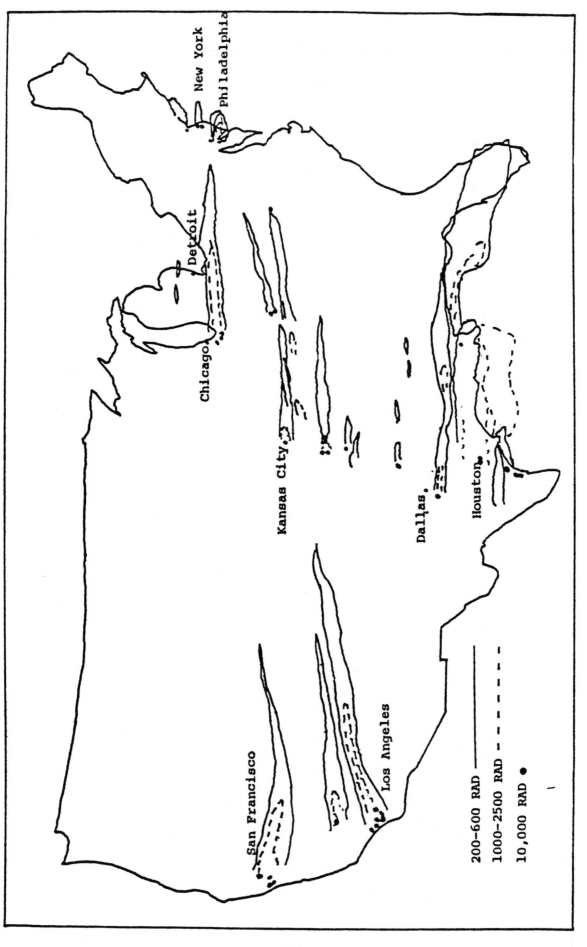

FALLOUT CONTOURS US

200-600 RAD ———
1000-2500 RAD - - - -
10,000 RAD ●

New York
Philadelphia
Detroit
Chicago
Kansas City
Dallas
Houston
San Francisco
Los Angeles

Figure 15

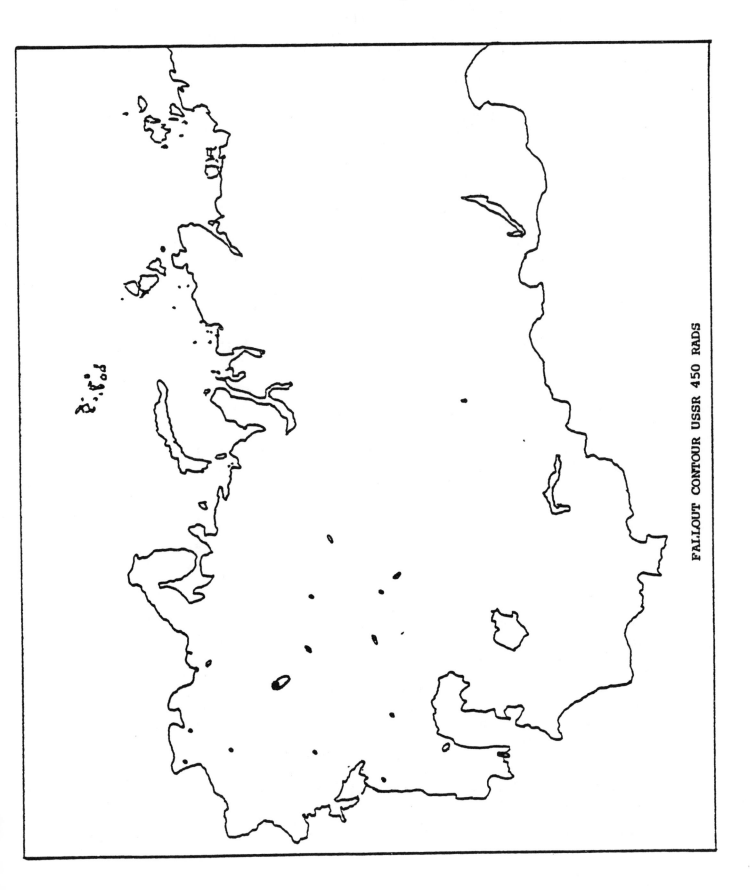

FALLOUT CONTOUR USSR 450 RADS

- <u>Fallout</u>. The general March wind pattern used to produce the general fallout contours shown in the preceeding section is subject to uncertainties. Higher velocity winds in the upper atmosphere would cause a more widespread distribution of fallout; however, while the area impacted would be larger, generally lower radiation levels would exist. Conversely, lower velocity winds in the upper atmosphere would reduce the radioactive area, but generally higher levels of radioactivity would exist in this reduced area. Additionally, as previously noted, local percipitation could cause irregularities and local "hot spots" in the fallout pattern.

- <u>Time/Date of Attack</u>: The calculation of collateral damage is predicated upon a nighttime distribution of the population. The reason for this time selection is discussed under demographic data. However, it may be assumed that in an attack at night a significantly lower number of workers would be present in industrial areas and at the oil refineries. A day time attack would, in addition to destroying the refineries, serve the purpose of killing a large proportion of oil refinery workers and workers in nearby industrial areas and thereby serve the purpose of further complicating recovery efforts. An attack occurring during the morning or evening rush hours would serve the purpose of catching many of the US urban areas in a condition where major and many minor roads need little to cause a massive disruption of traffic and access problems for emergency vehicles. It may be assumed that survivors already being on the move would attempt to get home and/or flee keeping the roads heavily congested from heavy traffic in addition to the large number of disabled vehicles resulting not only from the direct effects of the nuclear detonation but the accidents that would occur as a result of fright, etc.

- <u>Footprint Assumptions</u>. The assumptions of maximum footprint coverage used in the analysis affected the US ability to target refineries more severely than the Soviet targeting ability. If the assumed size of the POSEIDON weapon system is too large, actual US targeting capability would be reduced. For example, were the footprint reduced to 150 by 80 nautical miles, approximately six refineries representing about 10 to 16 percent of Soviet refining capacity could not be included in the attack without the assignment of additional weapons. Distances between targeted and untargeted refineries are of such a magnitude that the footprint assumption would have to be almost doubled before an additional refinery could be targeted. In the case of Soviet footprint, which is much larger, an error of assumption if as much as approximately five percent could be tolerated without significantly affecting the number of refineries targeted. The reason, in this case, is that US refineries tend to be clustered in one of several geographic areas and there are sufficient additional smaller refineries present in each footprint which were not targeted but which are within this smaller footprint. The percent of US national refining capacity destroyed, in such a case, would be lowered a small amount. With the exception of a few very

54

large US refineries, individual plants do not contribute more than fractionally to overall US refining capacity.

- Demographic Data. While it may be expected that overall US population data as derived from the 1975 census is quite accurate and more than adequate for analytic purposes that is not quite the case as is described below. Demographic data collected every ten years in the US nationwide census are probably the most accurate recording of this information anywhere in the world. However, data gathering is oriented toward persons residences. Little is known about the semi-daily shifts in population between work and residence. In addition, because of the data collection methodology, little information has been established about transient populations; hence anomalies exist in the data which represent empty hotels and unpopulated work areas which may in fact be fully and densly occupied. The accuracy of US demographic data cannot hope to be reached in the case of Soviet demographic data which are probably reasonably accurate for large urban areas and less accurate for small urban and rural areas which represent a large portion of the Soviet population. The calculation of collateral damage is heavily dependent upon knowledge of population distribution and type of building construction. Thus any inaccuracy or uncertainty in demographic data directly affects the accuracy and uncertainty of the calculated results.

- Sheltering. While many parameters take part in the calculation of fatalities from a nuclear explosion (yield, height of burst, fission fraction, etc.), the one ingredient of the equation to which the answer is most sensitive is sheltering. Unfortunately, this is also the one ingredient (besides weather) upon which we have the least control and the least knowledge. The decision to assume a warned vs. an unwarned population can mean a 10 to 20 fold difference in the fatality levels. Even once this is decided upon, the distribution of people between all being in single story buildings versus multi-story buildings can bring about a two-fold increase or decrease as can be seen in this analysis. As an excursion to the CCTC computer runs, a small research firm used their existing model and assumed a sheltering similar to that of the DCPA US population calculation. The number of people who were calculated to have died was one-tenth that of the original CCTC runs. Thus it is easy to see that the distribution of people within the sheltering environment between single story building, multi-story building, basements, underground shelters, etc., is a critical one, and any results must be viewed in light of this.

- Methods of Damage Calculation. The simplest method for calculating fatalities from a nuclear blast is the so-called "cookie-cutter" method. Using this method, a lethality criterion (based on overpressures for instance) is established and then one simply assumes that within that distance from the aimpoint all people have been killed. This method disregards weapon delivery accuracy as well as

55

the decreasing effectiveness of the weapon with distance from its ground zero. This last relationship stems from there really being no absolute killing criterion at the lower overpressures, etc., that are often used in these calculations. The other common method used in fatality calculations is that of the physical vulnerability system.[31] Under this system, delivery accuracy, the changing response of people to the nuclear effects (blast, heat, etc.) with distance from the explosion and the combined effects actually experienced in the nuclear environment are taken into account. While not as simple to compute, adequate computation aids (tables, nonographs, etc.) are in existance.

- Synergistic Weapon Effects. All of our knowledge of the effects of nuclear weapons is based upon a limited number of nuclear tests and the results of two attacks on Japanese cities. Few of these tests were conducted using the weapon yields used in the analysis. Hence, all of the results are calculated based upon scaling laws for nuclear weapons effects. There is thus some degree of uncertainty introduced by this process. In addition to this uncertainty, there is no information or data available concerning the results of multiple nuclear detonations in the same general vicinity. Consider the detailed description of the attack of refineries in Philadelphia. Two 1 megaton weapons are detonated in a very small area. One may presume that the effects of the first detonation will weaken many structures which are subsequently destroyed by the second weapon's effects. This cumulative or synergistic effect is not understood and generally ignored in analyses. The other synergistic effect which has not been considered is fratricide (where the first weapon detonation affects the detonation or tragetory of subsequent weapons).

- Uncertainties in Petroleum Data/Projections. Soviet petroleum refining capacity data was obtained from a source which required extensive footnotes to explain differences in its data sources. The projection of new planned/under construction refining capacity had the same general uncertainty. The assumption that each of the 15 individual refineries which were grouped in the data (and which together represent almost half of the total Soviet refining capacity) were the same size represents a great deal of additional uncertainty. US refinery data did not include refineries which are either under construction or planned nor did this data have an indication of planned expansion at existing refineries. This lack of projected US refining capacity introduces another uncertainty into the direct damage calculations. It has been estimated by the National Petroleum Refiners Council that almost all US refineries are operating at or nearly at 100 percent of their capacity. No excess capacity data are available concerning Soviet petroleum refineries. Loss of refining capacity is not as significant if a large excess in refining capacity is available.

---

[31] Physical Vulnerability Handbook.

- Secondary Effects.

    -- Mass Fires. Under some conditions the many individual fires
    created by a nuclear explosion can coalesce into mass fires.
    It is possible that "fire storms" and/or conflagrations may
    result in urban areas held under attack. Such mass fires are
    particularly insidious in the case of a nuclear explosion because
    remaining fire fighting personnel are hampered by losses of
    firefighting equipment, broken water mains, and reduced pressure.
    The uncertainties associated with mass fires are so large that
    little more can be said with the exception of being able to state
    the probability of their occurrence. According to Glasstone:[32]

        Furthermore, the conditions; e.g., weather, ignition-
        point density, fuel density, etc, under which a fire storm
        may be expected are not known. ....Conflagrations, as dis-
        tinct from fire storms, have moving fire fronts which can
        be driven by the ambient wind. The fire can spread as long
        as there is sufficient fuel.

    -- Electromagnetic Pulse (EMP). Nuclear EMP is a time-varying
    electromagnetic radiation which increases very rapidly to a
    peak value and then decays slowly. This pulse and its effects
    are very complex and are not understood in any great amount of
    detail. However, much electrical and electronic equipment is
    susceptible to EMP effects. It may be assumed that broadcasting
    stations, telephone equipment, electric generation and switching
    equipment and much computer controlled equipment near the blasts
    would be effected. These would contribute to the otherwise
    general localized failure of electric and communication networks
    in addition to whatever other damage is incurred.

    -- Panic/Flight. Little is known about the reaction of the American
    population to multiple disasters. That is, while we generally
    know what occurred during the Texas City disaster, it is only
    possible to conjecture what the reaction of eight simultaneous
    disasters many times larger than Texas City might cause. Recent
    experiences in the United States during a power failure in New
    York City and a major snow storm in Baltimore, Maryland suggest
    that a breakdown of law and order may accompany a major attack.
    In any event, it should be expected that the immediate reaction
    of the population may be to flee as fast as possible from the
    scene. This may lead to additional loss of life, injury, etc.
    especially if those agencies charged with maintenance of order
    and damage control are unable to function.

---

[32] The Effects of Nuclear Weapons, pp. 299-300.

LONG-TERM HEALTH EFFECTS FROM NUCLEAR ATTACK RADIATION EXPOSURES

March 5, 1979

Prepared for:

OFFICE OF TECHNOLOGY ASSESSMENT
United States Congress
Washington, D.C. 20510

Attention: Dr. Peter J. Sharfman

SUMMARY

The executive branch of government is currently pursuing SALT II agreements with the Soviet Union. To provide Congress information necessary for forming decisions on the ratification of agreements negotiated by the executive branch, the Office of Technology Assessment has been tasked to provide information on the effects of strategic nuclear weapons employment. The long-term adverse health effects resulting from radiation exposures constitute one of the informational requirements.

The more serious long-term effects of ionizing radiation exposures are induced cancer deaths, thyroid cancers and nodules, and genetic spontaneous abortions and other deleterious genetic disorders. This report provides the calculated numbers of these long-term effects that would probably occur for a set of nuclear attack scenarios, against the U.S. and the S.U., ranging from a single weapon attack on a city to a massive attack utilizing thousands of weapons. For the purpose of completeness and to provide comprehension on the wherewithal of the calculated results, explanation of the problem and assessment methodology covering the calculation processes and the assumptions and technical inputs used are also provided.

The calculative process is basically that of summing the exposure doses received by the surviving world population from all weapon burst produced radiation sources and then converting the total surviving population exposure dose to expected long-term effects with the use of risk factors. The exposure dose received by a population group depends on its location with respect to the various radiation sources, the radiation rate or concentration of these sources, the countermeasures used by the group to protect itself from these sources, and the period of time that it is exposed to these sources. The radiation sources are prompt radiation from the weapon burst point, fallout deposited on the ground and structural surfaces and fallout taken internally through inhalation and the consumption of food and water. Fallout includes local fallout that extends several

i

hundreds of miles downwind from surface bursts, and worldwide fallout from surface and air bursts that affect the world (mostly northern hemisphere) population. Established calculative procedures, along with data inputs estimated from past radiological research, and scenario inputs, such as, the shelters utilized by the population, shelter stay periods, decontamination effectiveness, and restrictions on the consumption of food and water, were used to estimate the exposure doses received by the population from these sources.

Representative results spanning the range of the calculated results are as follows:

1) Long-term effects from a 1 MT airburst over a city.

cancer deaths	200 to 1000
thyroid cancers	∿ 700
thyroid nodules	∿ 1000
spontaneous abortions	∿ 200
other genetic effects	∿ 700

2) Long-term effects from 72 - 40 KT airbursts on Soviet energy production and distribution systems.

cancer deaths	6000 to 30,000
thyroid cancers	∿ 50,000
thyroid nodules	∿ 80,000
spontaneous abortions	∿ 5,000
other genetic effects	∿ 10,000

3) Long-term effects from 78 - 1 MT surface bursts on U.S. energy production and distribution systems.

cancer deaths	300,000 to 3,000,000
thyroid cancers	300,000 to 2,000,000
thyroid nodules	500,000 to 3,000,000
spontaneous abortions	100,000 to 600,000
other genetic effects	300,000 to 2,000,000

4) Long-term effects from a counterforce attack on the S.U. with
1 air and 1 surface 100 KT burst on each of 1477 missile silos.

cancer deaths	300,000 to 2,000,000
thyroid cancers	2,000,000 to 3,000,000
thyroid nodules	~ 4,000,000
spontaneous abortions	200,000 to 300,000
other genetic effects	700,000 to 800,000

5) Long-term effects from a counterforce attack on the U.S. with
1 air and 1 surface 1 MT burst on each of 1054 missile silos.

cancer deaths	500,000 to 3,000,000
thyroid cancers	~ 2,000,000
thyroid nodules	2,000,000 to 3,000,000
spontaneous abortions	400,000 to 600,000
other genetic effects	1,000,000 to 2,000,000

6) Long-term effects of a mixed military and population attack on the
S.U. consisting of 5660 weapons with a total yield of 1307.2 MT.

cancer deaths	1,000,000 to 5,000,000
thyroid cancers	5,000,000 to 6,000,000
thyroid nodules	~ 8,000,000
spontaneous abortions	700,000 to 800,000
other genetic effects	2,000,000 to 3,000,000

7) Long-term effects of a mixed military and population attack on the
U.S. consisting of 3325 weapons with a total yield of 6500 MT.

cancer deaths	2,000,000 to 7,000,000
thyroid cancers	4,000,000 to 5,000,000
thyroid nodules	6,000,000 to 7,000,000
spontaneous abortions	~ 1,000,000
other genetic effects	4,000,000 to 5,000,000

In the above results, the uncertainties on cancer risks from radiation
exposures are such that the cancer deaths could be higher by a factor of 2
and the uncertainties on genetic risks are such that the genetic disorders

could be higher by a factor of 5. To provide perspective on the numerical results above, 5 million worldwide cancer deaths over a period of 40 years represent an increase of about 2 to 3 percent of the current cancer death rate. Also 5 million worldwide genetic anomalies over several generations represent an increase of about one percent of the current rate.

The more salient conclusions drawn from the calculated results are:

1) Several million latent cancer deaths could result from a massive nuclear attack on either the U.S. or the S.U. Without improved civil defense capabilities, the number of projected latent cancer deaths is small when compared with the total number of early fatalities. Similar magnitudes of thyroid cancers, thyroid nodules, and genetic disorders are also projected.

2) Except for one case, a limited attack where all the weapons were surface bursts, the total number of projected long-term adverse health effects is relatively insensitive to the shelter protection provided.

3) Because other factors, such as weapon size, height of burst, and type of target, all impact on the projected number of long-term adverse health effects, increasing the magnitude of the attack, that is, increasing the total nuclear yield, will not necessarily result in an increase in the number of long-term adverse health effects.

CONTENTS

INTRODUCTION

Background

The collateral damage effects of a strategic nuclear attack include the possible long-term adverse health effects resulting from population exposures to ionizing radiation. Because the results of past assessments of the effects of strategic nuclear attack scenarios have shown the early mortalities to be overwhelmingly high, little attention has been focused on the long-term adverse health effects from ionizing radiation exposures. For special nuclear attack scenarios where population centers are not targeted, however, the number of early mortalities could be substantially reduced. In such cases, the number of long-term adverse health effects, e.g., cancer deaths, resulting from these special scenarios could be relatively significant.

The Office of Technology Assessment is exploring the possible outcome resulting from a variety of hypothesized nuclear attack scenarios. Because the hypothesized attacks vary over an extremely wide range, it is essential that the total effects, including the long-term adverse health effects from ionizing radiation exposures, be quantified.

The numbers of the various long-term adverse effects are projected from estimates of the ionizing radiation exposure doses received by the surviving population. The sources of radiation exposures are "prompt" radiation that is emitted from the weapon bursts, radioactive fallout that is deposited on the ground and structural surfaces, and radioactivity that enters the body with the inhalation of suspended radioactive particles and with the consumption of fallout contaminated food and water. The exposure dose received by an organ, an individual, or a population group from a radiation source depends on the source strength, the distance between the source and the biological entity, the radiation shielding that exists between the source and the biological entity, and the period of the exposure.

1

For prompt radiation, the source strength is established by specifying the weapon yield. Furthermore, calculated data are available that relate weapon yields and distances to exposure doses. Thus if the locations of people with respect to each burst point and the prompt radiation shielding used by the people were known or specified, the prompt radiation exposure doses received by the people could be readily calculated.

Fallout, on the other hand, is deposited over large expanses in varying amounts and at different times. Substantial research over the past 25 years have been conducted to quantify the transport and deposition of fallout. The results of this research are methods and computerized systems for estimating the fallout deposition times and deposition distribution for various weapon yields and meteorology. Thus in this case it is necessary to match the number of people and the fallout radiation shielding used by the people with fallout deposition times and the fallout deposition quantities at the various locations to determine the exposure dose received by each population group. Also, since the deposited fallout will remain for a considerable time, unless physically removed, exposure periods must be specified before exposure doses could be calculated.

In areas of heavy fallout, e.g., close-in local fallout areas, the radiation rates are relatively high at early times after deposition but they also decay rapidly at early times. At later times after the shorter half-lived fission products have decayed to insignificance, the radiation rates are considerably lower and the decay rates are also slower. For this reason and because people can sustain higher chronically accumulated radiation doses than acute radiation doses without succumbing, civil defense planning prescribes the use of protective shelters providing adequate shielding against local fallout radiation at early times, e.g., for the first two weeks after an attack, and the performance of decontamination and other recovery tasks at later times, e.g., after two weeks, when the exposure rates have been significantly reduced by radioactive decay. Thus if it is assumed that civil defense plans are carried out, the local fallout exposure received by each population group is reduced by the radiation shielding provided by the shelter used by each group for the first two weeks. After the first two weeks, the exposure dose received by the group depends

2

upon the time spent out-of-doors each day, the amount of fallout that was removed from their environment by decontamination, and the radioactive decay and weathering rates.

For the calculation of internal exposure doses, past research has provided data on the persistence of fallout in the biosphere and data relating fallout deposition density to the amount of fallout that is inhaled and to the radioactivity concentrations in field crops and in dairy and flesh foods. It has also provided data on the uptake and elimination rates of the various fission product species by the various body organs and the resulting exposure doses that would be absorbed by the organ per unit amount of activity inhaled or consumed. Thus internal exposure doses can be readily calculated if the fallout deposition density at the location of each population group, the fallout deposition density at the location of their food sources, and their diet were known or specified.

Because the population within a country and the radiation shielding available to the population are non-uniformly distributed, and the burst points and local fallout depositions are also non-uniformly distributed, the calculation of population radiation exposure doses are normally accomplished with an electronic computer. The electronic computer facilitates rapid computation of the exposure environment at a very large number of sampling points that are associated with specified numbers of people and radiation shielding distributions. The computer inputs include: weapon and burst specifications, i.e., burst locations, burst heights, and yields; population location distributions, i.e., number at each location; population protection distribution, i.e., the blast protection, and the prompt and fallout shielding protection distribution at each location; crop production location distribution, i.e., the type and quantities of crops produced including pasturage and food animals at each location; meteorological data covering all fallout areas; and postshelter countermeasures such as shelter emergence times, decontamination effectiveness, and restrictions on contaminated food intake. With this computation method, even if all the other inputs could be accurately determined, however, the meteorological conditions at any future attack date could not, and thus the results obtained are expected results for the meteorological inputs. Since the meteorological conditions at the time of an actual attack could be

3

significantly different from those used in the computation, the resulting population exposures could also be significantly different.

Because the time available for this study was very limited, computerized methodology was not utilized and relatively coarse generalized calculative procedures were used. Essentially the same mathematical equations and established radiological relationships leading to quantifying exposure doses were used. The basic difference in the two procedures is the method used to arrive at local fallout total population exposure doses. The computerized methodology sums the results obtained from many thousands of disaggregated independent samples whereas the manual method uses a relatively small number of averaged inputs to compute the results. For example, computerized input would include population distributions in shelters providing a range of protection at each of thousands of locations, whereas a single different protection value was used for all the population by the manual method for each of three separate calculations.

The induction of long-term adverse health effects from ionizing radiation, however, is not limited to local fallout radiation. Nuclear burst debris that is not deposited as local fallout (arbitrarily defined as fallout depositing within 24 hours of burst) is called worldwide fallout. It is called worldwide fallout because parts of this fallout could circle the earth several times before depositing. Computerized methodology currently is not used to calculate worldwide fallout exposure doses rather the calculation of worldwide fallout exposure doses are more amenable to manual methods and established manual methods were used.

This study is an assessment of the possible long-term adverse health effects from radiation exposures resulting from several hypothesized nuclear attack scenarios. In the sections that follow, the nature of the problem and the calculative procedures are detailed and discussed along with the rationale for the assumptions and choice of inputs used, and the calculated results are presented along with their sensitivity to the assumptions and inputs used.

4

Nuclear Attack Scenarios

Long-term adverse health effects from ionizing radiation exposures were calculated for the following nuclear attack scenarios that were supplied by the Office of Technology Assessment.

1a   A 1 MT airburst at optimum altitude for industrial destruction over a U.S. city.

1b   A 1 MT airburst at optimum altitude for industrial destruction over a Soviet city.

1c   A 25 MT airburst at optimum altitude for industrial destruction over a U.S. city.

1d   A 9 MT airburst at optimum altitude for industrial destruction over a Soviet city.

1e   A pattern of 10 - 40 KT airbursts over a Soviet city.

2a   78 - 1 MT surface bursts on U.S. energy production and distribution systems.

2b   72 - 40 KT airbursts at optimum altitude on Soviet energy production and distribution systems.

3a   1 airburst and 1 surface burst on each of 1054 U.S. missile silos. Weapon yields are 1 MT.

3a-1   1 airburst and 1 surface burst on each of 1054 U.S. missile silos. Weapon yields are 550 KT.

3b   1 airburst and 1 surface burst on each of 1477 Soviet missile silos. Weapon yields are 100 KT.

4a   1 airburst and 1 surface burst on each of 1054 U.S. missile silos, 2 airbursts for each of 46 U.S. bomber bases and SSBN facility. Weapon yields are 550 KT.

4b   1 airburst and 1 surface burst on each of 1477 Soviet missile silos and on each of 9 other strategic facilities. For these targets the weapon yields are 100 KT. In addition, 10 - 40 KT airbursts for each of 30 Soviet bomber bases and Moscow.

5

5a A mixed military and urban/industrial attack on the U.S. The attack consists of 3325 weapons with a total yield of 6500 MT. The weapon yields are 1, 2, 5, and 25 MT. One-half of the total nuclear yield is burst on the surface.

5b A mixed military and urban/industrial attack on the Soviet Union. The weapon allocations are: 2865 - 40 KT airbursts and 415 - 40 KT surface bursts on urban/industrial targets, 1000 - 550 KT airbursts and 1000 - 550 KT surface bursts on missile silo sites, and 380 - 200 KT surface bursts on other military installations.

6

Potential Radiation Exposure Sources

The sources of radiation exposures to which populations may be subjected in a nuclear attack include the following:

1) prompt radiation

2) local fallout (fission products)
   a) early postattack, external sources
   b) long-term (chronic)
      i) external sources
      ii) internal sources

3) worldwide fallout (fission products)
   a) tropospheric
      i) external sources
      ii) internal sources
   b) stratospheric
      i) external sources
      ii) internal sources

4) induced radioactivity

Prompt radiation

The intensity (flux density) of prompt radiation falls off rapidly with distance from the burst point.[1] For high yield weapons, the range of high blast overpressures and high thermal fluxes are greater than the range of significant prompt radiation doses. Thus if out-of-doors, a person could succumb to blast and/or thermal insults and yet be at a distance where the prompt radiation dose is insignificant. For example, a 1 MT airburst provides a prompt radiation dose of 1 rem at 2.6 miles, whereas at this distance the maximum overpressure is about 11 psi and the thermal radiation is about 150 cal/cm^2.[1] For low yield weapons, the prompt radiation ranges are increased in significance when compared to the blast and thermal ranges. For example, the 11 psi range for a 40 KT weapon is about 0.9 miles, whereas the unshielded prompt radiation dose at 0.9 miles is 1000 rem.[1] If a protection factor against prompt radiation of 2 is assumed (PF=2),* then the 500 rem dose radius would be 0.9 miles and the 1 rem dose radius would be at 1.8 miles. A dose of 500 rems is

---

*It should be noted that because of source geometry and radiation energy differences, the PF for prompt radiation is different from the PF for fallout radiation.

7

sufficient to cause more than 50 percent early mortalities among a population so exposed. If it is assumed that all people beyond 0.9 miles survived (< 500 rem), the total prompt radiation dose among the survivors would be approximately 250 D_p, where D_p is the population density per square mile, and the projected latent cancer deaths would be 0.05 D_p. This may be compared with the projected number of early deaths, i.e., the population within 0.9 miles, of about 2.5 D_p.

Similar estimates can be made for higher prompt radiation protection factors. For example, if a PF=10 is used, the 500 rem dose radius is reduced to 0.8 miles and the 1 rem dose radius is reduced to 1.6 miles. In this case, if all the people beyond 0.8 miles survived (< 500 rem), the prompt radiation dose among the survivors is approximately 200 D_p and the projected number of latent cancers would be about 0.04 D_p. This in turn can be compared to the number of early deaths, i.e., the population within 0.8 miles, of about 2 D_p.

For surface bursts, the total prompt radiation population dose is relatively insignificant when compared to the local fallout population dose. An exception to this generality is where the population is assumed to be protected by shelters providing good shielding against fallout radiation and poor shielding against prompt radiation. Such an assumption, however, is not valid. Transmission factors for prompt radiation and fallout radiation for various sheltered locations are provided in Reference 1.

Since the total population exposure dose from prompt radiation among the survivors is estimated to be small relative to the population exposure doses from other radiation sources, they were not included in the calculation of exposure doses.

Local fallout

When nuclear weapons are detonated on or near the earth's surface, large quantities of soil are drawn into the nuclear fireball. Upon cooling, the fission products of nuclear fission are associated with the soil particles that vary over a wide range of sizes. The larger sized particles because of their faster falling velocity are returned to earth earlier than the smaller sized particles. The term "local fallout" is used to describe the fallout that is deposited at relatively early times. The remainder, that which is not deposited at early times, is referred to as worldwide fallout.

Fallout deposited within 24 hours after burst has been arbitrarily designated as local fallout. Using this definition, the local fallout is generally restricted to several hundred miles of the burst point. The fraction of nuclear debris in the local fallout has been found to vary widely. The UNSCEAR[2] report suggests a local fallout fraction of 0.8 for surface bursts. Thus for calculation purposes, it is more convenient to quantify the local fallout accordingly, regardless of the time required for its deposition. Also, by definition, the local fallout fraction for airbursts is zero.

The distribution of local fallout deposition is usually approximated through the use of computerized fallout models. Because the radiation rates in areas of heavy local fallout at early times could be lethal for even short exposures, shelters providing adequate radiation shielding are required to protect the public. Thus a nuclear scenario that includes civil defense measures would prescribe the use of fallout shelters by the people at early times. The population exposures from the deposited fallout are therefore reduced by various hypothesized shelter protection or radiation shielding factors. After a period in shelters, e.g., one or two weeks, the "safe" rehabitation of the areas with heavy fallout requires these areas be decontaminated. Upon rehabitation, the people will be subjected to additional external radiation exposures at reduced rates from the radioactivity remaining. During this later period, some amount of resuspended radioactive fallout will be inhaled and some amount of radioactivity will also be ingested with contaminated food and water. The radioactivity entering the body will provide internal organ exposures.

9

Worldwide fallout

That which is not local fallout is designated as worldwide fallout, e.g., fallout deposited after 24 hours after burst. Worldwide fallout is characterized by small particle sizes. The particle sizes are so small that in the absence of weather, the deposition time would be very long (years). The deposition of worldwide fallout is generally associated with precipitation. Thus the deposition of worldwide fallout originating from the troposphere, where weather exists, occurs earlier and the deposition of worldwide fallout originating from the stratosphere, where weather does not exist, occurs much later. Therefore, for calculative purposes, it is convenient to separate worldwide fallout into these two categories, i.e., tropospheric fallout and stratospheric fallout.

Worldwide fallout if originally injected into the northern hemisphere at latitudes greater than 30 degree will deposit almost entirely in the northern hemisphere. The deposition distributions of worldwide fallout have been found to be greater between 30 and 60 degrees north than at other latitudes.[2]

Because of the long deposition period of stratospheric fallout, the countermeasures that are used for reducing radiation exposures from local fallout are impractical for stratospheric fallout. For example, decontamination for stratospheric fallout would be required on a continuing basis for years. For tropospheric fallout, whose deposition period is measured in weeks, there are some countermeasures that can be effectively implemented, e.g., delaying the consumption of milk is an effective countermeasure for preventing high thyroid exposure doses.

Since the deposition period of tropospheric fallout is short (weeks) compared to the deposition period of stratospheric fallout (years), an important factor affecting the calculation of the worldwide fallout exposure doses is the fraction of the worldwide fallout assigned to each category. This assignment cannot be precise, however, because the altitude reached by the nuclear cloud for any yield can only be approximated since the altitude attained is also affected by atmospheric parameters as well as weapon yield. Also, the altitude of the tropopause varies with latitude and season.

10

Fallout partition fractions

Reference 2 suggests the following fallout partition fractions:

	Local	Tropospheric	Stratospheric
Surface bursts			
< 0.1 MT	0.8	0.2	0
0.1 – 2 MT	0.8 – 0.79	0.2 – 0.01	0 – 0.2
> 2 MT	0.79	0.01	0.2
Airbursts			
< 0.1 MT	0	1.0	0
0.1 – 2 MT	0	1.0 – 0.01	0 – 0.99
> 2 MT	0	0.01	0.99

Alternatively the nuclear cloud top and nuclear cloud base altitudes can be estimated for various yields and burst heights (HOB) and compared to the tropopause altitude to obtain estimates of the fallout fractions in the troposphere and the stratosphere. For airbursts, all of the fallout debris in the nuclear cloud are small particles and the total becomes worldwide fallout. For surface bursts, the worldwide fallout is taken to be 20 percent of the total fission activity produced. Since the altitude of the tropopause at latitudes greater than 30 degrees is typically between 10 and 13 km, a tropopause altitude of 11 km was used to calculate the tropospheric and stratospheric fallout fractions.

Nuclear cloud altitudes, cloud top and cloud base, for various yields and burst heights were calculated from equations provided in Reference 3. Also for low airbursts, that is the transition zone between surface bursts and airbursts, an estimated adjustment factor is calculated with an equation provided in Reference 4 for this purpose. The adjustment factor obtained is then multiplied by 0.8 for all bursts altitudes between 0 and 180 $W^{0.4}$ feet to obtain the local fallout fraction. Reference 4 also provides the data and procedure for calculating the height of burst (HOB) that maximizes the range for any overpressure for any weapon yield.

11

Radioactivity production

The radioactivity produced by a nuclear burst and the fission product mix depends on the type of weapon as well as the nuclear yield. For a weapon whose yield is predominantly from the fission of U-238, the total fission product radioactivity is about 440 MCi/KT fission at 1 hour after burst. If deposited over a smooth infinite plane, this would be equivalent to about 3000 R/hr/KT/mi^2 at 1 hour after burst.[5]

In addition to the fission product activity, about 2×10^{26} C-14 atoms are formed per MT of total yield for airbursts and about 1×10^{26} C-14 atoms are formed per MT of total yield for surface bursts.[2]

Exposure Doses

External radiation

External radiation rates from deposited fallout are decreased by radioactive decay and natural weathering. The weathering process decreases the radiation rate emanating from a contaminated surface by the removal of deposited fallout to other locations and by the settling of the fallout into the soil. External radiation exposure doses can also be reduced by radiation shielding and the deposited fallout can also be reduced by decontamination.

To facilitate the calculation of long-term health effects, the following countermeasures are assumed for local fallout:

1) people will be in shelters providing specified protection factors (PF) against fallout radiation for the first two weeks after the attack,

2) decontamination operations by emergency personnel will have reduced the fallout activity by a factor of 0.1 at the time of shelter emergence.

It is also assumed that the total dose (person-rems) received by decontamination personnel is relatively low when compared with the total population dose (person-rems) received while in shelters and after emerging from shelters. The recontamination of decontaminated areas by weathering is not separately considered.

12

For worldwide fallout it is assumed that no special countermeasures will be taken.

The external radiation dose from local fallout is estimated by:

$$D_1 = \sum^i \sum^j \sum^k \sum^\ell P_s^i R_1^j M_1^k F_s / (PF)_1^\ell \tag{1}$$

for the shelter period, and

$$D_3 = \sum^i \sum^j P_s^i R_1^j M_3 F_s f_d / (PF)_3 \tag{2}$$

for the postshelter period, where

P_s^i is the surviving population in group i that is in a reference radiation field R_1^j and shelter protection $(PF)_1^\ell$,

M_1^k and M_3 are the reference-dose-rate multipliers for each period that converts the decaying dose rate to integrated dose for the exposure period.

F_s is the body organ screening factor, and

f_d is the decontamination factor.

$(PF)_3$, the effective protection factor for the postshelter period, is estimated by considering the time spent by the population indoors, where the protection afforded depends on the structure characteristics, and the time outdoors, where the estimated protection factor is about 1.5.

R_1^j, the standard intensity at location j, is normally calculated with a computerized fallout model and M_1^k is determined for various effective fallout arrival times for each location. Since computerized methods were not feasible for this study because of time constraints, single weapon and multi-weapon local fallout iso-dose-rate areas were used with assumed uniform population densities to estimate the population and dose-rate multipliers associated with the various R_1^j areas. Also, because computerized methods were not used, shelter exposure doses were separately calculated for specific PF_1 values rather than for a mixture of PF_1^ℓ values. Finally although M_1^k, at any location, depends on the time of fallout arrival (which is influenced by the wind velocity) and the time of shelter exit, the value of M_3 is fixed for a specified shelter exit time.

For scenario 2a and 5a, the Defense Civil Preparedness Agency (DCPA) provided print-outs of the distribution of sheltered (inside) exposure doses among the surviving population and the distribution of outside exposure doses among the surviving population. For these two cases, the shelter doses were summarized and used, and the outside exposure doses were converted to R_1^j values and used to estimate the postshelter population exposure doses. The R_1^j values were also used with estimated M_1^k to calculate the shelter doses for shelter protection factors of 5, 10, and 40.

The scenario 2a attack consisted of 78 - 1 MT surface bursts. Because of the relatively small number of weapons used, the target points were assumed to be sufficiently separated so that the local fallout patterns could be treated as non-overlapping. Also, since all the weapon yields were 1 MT, a 1 MT fallout pattern was used to estimate R_1^j and M_1^k values. The 5a scenario, on the other hand, was a very large attack with over a thousand (1450) surface bursts. For this case, it was assumed that the ERD (Equivalent Residual Dose) distribution provided in the print-outs represented contributions from 3 overlapping local fallout patterns. Also, because of the mix of weapon yields, fallout patterns from 2 MT weapons with a suitable fission fraction were considered appropriate for estimating the R_1^j and M_1^k values. The other assumptions used to obtain the R_1^j and corresponding M_1^k values for the surviving population groups for both scenarios were:

1) The average dose within each population group is at the 35 percentile of the dose range. The 35 percentile is used because within a given dose range, the number of people below the median dose is larger than the number of people above the median dose.

2) The outside ERD (ranges) is approximately equal to a four-day dose. The print-out of radiation exposures were in ERD (Equivalent Residual Dose) units. ERD is calculated by assuming a dose recovery rate (injury recovery rate) of 2.5 percent per day of 90 percent of the exposure dose received.

3) The effective wind speed is 20 miles per hour.

14

The 5b attack scenario also had over a thousand (1815) surface bursts, but the weapon yields were lower than those of scenario 5a. In this case, since no dose distribution data were provided, the scenario 5a data were adjusted for the differences in the number of survivors, the size of the attack, and the type of weapons used. As was the case for scenario 5a, it was assumed that the ERD distribution ranges represented contributions from 3 overlapping fallout patterns. In this case, however, fallout patterns from 360 KT weapons with a suitable fission fraction were considered to be representative for the weapon mix. These fallout patterns consisting of standard intensity or dose-rate contours (R_1 contours) for a wind speed of 20 mph were then used along with estimated effective fallout arrival times to obtain R_1^j and M_1^k values for the various areas within each standard intensity contour. The values were then used to obtain estimated fallout arrival times and R_1^j values correlating to the dose ranges of the print-outs.

The remaining adjustments are a proportional increase in the number of survivors in each dose range to account for the estimated larger number of survivors, and then a redistribution of the number of people in each dose range according to the area ratios of the 360 KT patterns to the 2 MT patterns for each dose range.

The external radiation dose from worldwide fallout is estimated by:

$$D_t = P_N C_r W_f f_t M_t F_s F_g /(PF) A \qquad (3)$$

for tropospheric fallout, and

$$D_s = 9.3 P_N F_t^i f_s C_r^i F_s /(PF) A \qquad (4)$$

for stratospheric fallout (where weapon bursts are limited to the U.S. and the S.U.). In the above equations:

P_N is the northern hemisphere population (surviving),

C_r^i is the conversion factor (nuclide i), Ci/km^2 to rad/yr,

W_f is the fission yield,

f_t and f_s are the tropospheric and stratospheric fractions,

M_t is the dose rate multiplier for the exposure period,

F_g is the geographical factor for greater deposition density at latitudes of higher population densities,

F_t^i is the yield of radionuclide i (Cs-137)

A is the area of the northern hemisphere, and

the other notations have been previously defined.

To simplify the calculations, a time of deposition for tropospheric fallout was set at thirty days whereas the deposition of tropospheric actually stretches over a period of several weeks. Tropospheric fallout deposition depends on the co-location of nuclear debris in the atmosphere and weather conditions that would cause it to be removed from the atmosphere. Thus it could be deposited earlier or later than 30 days, however, an atmospheric half-removal time of about 30 days is considered to be realistic.[2] Using an arrival time of 30 days, the appropriate dose-rate multiplier for tropospheric fallout external exposures would be approximately 0.5, i.e., $M_t = 0.5$.

The constant, 9.3, in equation 4, specifically applies to C-137 and is obtained by including radioactive decay with a stratospheric removal half-time of 5 years, a weathering half-life of 10 years for the deposited radioactivity, and a geographical factor of 2.[2] Equations 3 and 4 can be used to estimate the exposure doses received by the U.S. or Soviet population by substituting the surviving population in the U.S. or S.U. for P_N and substituting the appropriate (PF) for the two countries.

Internal Radiation

Internal radiation to various internal organs will occur with the inhalation and ingestion of radioactivity. Because inhaled and ingested radioactivity results in different internal organ exposure doses, they are separately calculated. Also, because the radionuclides entering the body expose internal organs differently according to species, the internal organ exposures are separately calculated for each radionuclide. Internal exposure doses were calculated for the following organs: bone marrow, lung, lower large intestine, thyroid, bone, "other soft tissue," and "whole body." Exposure doses were calculated only for those radionuclides that contributed significantly to the total dose received by the various organs. These radionuclides were: Sr-89, Sr-90, Zr-95, Mo-99, Ru-103, Ru-106, Sb-127, Te-127m, Te-132, I-131, Cs-137, Ba-140, La-140, Ce-141, and Ce-144.

Internal radiation organ doses are calculated by

$$RD_j = \sum^i \sum^k DC_k^i \int (IHR)(SD_o^i)(K_o e^{-\lambda t} + K_e^{-\lambda^i t}) \, dt \tag{5}$$

for local fallout inhalation,

$$RD_T = \sum^i (SD^i)(CF^i)(DC^i) \tag{6}$$

for local fallout ingestion,

$$RD_j = \sum^i \sum^k DC_k^i \int (IHR)(F_d^i(t)/A)(K_o e^{-\lambda t} + K_e)(e^{-\lambda^i t}) \, dt \tag{7}$$

for worldwide fallout inhalation, and

$$RD_T = \sum^i (CF^i)(DC^i) F_d^i f_W (1-e^{-\lambda t})(e^{-\lambda^i t})/A \tag{8}$$

for worldwide fallout ingestion.

17

In the above equations:[6]

DC$_k^i$ is the dose conversion factors for radionuclide i for exposure period k (for various organs),

SD^i and F$_d^i$ are different notations for the deposition density,

(IHR) is the inhalation rate,

(CF^i) is the ingestion concentration factor,

λ^i is the radionuclide decay constant,

K$_o$, K$_e$ and λ are empirical constants,

F^i is the total yield of radionuclide i, and

f$_w$ is the worldwide fallout fraction.

For induced radiation exposures, only C-14 is considered and the C-14 exposure dose is estimated by:[2]

$$D_\infty^{C-14} = 4.25 \times 10^{-27} \, r_o \, Q \, P_w \qquad (9)$$

where r_o is the annual dose from naturally occurring C-14, and Q is the number of atoms of C-14 formed.

The variables used with Equations 1 through 9 above include the following:

M_1 -- The value of M_1 depends on the fallout arrival time and the shelter exit time. The shelter exit time for all scenarios was specified at 2 weeks. The fallout arrival times for different local fallout deposition density areas were estimated from single weapon and multiweapon deposition patterns for 10 and 20 mph wind velocities.

(PF)$_1$ -- The shelter protection factors used are scenario dependent and (PF)$_1$ distributions are normally used in computerized computations. Single values, i.e., (PF)$_1$ = 5, (PF)$_1$ = 10, and (PF)$_1$ = 40 were used in this study. For scenarios 2a and 5a, computer print-out exposure dose distributions reflecting (PF)$_1$ distributions among large numbers of population groupings were utilized.

18

R_1 --   The standard intensity or dose-rate for local fallout associated with an area or a population group depends on the weapon(s) yield(s), burst height(s), the meteorology, and the relative location of the population group or area with respect to the burst point(s). Normally the standard dose-rate at any location for a nuclear attack scenario is estimated with the use of computerized fallout models that take into account the variables cited above. In the absence of computerized output, R_1(s) are estimated for various populations from single weapon and multiweapon deposition patterns.

f_s --   The stratospheric fallout fraction depends on the weapon yield and the burst height. It is calculated by determining the worldwide fallout fraction, i.e., 1 minus the local fallout fraction, and calculating the fraction of the nuclear cloud extending into the stratosphere. For this study, a tropopause altitude of 11 km was used. Also, nuclear cloud top and cloud base altitudes were calculated from equations taken from Reference 3.

f_t --   The tropospheric fallout fraction depends on the weapon yield and the burst height. It is calculated by multiplying the worldwide fallout fraction by the fraction of the stabilized nuclear cloud that is below the tropopuase. A minimum tropospheric fraction for all bursts below the tropopause was set at 0.01.

The constants used with Equations 1 through 9 above and their sources are listed below:

F_s = 0.6   The body screening factor depends on the source geometry, the gamma energy, and the organ. Reference 2 suggests the use of F_s = 0.6.

M_3 = 0.7 M_3 is calculated from the decay of fission products. The exposure period for M_3 is from 2 weeks to 2×10^4 hours. Additional exposures after 2×10^4 hours is relatively insignificant.

M_t = 0.5   As previously discussed, M_t = 0.5 is the appropriate dose-rate multiplier for fallout (tropospheric) deposition at 30 days after burst.

19

$(PF)_3$ = 3 for the U.S., 2.5 for the S.U., and 2 for the northern hemisphere. These $(PF)_3$ values were estimated with the use of the following equation:

$$D_{24} = \frac{R\, t_o}{(PF)_o} + \frac{R(24-t_o)}{(PF)_i} = \frac{24R}{(PF)_3}$$

where: R is the infinite smooth plane dose rate,

t_o is the hour spent outdoors each day,

$(PF)_o$ is the equivalent outdoors protection factor, which is equal to 1.5, and

$(PF)_i$ is the indoors protection factor.

After cancelling and rearranging:

$$(PF)_3 = \frac{36(PF)_i}{t_o(PF)_i + 1.5(24-t_o)}$$

The following values were used to estimate $(PF)_3$:

    U.S. -- $(PF)_i$ = 4; t_o = 5 hours,
    S.U. -- $(PF)_i$ = 3.8; t_o = 8 hours,
    N.H. -- $(PF)_i$ = 3; t_o = 12 hours.

f_d = 0.1 This decontamination factor was assumed to be appropriate for a postattack situation. Although f_d < 0.1 were obtained in decontamination experiments on some surfaces and some methods, f_d > 0.1 also resulted for other surfaces and methods.[7] Also these decontamination experiments were conducted under relatively ideal conditions. The use of a f_d << 0.1 would only reduce the total number of effects by a small amount because the postshelter local fallout population exposure dose is only a small fraction of the total population exposure dose.

20

$F_g = 2$ Reference 2 stated that the population weighted mean world geographical factor had risen from 1.6 to 1.9 in the years 1955 - 1960. Because nuclear bursts in the U.S. and/or the S.U. would be at latitudes of higher population densities (than those detonated by the U.S. and the French in the Pacific), a rounded value of 2 was used for F_g.

$A = 2.6 \times 10^8 \text{ km}^2$ (area of northern hemisphere)

$W_f = 3000 \text{ R/hr/KT(fission)/mi}^2$ (Reference 5)

$(IHR) = 7300 \text{ m}^3$ per year for adults   (Reference 6)

$K_o. = 10^{-5}$ per m   (Reference 6)

$K^e = 10^{-9}$ per m   (Reference 6)

$\lambda = 0.677$ (Reference 6)

$r_o = 1.64$ mrem/yr for bone, 1.06 mrem/yr for the whole body, and 0.71 mrem/yr for marrow and soft tissue.   (Reference 2)

$Q = 2 \times 10^{26}$ atoms of C-14 per MT for airbursts and 1×10^{26} atoms of C-14 per MT for surface bursts were used (Reference 2). Reference 2 also states that for fusion devices, the value of Q could be considerably higher.

$P_{(U.S.)} = 2.2 \times 10^8$. Although this is the estimated current population, only the surviving population should be used when calculating the long-term effects.

$P_{(S.U.)} = 2.6 \times 10^8$

$P_N = 3.5 \times 10^9$. This is the estimated current population in the northern hemisphere.

$P_W = 4 \times 10^9$. The estimated world population in 1976 was 4.04×10^9. This was rounded to 1 significant number. If 4.1×10^9 were used as the current world population, the health effects from C-14 exposures would be increased by 2.5 percent.

DC_k^i and CF^i. The dose conversion factors and the ingestion concentration factors used were those provided in Reference 6 for the various radionuclide-organ combinations. For the calculation of inhalation doses, the resulting exposure doses were calculated for the previously listed radionuclides. For the ingested dose, DC_k^i and CF^i only for Sr-89, Sr-90, I-131, I-133, Cs-134, Cs-136, and Cs-137 were available. However, they represent the predominent contributors to organ exposures from fallout activity through ingestion. The activity ingested depends on the food consumed. The calculations of ingested exposure doses were based on the following assumptions: 1) standing crops at the time of the attack that are contaminated by local fallout will not be consumed, 2) contaminated milk and meat (from animals in contaminated pastures) also will not be consumed for the first three months after the attack, 3) root-uptake is the only path of crop contamination (succeeding crops) for local fallout, 4) foliar and root-uptake contamination occurs with worldwide fallout, and 5) one-third of the northern hemisphere population are milk-consumers (similar to the U.S.) and two-thirds are not.

λ^i Appropriate decay constants were used for the various fission products.

Latent Health Effects

Considerable controversy exists in the scientific community on the method and parameters for estimating latent health effects from radiation exposures. The subject is thoroughly discussed in the BEIR report,[8] in Reference 2 and many other published papers and reports. The subject was also discussed in a recent ARACOR report.[9] The major controversial areas that can significantly affect the number of projected latent adverse health effects include the following:

1)   the absolute risk model versus the relative risk model as the appropriate calculative model,

2)   the presence or absence of a threshold exposure dose for incurring latent health effects, and

3)   the relative effectiveness of low exposure rates and/or low radiation exposure doses for incurring latent health effects.

Absolute risk is defined as the product of assumed relative risks times the total population at risk. Relative risk is defined as the ratio of the risk in those exposed to the risk to those not exposed. The difference between the two risk models leading to major differences in the projected number of cancer deaths lies in the calculated excess of cancers arising from the 0 - 9 years age group at the time of irradiation. Because data on relative risks are sparse and inconclusive, and more data exist supporting the absolute model, the absolute model was used to calculate the latent health effects. Also, because the effectiveness of low exposure rates and/or low radiation exposure doses for producing late health effects remains unresolved, projected cancer deaths were calculated with dose effectiveness factors (DEF) of 1.0 and 0.2 for low exposure rates and doses.[*] Also, because there is insufficient data to warrant limiting the risk plateau period to 30 years, a 40 year risk period was used.[9] Estimates of radiation genetic risks are also uncertain. Reference 8 estimates that the doubling dose for genetic risks to be between 20 and 200 rems although the possibility of it being lower than 20 rems or higher than 200 rems is not dismissed. Since a doubling dose of 100 rems was suggested by Reference 6 and it is within the estimated range of Reference 8, it was used to project the genetic risks. It follows that if the doubling dose is 20 rems then the projected number of genetic disorders (spontaneous abortions and "other genetic effects") should be multiplied by 5, and if the doubling dose is 200 rems then the projected number of genetic disorders should be halved. The resulting projected latent health effects from radiation exposures using a DEF=1 for cancer deaths are as follows:

Effects	Number per 10^6 person rems
Cancer deaths[*]	194.3
Thyroid cancers	134.1
Thyroid nodules	197.4
Spontaneous abortions	42
Other genetic effects	132.4

---

[*]Multiply by 0.2 for DEF = 0.2.

---

[*]A DEF=0.2 implies that the radiation received is only one-fifth as effective per unit of dose for producing latent effects when compared to a high dose received over a short period of time.

The projected latent cancer deaths from internal organ exposures are as follows:

Organ	Cancer deaths per 10^6 organ rems
Marrow	45.4
Lung	35.5
Digestive	27.1
Bone	11
Others	75.3

Also, for thyroid exposures from ingested I-131, the effectiveness of the exposure is estimated to be one-tenth that of an external (gamma) exposure.[6]

24

CALCULATED RESULTS

(All results should be rounded to one significant number)

CASE 1a: A 1 MT AIRBURST OVER A U.S. CITY

1)   ASSUME HOB FOR 10 psi MAX. RANGE

$$HOB = 750 (W^{1/3}) = 7500 \text{ ft} = 2286 \text{ m}$$

$$\text{CLOUD BASE} = 1350 W^{0.2961} + 2286 = 12724 \text{ m}$$

$$\therefore \text{CLOUD BASE ABOVE TROPOPAUSE (11000 m)}$$

2)   ASSUME 1% TROPOSPHERIC FALLOUT
            99% STRATOSPHERIC FALLOUT

LONG–TERM HEALTH EFFECTS	TROPOS FP		STRATOS FP		C–14		TOTAL	
	Total	U.S.	Total	U.S.	Total	U.S.	Total	U.S.
CANCER DEATHS*	54.3	2.8	410	24.3	592	32.6	1056	60
THYROID CANCERS	91.5	4.8	320	53.2	322	17.7	734	76
THYROID NODULES	135	7.1	472	78.4	474	26.1	1081	112
SPONTANEOUS ABORTIONS	7.5	0.34	50	2.83	151	8.32	209	12
OTHER GENETIC EFFECTS	23.6	1.06	157	8.88	477	26.2	658	36

———————————

*CANCER DEATHS FOR DEF = 1.0. MULTIPLY BY 0.2 FOR DEF = 0.2

CASE 1b: A 1 MT AIRBURST OVER A S.U. CITY

    (RESULTS SAME AS 1a ABOVE)

CASE 1c: A 25 MT AIRBURST OVER A U.S. CITY

    RESULTS: LONG–TERM HEALTH EFFECTS ARE 25 TIMES GREATER THAN THE
              1a RESULTS.

26

CASE 1d: A 9 MT AIRBURST OVER A U.S. CITY

RESULTS: LONG–TERM HEALTH EFFECTS ∿ 9 x 1a RESULTS

CASE 1e: 10 – 40 KT AIRBURSTS OVER A S.U. CITY

1) ASSUME HOB FOR 10 psi MAX. RANGE

THE CALCULATED CLOUD TOP = 10275 m, ∴ ALL FO IS TROPOSPHERIC.

HEALTH EFFECTS	TOTALS		U.S. ONLY	
	DEF = 1	DEF = 0.2	DEF = 1	DEF = 0.2
CANCER DEATHS	4582	916	215	43
THYROID CANCERS	7450		394	
THYROID NODULES	10968		579	
SPONTANEOUS ABORTIONS	660		27	
OTHER GENETIC EFFECTS	2082		86	

27

CASE 2a: 78 - 1 MT SURFACE BURSTS ON U.S. ENERGY PRODUCTION AN
           DISTRIBUTION SYSTEMS

           CLOUD TOP = 19870 m, CLOUD BASE = 10480
           LOCAL FO   = 80%
           TROPOSPHERIC FO FISSION   = 1%
           STRATOSPHERIC FO FISSION   = 19%

LOCAL FO EXTERNAL EXPOSURE EFFECTS

	PF=5	PF=10	PF=40
CANCER DEATHS (DEF=1.0)	2,636,000	1,364,000	410,000
(DEF=0.2)	2,036,000	1,053,300	284,600
THYROID CANCERS	1,819,000	941,000	283,000
THYROID NODULES	2,678,000	1,385,000	417,000
SPONTANEOUS ABORTIONS	570,000	295,000	89,000
OTHER GENETIC EFFECTS	1,796,000	929,000	279,000

LOCAL FO INTERNAL EXPOSURE EFFECTS

	DEF=1	DEF=0.2
CANCER DEATHS	52,091	10,418
THYROID CANCERS	2,850	
THYROID NODULES	4,195	
SPONTANEOUS ABORTIONS	3,416	
OTHER GENETIC EFFECTS	10,768	

WORLDWIDE FO HEALTH EFFECTS

	TROPOS FO	STRATOS FO	C-14	TOTAL
CANCER DEATHS[*]	8,472	10,979	23,088	42,549
THYROID CANCERS	14,277	8,579	12,558	35,414
THYROID NODULES	21,017	12,636	18,486	52,140
SPONTANEOUS ABORTIONS	1,170	1,339	5,897	8,406
OTHER GENETIC EFFECTS	3,687	4,203	18,564	26,454

---

[*]DEF=1, MULTIPLY BY 0.2 FOR DEF=0.2.

28

CASE 2a (CONCLUDED)

TOTAL LATENT HEALTH EFFECTS

	PF=5	PF=10	PF=40
CANCER DEATHS (DEF=1.0)	2,731,000	1,459,000	504,600
(DEF=0.2)	2,055,000	1,072,000	303,500
THYROID CANCER	1,857,000	979,300	321,300
THYROID NODULES	2,734,000	1,441,000	472,300
SPONTANEOUS ABORTIONS	581,800	306,800	100,300
OTHER GENETIC EFFECTS	1,830,000	966,200	316,200

TOTAL LATENT HEALTH EFFECTS OUTSIDE OF THE U.S.

	DEF=1	DEF=0.2
CANCER DEATHS	40,383	8,077
THYROID CANCERS	32,735	
THYROID NODULES	48,443	
SPONTANEOUS ABORTIONS	7,995	
OTHER GENETIC EFFECTS	25,160	

CASE 2b: 72 - 40 KT AIRBURSTS ON S.U. ENERGY PRODUCTION AND DISTRIBUTION
SYSTEMS

1)   ASSUME HOB FOR 30 psi MAX. RANGE

$$HOB = 550 \ W^{1/3} = 1880 \text{ ft.}$$

FALLOUT IS ALL TROPOSPHERIC (SEE CASE 1e)

LATENT HEALTH EFFECTS

	TROPOS FO	C-14	TOTAL	U.S. ONLY
CANCER DEATHS*	31,283	1,705	32,988	1,463
THYROID CANCERS	52,716	927	53,643	2,788
THYROID NODULES	77,602	1,365	78,967	4,104
SPONTANEOUS ABORTIONS	4,320	435	4,755	176
OTHER GENETIC EFFECTS	13,614	1,374	14,988	553

----

*CANCER DEATHS ARE FOR DEF=1.   MULTIPLY TOTAL BY 0.2 FOR DEF=0.2.

30

CASE 3a   A COUNTERFORCE ATTACK ON THE U.S.

　　　　　1 AIR AND 1 SURFACE 1 MT WEAPON ATTACK ON EACH OF 1054

　　　　　MISSILE SILOS

1) ASSUME AIRBURST HOB MAXIMIZE RANGE FOR 100 psi

$$HOB = 200 \ W^{1/3} = 2000 \ ft$$

FO ADJUSTMENT FACTOR: $f_a = (180 - \frac{2000}{W^{.4}})^2 (360 + \frac{2000}{W^{.4}})/180^2 \times 360$

$$f_a = 0.1207$$

LOCAL FO FRACTION $= 0.8 \times 0.1207 = 0.09655$

WORLDWIDE FO FRACTION $= 1 - 0.09655 = 0.90345$

CLOUD TOP $= 4200 \ W^{0.225} + 610 = 20482 \ m$

CLOUD BASE $= 1700 \ W^{0.2634} - 333 \ W^{-.5} + 610 = 11086 \ m$

TROPOSPHERIC FO FRACTION $= 0.01$

STRATOSPHERIC FO FRACTION $= 0.89345$

2) LET POPULATION DENSITY = AVERAGE OF ARIZ, ARK, COLO, IDA, KAN,

MONT, MO, NEBR, ND, SD, AND WYO.

$$D_p = 17/mi^2$$

LOCAL FO EXTERNAL EXPOSURE EFFECTS

	PF=5	PF=10	PF=40
CANCER DEATHS (DEF=1.0)	903,800	487,300	177,900
(DEF=0.2)	690,000	275,900	59,700
THYROID CANCERS	623,700	336,300	122,800
THYROID NODULES	918,200	495,100	180,700
SPONTANEOUS ABORTIONS	195,400	105,300	38,400
OTHER GENETIC EFFECTS	615,800	332,100	121,200

31

CASE 3a (CONCLUDED)

LOCAL FO INTERNAL EXPOSURE EFFECTS

	PF=5 or PF=10	PF=40
CANCER DEATHS (DEF=1.0)	59041	67099
DEF=0.2)	11815	13413
THYROID CANCERS	3213	3672
THYROID NODULES	4760	5406
SPONTANEOUS ABORTIONS	3876	4403
OTHER GENETIC EFFECTS	12206	13872

WORLDWIDE FO HEALTH EFFECTS

	TROPOS FO	STRATOS FO	C-14	TOTAL
CANCER DEATHS*	217,900	850,100	936,000	2,004,000
THYROID CANCERS	367,200	664,300	509,100	1,540,600
THYROID NODULES	540,500	978,400	749,400	2,268,300
SPONTANEOUS ABORTIONS	30,100	103,700	238,700	372,500
OTHER GENETIC EFFECTS	94,800	325,500	754,100	1,174,400

*DEF=1, MULTIPLY BY 0.2 FOR DEF=0.2.

TOTAL LATENT HEALTH EFFECTS

	PF=5	PF=10	PF=40
CANCER DEATHS (DEF=1.0)	2,966,800	2,550,300	2,249,000
(DEF=0.2)	1,102,600	688,500	473,900
THYROID CANCERS	2,167,500	1,880.100	1,667,100
THYROID NODULES	3,191,300	2,768,700	2,454,400
SPONTANEOUS ABORTIONS	571,800	481,700	415,300
OTHER GENETIC EFFECTS	1,802,400	1,518,700	1,309,500

TOTAL LATENT HEALTH EFFECTS OUTSIDE OF THE U.S.

	DEF=1	DEF=0.2
CANCER DEATHS	1,901,000	380,200
THYROID CANCERS	1,395,000	
THYROID NODULES	2,054,000	
SPONTANEOUS ABORTIONS	354,000	
OTHER GENETIC EFFECTS	1,116,000	

CASE 3a-1   A COUNTERFORCE ATTACK ON THE U.S.

1 AIR AND 1 SURFACE 550 KT WEAPON ATTACK ON EACH OF 1054

MISSILE SILOS

1) ASSUME AIR BURSTS MAXIMIZE RANGE FOR 100 psi

$$HOB = 200 \ W^{1/3} = 1600 \ ft$$

FO ADJUSTMENT FACTOR: $f_a = (180 - \frac{1600}{W^{.4}})^2 (360 + \frac{1600}{W^{.4}})/180^2 \ x \ 360$

$$f_a = 0.1122$$

LOCAL FO FRACTION = 0.8 x 0.1122 = 0.09

WORLDWIDE FO FRACTION = 1 - 0.09 = 0.91

CLOUD TOP = $4200 \ W^{0.225} + 488$ = 17859 m

CLOUD BASE = $1700 \ W^{0.2634} - 333 \ W^{-0.5} + 488$ = 9433 m

TROPOSPHERIC FO FRACTION = 0.17

STRATOSPHERIC FO FRACTION = 0.74

2) LET POPULATION DENSITY = $17/mi^2$ (SAME AS CASE 3a)

LOCAL FO EXTERNAL EXPOSURE EFFECTS

	PF=5	PF=10	PF=40
CANCER DEATHS (DEF=1.0)	670,000	359,000	126,000
(DEF=0.2)	474,000	172,000	25,100
THYROID CANCERS	462,000	248,000	86,700
THYROID NODULES	681,000	365,000	128,000
SPONTANEOUS ABORTIONS	145,000	77,600	27,100
OTHER GENETIC EFFECTS	457,000	245,000	85,600

CASE 3a-1 (CONCLUDED)

LOCAL FO INTERNAL EXPOSURE EFFECTS

	DEF=1.0	DEF=0.2
CANCER DEATHS	27189	5438
THYROUD CANCERS	1490	
THYROID NODULES	2190	
SPONTANEOUS ABORTIONS	1783	
OTHER GENETIC EFFECTS	5620	

WORLDWIDE FO HEALTH EFFECTS

	TROPOS FO	STRATOS FO	C-14	TOTAL
CANCER DEATHS*	1,247,000	384,000	515,000	2,146,000
THYROID CANCERS	2,101,000	300,000	280,000	2,681,000
THYROID NODULES	3,093,000	443,000	412,000	3,948,000
SPONTANEOUS ABORTIONS	172,000	47,000	131,000	350,000
OTHER GENETIC EFFECTS	543,000	147,000	415,000	1,105,000

---

*DEF=1, MULTIPLY BY 0.2 FOR DEF=0.2.

TOTAL LATENT HEALTH EFFECTS

	PF=5	PF=10	PF=40
CANCER DEATHS (DEF=1.0)	2,843,000	2,532,000	2,299,000
(DEF=0.2)	909,000	607,000	460,000
THYROID CANCERS	3,140,000	2,930,000	2,790,000
THYROID NODULES	4,630,000	4,320,000	4,080,000
SPONTANEOUS ABORTIONS	497,000	429,000	379,000
OTHER GENETIC EFFECTS	1,568,000	1,356,000	1,196,000

TOTAL LATENT HEALTH EFFECTS OUTSIDE OF THE U.S.

	DEF=1	DEF=0.2
CANCER DEATHS	2,041,000	408,000
THYROID CANCERS	2,511,000	
THYROID NODULES	3,697,000	
SPONTANEOUS ABORTIONS	334,000	
OTHER GENETIC EFFECTS	1,055,000	

CASE 3b: A COUNTERFORCE ATTACK ON THE S.U.
           1 AIR AND 1 SURFACE 100 KT BURST ON EACH OF 1477 MISSILE SILOS

1)   ASSUME AIRBURSTS FOR 100 psi MAX. RANGE

$$\text{AIRBURST HOB} = 200\ W^{1/3} = 928\ \text{ft} = 283\ \text{m}$$

$$\text{FO ADJUSTMENT FACTOR} = f_a = 0.047$$

$$\text{AIRBURST LOCAL FO FRACTION} = 0.8 \times 0.047 = 0.0376$$

$$\text{WORLDWIDE FRACTION} = 0.9624$$

$$\text{CLOUD TOP} = 4200\ W^{0.225} + 283 = 12120\ \text{m}$$

CLOUD BASE	= 5968 m
TROPOSPHERE FRACTION	= 0.7872
STRATOSPHERE FRACTION	= 0.1752
SURFACE BURST LOCAL FRACTION	= 0.8
TROPOSPHERE FRACTION	= 0.173
STRATOSPHERE FRACTION	= 0.027

2)   LET POPULATION DENSITY $= 10/\text{mi}^2$

LOCAL FO EXTERNAL EXPOSURE EFFECTS

	PF=5	PF=10	PF=40
CANCER DEATHS (DEF=1.0)	108,200	58,000	20,400
(DEF=0.2)	70,600	24,300	4,100
THYROID CANCERS	74,700	40,000	14,100
THYROID NODULES	109,900	58,900	20,700
SPONTANEOUS ABORTIONS	23,400	12,500	4,400
OTHER GENETIC EFFECTS	73,700	39,500	13,900

LOCAL FO INTERNAL EXPOSURE EFFECTS

	DEF=1	DEF=0.2
CANCER DEATHS	3699	740
THYROID CANCERS	202	
THYROID NODULES	298	
SPONTANEOUS ABORTIONS	242	
OTHER GENETIC EFFECTS	765	

35

CASE 3b (CONCLUDED)

WORLDWIDE FO HEALTH EFFECTS

	TROPOS FO	STRATOS FO	C-14	TOTAL
CANCER DEATHS*	1,386,000	22,300	131,200	1,539,500
THYROID CANCERS	2,336,000	17,400	71,300	2,424,700
THYROID NODULES	3,439,000	25,600	105,000	3,569,600
SPONTANEOUS ABORTIONS	191,500	2,700	33,500	227,700
OTHER GENETIC EFFECTS	603,400	8,500	105,700	717,600

---

*DEF=1, MULTIPLY BY 0.2 FOR DEF=0.2

TOTAL LATENT HEALTH EFFECTS

	PF=5	PF=10	PF=40
CANCER DEATHS (DEF=1.0)	1,650,000	1,600,000	1,560,000
DEF=0.2)	379,000	333,000	313,000
THYROID CANCERS	2,500,000	2,470,000	2,440,000
THYROID NODULES	3,680,000	3,630,000	3,590,000
SPONTANEOUS ABORTIONS	251,000	240,000	232,000
OTHER GENETIC EFFECTS	792,000	758,000	732,000

TOTAL LATENT HEALTH EFFECTS IN THE U.S. ONLY

	DEF=1	DEF=0.2
CANCER DEATHS	72,598	14,520
THYROID CANCERS	129,750	
THYROID NODULES	191,000	
SPONTANEOUS ABORTIONS	9,601	
OTHER GENETIC EFFECTS	30,218	

CASE 4a: A COUNTERFORCE ATTACK ON THE U.S. -- 1054 SILOS, 46 BOMBER BASES,

2 SSBN FACILITIES, 1 AIR AND 1 SURFACE 550 KT BURST PER SILO,

2 550 KT AIRBURSTS FOR EACH BOMBER BASE AND SSBN FACILITY,

AIRBURST ALTITUDE FOR SILOS IS 1600 ft (SEE CASE 3a).

AIRBURSTS FOR BOMBER BASES AND SSBN FACILITIES AT

ALTITUDE FOR MAXIMUM RANGE FOR 20 psi, e.g., $600\ W^{1/3}$ = 4900 ft.

CLOUD TOP	=	18,869 m
CLOUD BASE	=	10,445 m
LOCAL FO FRACTION =	0	
TROPOSPHERIC FO FRACTION	=	0.066
STRATOSPHERIC FRACTION	=	0.934
TOTAL YIELD =	(96)(0.55)	52.8 MT

ADDITIONAL LATENT HEALTH EFFECTS (TO CASE 3a) FOR 96 ADDITIONAL AIRBURSTS

	TROPOS FO	STRATOS FO	C-14	TOTAL
CANCER DEATHS*	34063	36750	31258	102071
THYROID CANCERS	57401	28716	17002	103119
THYROID NODULES	84500	42280	25027	151807
SPONTANEOUS ABORTIONS	4704	4483	7973	17160
OTHER GENETIC EFFECTS	14824	14070	25186	54080

*FOR DEF=1, MULTIPLY BY 0.2 FOR DEF=0.2.

CASE 4a (CONCLUDED)

TOTAL LATENT HEALTH EFFECTS

	PF=5	PF=10	PF=40
CANCER DEATHS (DEF=1.0)	2,950,000	2,634,000	2,401,000
(DEF=0.2)	929,000	627,000	480,000
THYROID CANCERS	3,247,000	3,033,000	2,872,000
THYROID NODULES	4,783,000	4,467,000	4,230,000
SPONTANEOUS ABORTIONS	514,000	446,000	396,000
OTHER GENETIC EFFECTS	1,622,000	1,410,000	1,250,000

TOTAL LATENT HEALTH EFFECTS OUTSIDE OF THE U.S.

	DEF=1.0	DEF=0.2
CANCER DEATHS	2,138,000	427,000
THYROID CANCERS	2,606,000	
THYROID NODULES	3,845,000	
SPONTANEOUS ABORTIONS	350,300	
OTHER GENETIC EFFECTS	1,106,000	

38

CASE 4b: AN ATTACK ON THE S.U. COUNTERFORCE AND ON MOSCOW --
           1477 SILOS, 1 AIR AND 1 SURFACE 100 KT BURST EACH;
           30 BOMBER BASES, 10-40 KT AIRBURSTS EACH; 9 OTHER SITES,
           1 AIR AND 1 SURFACE 100 KT BURST EACH; MOSCOW, 10-40 KT AIR BURSTS.

1)   LET HOB FOR BOMBER BASES = 2052 ft = 625 m,

        $HOB > 180 \ W^{.4}$; $\therefore$ NO LOCAL FO

        CLOUD TOP < 11,000 m; $\therefore$ ALL TROPOSPHERIC FALLOUT

2)   LET HOB FOR OTHER SITES = 2785 ft = 849 m

        $HOB > 180 \ W^{.4}$; $\therefore$ NO LOCAL FALLOUT

        CLOUD TOP = 12686 m (AIRBURSTS); 11837 (SURFACE BURSTS)

        CLOUD BASE = 6534 m (AIRBURSTS): 5685 (SURFACE BURSTS)

        TROPOSPHERIC FRACTION = 0.73 (AIR)   0.173 (SURFACE)

        STRATOSPHERIC FRACTION = 0.27 (AIR)   0.027 (SURFACE)

3)   LET HOB FOR MOSCOW = HOB FOR BOMBER BASES

4)   LET POPULATION DENSITY AT BOMBER BASES AND OTHER SITES = 500/mi^2

5)   LET POPULATION DENSITY OF MOSCOW = 10,000/mi^2

39

Case 4b (CONTINUED)

PROMPT RADIATION LATENT HEALTH EFFECTS

MOSCOW

OVERPRESSURE FOR BLAST MORTALITY	10 psi*			5 psi†		
PROMPT RADIATION PF	2	5	10	2	5	10
CANCER DEATHS	4663	1846	933	233	95	47
THYROID CANCERS	3218	1287	644	193	77	39
THYROID NODULES	4738	1895	948	237	95	47
SPONTANEOUS ABORTIONS	1008	403	202	50	20	10
OTHER GENETIC EFFECTS	3178	1271	636	159	64	32

BOMBER BASES

OVERPRESSURE FOR BLAST MORTALITY	10 psi*			5 psi†		
PROMPT RADIATION PF	2	5	10	2	5	10
CANCER DEATHS	6995	2798	1399	350	140	70
THYROID CANCERS	4828	1931	966	241	97	48
THYROID NODULES	7106	2843	1421	355	142	71
SPONTANEOUS ABORTIONS	1512	605	302	76	30	15
OTHER GENETICS EFFECTS	4766	1907	953	238	95	48

OTHER FACILITIES

OVERPRESSURE FOR BLAST MORTALITY	10 psi*			5 psi†		
PROMPT RADIATION PF	2	5	10	2	5	10
CANCER DEATHS	331	132	66	2.3	0.9	0.5
THYROID CANCERS	229	92	46	1.6	0.6	0.3
THYROID NODULES	337	135	67	2.3	0.9	0.5
SPONTANEOUS ABORTIONS	72	29	14	0.5	0.2	0.1
OTHER GENETIC EFFECTS	226	90	45	1.6	0.6	0.3

---

*NUMBERS USED IN TOTAL EFFECTS.

†NUMBERS NOT USED IN TOTAL EFFECTS.

40

Case 4b (CONTINUED)

LOCAL FALLOUT - ADDITIONAL LATENT HEALTH EFFECTS (TO CASE 3b)

	PF=5		PF=10		PF=40	
	DEF=1	DEF=0.2	DEF=1	DEF=0.2	DEF=1	DEF=0.2
CANCER DEATHS	32560	20760	17950	7288	7013	1413
THYROID CANCERS	21800		11700		4163	
THYROID NODULES	32060		17230		6113	
SPONTANEOUS ABORTIONS	6875		3713		1350	
OTHER GENETIC EFFECTS	21680		11710		4263	

WORLDWIDE FALLOUT - ADDITIONAL LATENT HEALTH EFFECTS (TO CASE 3b)

	TROPOS FO	STRATOS FO	C-14 AIR	C-14 SURFACE	TOTAL
CANCER DEATHS*	142618	199	7874	266	150957
THYROID CANCERS	240332	155	4283	145	244915
THYROID NODULES	353788	229	6304	213	360534
SPONTANEOUS ABORTIONS	19695	24	2008	68	21795
OTHER GENETIC EFFECTS	62066	76	6344	214	68700

---

*DEF=1.0, MULTIPLY BY 0.2 FOR DEF=0.2

TOTAL LATENT HEALTH EFFECTS

	FO-PF=5,PR-PF=2	FO-PF=10,PR-PF=5	FO-PF=40,PR-PF=10
CANCER DEATHS (DEF=1.0)	1,845,000	1,774,000	1,720,000
(DEF=0.2)	442,000	378,000	348,000
THYROID CANCERS	2,775,000	2,730,000	2,691,000
THYROID NODULES	4,082,000	4,013,000	3,959,000
SPONTANEOUS ABORTIONS	282,000	267,000	256,000
OTHER GENETIC EFFECTS	891,000	842,000	807,000

41

Case 4b (CONCLUDED)

TOTAL LATENT HEALTH EFFECTS IN THE U.S. ONLY

	DEF = 1	DEF = 0.2
CANCER DEATHS	79686	15937
THYROID CANCERS	142705	
THYROID NODULES	210070	
SPONTANEOUS ABORTIONS	10507	
OTHER GENETIC EFFECTS	33070	

42

Case 5a   A MIXED MILITARY AND POPULATION ATTACK ON THE U.S.

TOTAL YIELD: 6500 MT

WEAPON MIX: 1 MT TO 25 MT.

COMPUTER PRINT-OUT OF SURVIVOR DOSE DISTRIBUTION

AND OUTSIDE DOSE DISTRIBUTION AT SURVIVOR LOCATION WERE

PROVIDED BY DCPA.

THE PRINT-OUT REFLECTS POPULATION USE OF SHELTERS

WITH A WIDE RANGE OF PROTECTION FACTORS

ASSUMED WEAPON ALLOCATION

YIELD (MT)	HOB (m)	NUMBER OF WEAPONS
1	0	1250
1	610	1100
2	2880	575
5	0	150
5	3260	200
25	0	50

TOTAL   3325

TOTAL YIELD -- SURFACE BURST = 3250 MT

TOTAL YIELD -- AIR BURST   = 3250 MT

43

LOCAL FALLOUT HEALTH EFFECTS

	PFs=5	PFs=10	PFs=40	Mixed PFs
External Exposure				
ADDITIONAL SHELTER FATALITIES	21,712,000	9,441,000	327,200	---
CANCER DEATHS (DEF=1)	2,390,000	2,099,000	1,005,000	1,720,000
CANCER DEATHS (DEF=0.2)	2,359,000	2,082,000	993,800	1,700,000
THYROID CANCERS	1,650,000	1,449,000	693,500	1,190,000
THYROID NODULES	2,429,000	2,132,000	1,021,000	1,750,000
SPONTANEOUS ABORTIONS	516,700	453,700	217,200	372,000
OTHER GENETIC EFFECTS	1,629,000	1,430,000	684,700	1,170,000
Internal Exposure				
CANCER DEATHS (DEF=1)	47,200	80,200	127,800	132,000
CANCER DEATHS (DEF=0.2)	9,400	16,000	25,600	26,400
THYROID CANCERS	2,600	4,400	7,000	7,200
THYROID NODULES	3,800	6,500	10,300	10,600
SPONTANEOUS ABORTIONS	3,100	5,300	8,400	8,700
OTHER GENETIC EFFECTS	9,800	16,600	26,400	27,300

44

WORLDWIDE FALLOUT HEALTH EFFECTS

	TROPOS	STRATOS	C-14	TOTAL
CANCER DEATHS (DEF=1)	360,100	1,543,000	2,886,000	4,789,000
CANCER DEATHS (DEF=0.2)	72,000	308,600	577,200	957,800
THYROID CANCERS	606,800	1,206,000	1,570,000	3,383,000
THYROID NODULES	893,200	1,776,000	2,311,000	4,980,000
SPONTANEOUS ABORTIONS	49,700	188,200	736,500	974,400
OTHER GENETIC EFFECTS	156,700	590.800	2,324,000	3,072,000

TOTAL LATENT HEALTH EFFECTS

	PFs=5	PFs=10	PFs=40	Mixed PFs
ADDITIONAL SHELTER FATALITIES	21,712,000	9,441,000	327,200	----
CANCER DEATHS (DEF=1)	7,226,000	6,968,000	5,922,000	6,640,000
CANCER DEATHS (DEF=0.2)	3,326,000	3,056,000	1,977,000	2,680,000
THYROID CANCERS	5,036,000	4,836,000	4,084,000	4,580,000
THYROID NODULES	7,413,000	7,119,000	6,011,000	6,730,000
SPONTANEOUS ABORTIONS	1,494,000	1,433,000	1,200,000	1,360,000
OTHER GENETIC EFFECTS	4,711,000	4,515,000	3,783,000	4,270,000

TOTAL LATENT HEALTH EFFECTS OUTSIDE OF THE U.S.

	DEF=1	DEF=0.2
CANCER DEATHS	4,545,000	909,000
THYROID CANCERS	3,254,000	
THYROID NODULES	4,549,000	
SPONTANEOUS ABORTIONS	926,000	
OTHER GENETIC EFFECTS	2,919,000	

45

Case 5b   A MIXED MILITARY AND POPULATION ATTACK ON THE S.U.

TOTAL YIELD: 1307.2 MT

WEAPON MIX: 40 KT TO 550 KT.

EARLY FATALITIES WERE ESTIMATED

SURVIVOR DOSE DISTRIBUTIONS WERE ESTIMATED.

ASSUMED WEAPONS ALLOCATION

YIELD (KT)	FISSION FRAC	HOB (m)	NUMBER OF WEAPONS
40	1.0	782	1725
40	1.0	636	1140
40	1.0	0	415
200	0.9	0	380
550	0.9	500	980
550	0.9	0	1020
TOTAL			5660

TOTAL YIELD — SURFACE BURST = 653.6 MT

TOTAL YIELD -- AIR BURST   = 653.6 MT

46

CASE 5b (CONTINUED)

LOCAL FALLOUT HEALTH EFFECTS

External Exposure	PF=5	PF=10	PF=40	Mixed PF*
ADDITIONAL SHELTER FATALITIES[†]	14,050,000	6,420,000	101,000	----
CANCER DEATHS (DEF=1)	1,175,000	1,110,000	557,100	752,500
CANCER DEATHS (DEF=0.2)	1,076,000	1,079,000	545,300	736,800
THYROID CANCERS	810,700	765,800	384,500	519,300
THYROID NODULES	1,193,000	1,127,000	566,000	764,500
SPONTANEOUS ABORTIONS	253,900	239,900	120,400	162,700
OTHER GENETIC EFFECTS	800,400	756,100	379,600	512,800

Internal Exposure Effects				
CANCER DEATHS (DEF=1)	23,200	42,400	70,800	71,800
CANCER DEATHS (DEF=0.2)	4,600	8,500	14,200	14,400
THYROID CANCERS	1,300	2,300	3,900	3,900
THYROID NODULES	1,900	3,400	5,700	5,800
SPONTANEOUS ABORTIONS	1,500	2,800	4,600	4,700
OTHER GENETIC EFFECTS	4,800	8,800	14,600	14,800

*PF VALUES RANGE FROM 5 TO 5000. AN AVERAGE PF OF 28, DERIVED FROM 5a SURVIVOR DOSE DATA, WAS USED FOR THESE CALCULATIONS.

[†]ADDITIONAL SHELTER FATALITIES ARE CALCULATED ASSUMING THAT ALL SURVIVORS ARE IN SHELTERS WITH PF INDICATED.

47

CASE 5b (CONCLUDED)

WORLDWIDE FALLOUT HEALTH EFFECTS

	TROPOS	STRATOS	C-14	TOTAL
CANCER DEATHS (DEF=1)	2,531,000	369,200	580,400	3,481,000
CANCER DEATHS (DEF=0.2)	506,300	73,800	116,100	696,200
THYROID CANCER	4,266,000	288,500	315,700	4,870,000
THYROID NODULES	6,280,000	425,000	464,700	7,170,000
SPONTANEOUS ABORTIONS	349,500	45,000	148,100	542,600
OTHER GENETIC EFFECTS	1,102,000	141,400	467,300	1,711,000

TOTAL LATENT HEALTH EFFECTS

	PF=5	PF=10	PF=40	Mixed PF
ADDITIONAL SHELTER FATALITIES	14,050,000	6,420,000	101,000	----
CANCER DEATHS (DEF=1)	4,679,000	4,633,000	4,109,000	4,300,000
CANCER DEATHS (DEF=0.2)	1,777,000	1,784,000	1,256,000	1,447,000
THYROID CANCERS	5,682,000	5,638,000	5,258,000	5,393,000
THYROID NODULES	8,365,000	8,300,000	7,742,000	7,941,000
SPONTANEOUS ABORTIONS	798,000	785,300	667,600	710,000
OTHER GENETIC EFFECTS	2,516,000	2,476,000	2,105,000	2,238,000

TOTAL LATENT EFFECTS ON THE U.S. ONLY

	DEF=1	DEF=0.2
CANCER DEATHS	167,300	33,500
THYROID CANCERS	285,000	
THYROID NODULES	419,500	
SPONTANEOUS ABORTIONS	23,900	
OTHER GENETIC EFFECTS	75,500	

48

Individual Cases

The calculated latent adverse health effects, i.e., cancer deaths, thyroid cancers, thyroid nodules, genetic spontaneous abortions and other genetic disorders, were presented in the previous section for 14 attack scenarios. The results from each attack scenario are separately discussed as individual cases below.

Case 1a

The numbers of the various more serious latent adverse health effects are relatively small. The total number of cancer deaths calculated for the U.S., i.e., 60 over a span of 40 years, may be compared with the current rate of about 390,000 per year. The reason for the small numbers are that the initial or prompt radiation population dose among the survivors is minimal, the amount of local fallout is insignificant and the amount of tropospheric fallout is minimal. For a 1 MT airburst, the 10 psi range is about 2.7 miles. At 2.7 miles, the unshielded initial or prompt radiation dose is less than 1 rem. Consequently, if the blast mortality criterion is 10 psi, the prompt radiation dose among the survivors, i.e., people located beyond 2.7 miles, would not be significant. In an actual case, depending on the structural characteristics of the city, blast mortalities can be expected beyond the 5 psi range, and survivors can be expected within the 10 psi range. However, the blast survivors within the 10 psi range would be those within strong structures and these structures would also provide shielding against prompt radiation.

The amount of local fallout is insignificant because the height of burst exceeds $180 \ W^{0.4}$ feet, which is the minimum altitude of significant local fallout. The amount of tropospheric fallout is minimal because the nuclear cloud base was calculated to be above the tropopause. Because the prompt radiation population dose among the survivors is relatively insignificant and the fallout is almost entirely stratospheric, the city used for estimating the long-term latent effects is not important.

49

Case 1b

The only difference between Case 1a and 1b is the location of the city, that is, in the Soviet Union instead of the United States. Since the adverse health effects in Case 1a were attributed entirely to radiation exposures from worldwide fallout, the results for Case 1b will be the same as those calculated for 1a.

Case 1c

The number of adverse health effects for this case would be about 25 times greater than those of Case 1a. In this case, the height of burst would also exceed the burst altitude of significant local fallout and the nuclear cloud base would also be above the tropopause. However, the nuclear cloud would attain a greater altitude (into the stratosphere) than the 1 MT burst of Case 1a. Consequently, it can be expected that the stratospheric residence time for the fallout from the 25 MT burst of Case 1c will be greater than that from the 1 MT burst of 1 MT. However, because deposited stratospheric fallout only consists of long-lived radionuclides, the net results are that the number of adverse health effects would be only slightly less than 25 times greater than those of Case 1a.

Case 1d

The number of adverse health effects for this case would be about 9 times greater than those of Case 1a. The statements above regarding Case 1c are also applicable to this case.

Case 1e

In this case, the weapon yields (40 KT) are sufficiently low so that at the 10 psi range of 0.94 miles, the unshielded initial or prompt radiation dose is 1000 rem. The unshielded radiation dose is reduced to 1 rem at about 1.94 miles. Thus in this case, the prompt radiation dose among the surviving population within this annulus of area could be significant. If a protection factor of 2 is used for the prompt radiation and a population density of 10,000 per square mile is used for the Soviet city, the calculated number of latent cancer deaths, from the prompt radiation of a single 40 KT burst, would be 466. Thus for 10 non-overlapping

1.94 mile radii, the estimated number of latent cancer deaths would be about 4660. The expected number will be lower however, because overlapping patterns are likely as are prompt radiation protection factors greater than 2 (for a city with a population density of 10,000 per square mile). Because the number of long-term adverse health effects from prompt radiation exposures are scenario dependent, e.g., the population density, the prompt radiation protection distribution, the relative burst points of each weapon, and the criteria for early fatalities, they were not included in the results listed for Case 1e.

Case 2a

The numbers of latent effects are relatively large because a large fraction of the fallout is deposited early (local fallout). As can be seen, the local fallout radiation exposures are the cause of the bulk of the latent effects and this is especially the case for low fallout shelter protection factors. In this case, DCPA provided computer printouts of surviving population distributions in unshielded local fallout dose ranges. These dose distributions were then converted to deposition distributions. DCPA also provided the shielded dose distributions among the survivors. If these were directly used to calculate the latent effects from shelter period exposures, they would be slightly lower than that shown for the 40 PF case.

The DCPA computer printout for this scenario showed 208.3 million survivors out of an initial population of 211.8 million. The number of early fatalities, therefore, was 3.5 million. For comparative purposes, the 3.5 million early fatalities could be considered relevant to the 40 PF case. It was estimated that the protection provided by the mixed shelter distribution among the surviving population, in this case, was equivalent to a protection factor of 50. Thus if it is assumed that the population were provided less protection, e.g., PF=5, PF=10, or PF=40, additional early fatalities would have resulted. For the PF=5 case, there would be about 3 million additional early fatalities. Thus, in this case, the 2 to 2.7 million latent cancer deaths (for PF=5) could be compared with about 6.5 million early fatalities. Two million cancer deaths over a period of 40 years is equivalent to 50,000 per year, which is about 13 percent of the current U.S. annual rate.

51

Case 2b

The numbers of latent health effects are very low when compared to those of Case 2a because: 1) the total fission yield is considerably lower, and 2) there is no local fallout in this case, that is, the burst altitude was greater than $180\ W^{0.4}$ feet. Because there is no local fallout, it was not necessary to list the results for different local fallout protection factors, i.e., the results would be the same.

As discussed for Case 1e, survivors with prompt radiation exposures can be anticipated for low yield bursts in the 40 KT range. Since the population densities at Soviet energy production and distribution systems and the available prompt radiation shielding are not known, they were not calculated and consequently are not included in the results. If a prompt radiation protection factor of 2 is used with a population density of 1000 per square mile, the number of expected latent cancer deaths from prompt radiation exposures would be about 3400 for the 72 bursts.

Case 3a

In this case, a single 1 MT surface burst fallout standard iso-dose-rate contour pattern was used along with estimated fallout arrival times and a specified population density to estimate the local fallout population exposure dose. Were overlapping fallout patterns to occur, the number of survivors (not specified) would be different. In some areas where people would have succumbed to the fallout exposures from a single burst, additional fallout from other bursts would not produce additional fatalities. In other areas where people would have survived the fallout exposures from a single burst, the additional fallout from other bursts would be sufficient to cause fatalities. In any event, an increase in early fatalities would result in a decrease in the number of latent health effects and a decrease in early fatalities would result in an increase in the number of latent health effects. It is estimated, however, that the overlapping of fallout patterns would not change the number of expected latent health effects from local fallout exposures significantly, much less the total number of latent health

effects from all exposures. The local fallout population exposure
dose could be significantly increased, however, if the winds aloft
caused several large cities such as Kansas City, St. Louis, and Minneapolis
to be significantly contaminated by local fallout.

Case 3a-1

The scenario of this case is the same as Case 3a, except that the
total yield of each weapon was changed from 1 MT to 550 KT. The results
show that the numbers of the latent effects were not proportionally
decreased. The reason they were not proportionally decreased is that
the lower weapon yield sent a smaller fraction of the worldwide fallout
into the stratosphere. This resulted in a considerable increase of
tropospheric fallout. Thus whereas tropospheric fallout was a minor
contributor to latent health effects in Case 3a, it was a major contributor
to latent health effects in Case 3a-1. The net result was a small decrease
in the total number of cancer deaths and genetic effects, and a larger
increase in the total number of thyroid cancers and nodules.

Case 3b

The scenario for this case is also similar to that of Case 3a.
The differences are: the missile silos attacked are in the S.U. instead
of the U.S., the number of silos is larger, and the weapons used are
considerably smaller. The increase in the number of air and surface
bursts from 1054 each to 1477 each, and the decrease in weapon size from
550 KT to 100 KT resulted in a factor of 4 decrease in local fallout,
a slight increase in tropospheric fallout, and a factor of 17 decrease
in stratospheric fallout. In addition, a population density of 10 people
per square mile was assumed in this case whereas 17 people per square mile
was assumed in Case 3a. Also, an effective postshelter PF of 2.5 was
assumed for the S.U. whereas an effective postshelter PF of 3 was assumed
for the U.S. Those differences account for the different numbers of latent
health effects from local, tropospheric, and stratospheric fallout. The
difference in the numbers of latent health effects from C-14 is due to the
difference in total nuclear yield.

53

Case 4a

The difference in this scenario from that of Case 3a-1 is that an additional 46 bomber bases and 2 SSBN facilities are targeted. If it is assumed that the additional bursts did not interact to change the outcome of the attack on the 1054 missile silos then the results of an "independent" attack on the 48 additional targets could be added to the results obtained for Case 3a-1. Since the additional deployment were airbursts, it is safe to assume that the 48 additional bursts could be treated as an independent additional attack. As can be expected a slight increase in the total number of latent health effects over that of Case 3a-1 resulted.

Case 4b

The difference in this scenario from that of Case 3b is that it includes 40 additional targets. The additional weapons and targets are: 10 - 40 KT airbursts on each of 30 bomber bases, 1 air and 1 surface 100 KT burst on each of 9 nuclear weapon production and strategic C^3 sites, and 10 - 40 KT airbursts on Moscow. As in Case 4a, the attack on these additional targets were treated as an additional independent attack and the additional latent effects were added to those of Case 3b.

The attack on Moscow is similar to Case 1e. The number of latent effects from prompt radiation exposures which were calculated for blast mortality criteria of 10 and 5 psi for prompt radiation protection factors of 2, 5, and 10, are insignificant when compared to the total number of latent effects for the entire attack. The same could be said for the number of latent effects from prompt radiation for the attacks on the bomber bases and the other 9 strategic sites. Also, as can be expected, a small increase in the total number of latent health effects over that of 3b resulted.

Case 5a

In this case, as in Case 2a, DCPA provided printouts on specific facets of the attack. They included the exposure dose distribution among the survivors and the surviving population distribution in unshielded local fallout dose ranges. The attack consisted of 3325 weapons with a total yield of 6500 MT. The targets included population centers as well as military facilities. For the mixture of shelters (providing protection against blast as well as radiation) assumed, the results showed a total of 97.8 million early fatalities. Compared to this number a total of 2.7 to 6.6 million additional latent cancer deaths occurring over a span of 40 years would appear to be relatively insignificant. (6.6 million cancer deaths in 40 years is about 40 percent of the current U.S. annual rate.)

Because the bulk of the latent cancer deaths were from worldwide fallout exposures and additional early fatalities occurred with the use of shelters providing less protection, the differences in the latent health effect totals for poorer protection factors were minimal.

Case 5b

In this case, it was assumed that for the mixed shelter protection posture that 35 percent of the Soviet population or about 91 million were early fatalities. The total number of latent cancer deaths were calculated to be between 1.4 and 4.3 million. As was with Case 5a, the total number of 1.4 to 4.3 million latent cancer deaths accrued over a 40 year period would appear to be relatively insignificant.

Whereas tropospheric fallout contributed to only about 5 percent of the total latent cancer deaths in Case 5a, troposphere fallout contributed to over 50 percent of the total latent cancer deaths in this case. The reason is that the combination of small weapons and a lower total yield reduced the local fallout by 62 percent and the stratospheric fallout by 76 percent, but increased the tropospheric fallout by 700 percent. The net results were that although the total nuclear yield of the 5b attack was only one-fifth that of the 5a attack and the fission yield of the 5b attack was only about one-third that of the 5a attack, the number of cancer deaths from the 5b attack was about one-half to two-thirds that of the 5a attack. In addition, the number of thyroid anomalies from the 5b attack exceeded those from the 5a attack.

55

The reason for the greater number of thyroid anomalies is the increase in tropospheric fallout. I-131 is a major contributor to thyroid exposure doses. Since it is assumed that crops directly contaminated by local fallout would not be harvested (as well as animal products from animals consuming directly contaminated forage), and the decay rate of I-131 is sufficiently fast that only insignificant amounts would remain in deposited stratospheric fallout, tropospheric fallout is the major source of I-131 that enters the body.

Exposure doses

Several factors can combine to increase or decrease the population dose from fallout. For local fallout, they include the following:

1) The local fallout distribution is affected by meteorological factors which at the time of an actual attack could be different from that assumed and used in the calculations. Different wind speeds and directions could cause the local fallout to be deposited over higher or lower population density areas and thus affect the population exposure dose. Under precipitation conditions, either existing or induced, could result in "rainout" and/or "washout" which would cause the airborne nuclear debris to be deposited faster.

2) The shelter protection utilized by the population was assumed. This is usually a scenario input and can be increased or decreased. The assigned protection factors to currently available shelter spaces have only been roughly estimated. Also, the intrusion of fallout into structures through broken windows could decrease the protection provided by some shelters.

3) The location of the population at the time of attack and after the attack was assumed. The relocation of people before the attack could reduce the early fatalities if urban centers are targeted. However, depending on their location with respect to the fallout and their fallout protection, the relocation of people could also result in increased latent health effects.

4) A shelter period of two weeks was assumed. Depending on the circumstances, the shelter period could be extended. Extending the shelter period would reduce the postshelter exposure doses. However, the calculations have shown that with a decontamination factor of 0.1 or better, the postshelter external exposure dose is only a minor contributor (especially for the poor shelter case) to latent health effects. Conversely, it may be necessary in many cases to leave the shelter earlier, e.g., people may be

57

driven from shelters by fire or smoke. Leaving shelters earlier could increase the population dose significantly. However, very short shelter stays would increase the number of fallout radiation early fatalities.

5) The postshelter countermeasures are scenario dependent. For example, an alternative scenario could have survivors in heavy fallout areas relocated to less contaminated areas. Another scenario could include no decontamination for a considerable period of time because of the unavailability of resources, or no decontamination at all. Although the calculations have shown that, with decontamination factors of 0.1 or better, the postshelter external exposure dose would only be a minor contributor to latent health effects, without decontamination the postshelter external exposure dose could be a major contributor to latent health effects. People could sustain relatively large radiation exposure doses without apparent effects if the exposure rate is low. Thus if the fallout is heavy and people are in high PF shelters for the first two weeks, the postshelter population dose without decontamination could be very large. For example, without decontamination, the postshelter dose could be about three times greater than that received in shelters with a protection factor of 40.

6) The ingestion of radioactivity is scenario dependent. The controls on contaminated water and food intake, depending on the postattack circumstances, could be stricter or more lenient. The projected incidence of thyroid cancers and nodules is particularly sensitive to earlier ingestion of radioactivity.

With respect to worldwide fallout, the partitioning between tropospheric and stratospheric fractions could vary considerably depending on the altitude of the tropopause and the meteorological factors that affect the altitude reached by the nuclear cloud. The results show that for the same amount of fission products in each spatial category, the adverse effects from tropospheric fallout are more than a magnitude greater than that from stratospheric fallout.

The C-14 produced by fusion weapons could be considerably higher than those used in the calculations. Although those used in the calculations are representative of a concensus of estimates, a range of up to a factor of 10 higher for some fusion devices (estimated by a Soviet scientist) was cited.[2] Since the latent health effects from C-14 exposures constituted a large fraction of the total, in some cases, the number of latent effects could be significantly larger than those shown for the cases where fusion constituted a large fraction of the total nuclear yield

The adult thyroid was used to estimate thyroid exposure doses. The thyroids of infants and children would receive higher exposure doses per unit of radioiodine ingested. On the other hand, the ingestion of milk from dairy cattle eating contaminated forage (which is a primary pathway for radioiodine ingestion) could be delayed until the concentration of I-131 is considerably reduced.

Health effects

Several factors can combine to increase or decrease the projected number of latent health effects from population exposures. The numbers obtained from using a dose effectiveness factor of 0.2 (DEF=0.2) for chronic exposures and low doses as well as DEF=1 for all exposures are shown in the results. Other uncertainties include the following:

1) If the relative risk model is really the more appropriate model and is used instead of the absolute risk model, the number of projected cancer deaths would be doubled.

2) If the appropriate risk plateau period is indeed 30 years instead of 40 years, the number of cancer deaths would be decreased by a factor of 1.6.

3) If the doubling dose for genetic disorders is 20 rems, the number of genetic disorders would be increased by a factor of 5; if the doubling dose is 200 rems, the number of genetic disorders would be halved.

59

Calculative procedures

When compared to the cited factors affecting the population exposure dose, the calculative procedures are relatively accurate. That is, the inaccuracies of the calculative processes associated with an electronic computer system arises from the non-representative inputs that may be used. In this case, where an electronic computer is not used, the basic calculative procedures are similar except that averaged and representative inputs are used instead of large quantities of distributive inputs. The inaccuracies of the manual process also arises from the use of non-representative inputs. However, since the number of latent health effects calculated are less sensitive to the inputs selected than the number of early casualties, the relative accuracies of the manual method for calculating latent health effects and the electronic computer method for calculating early casualties are comparable. Moreover, the manual calculations included separate results for different shelter protection factors and different dose-effectiveness-factors, and the effects of using different risk models and risk factors for converting exposure doses to latent effects, e.g., doubling the cancer deaths for the relative risk model or dividing by 1.6 for the shorter risk period of 30 years can be readily visualized for each case.

60

CONCLUSIONS

The long-term major adverse health effects resulting from hypothesized nuclear scenarios covering a nuclear employment range from a single weapon to a massive attack utilizing thousands of nuclear weapons were calculated. The general findings were as follows:

1. Several million latent cancer deaths could result from a massive nuclear attack directed at urban-industrial, military, and counterforce targets.* However, without improved civil defense capabilities, the number of projected latent cancer deaths is small when compared with the total number of early fatalities. Similar magnitudes of thyroid cancers, thyroid nodules, and genetic anomalies are also projected.

2. For limited attacks where the target points are in relatively low population density areas, the resulting number of latent cancer deaths could be large when compared with the total number of early fatalities.

3. For nuclear employments that are dominated by airbursts, the projected number of long-term adverse health effects that would occur in the attacked country is only a small percentage of the projected worldwide total.

4. For airbursts, the resulting number of long-term adverse health effects are larger for low yield weapons (40 KT) than for high yield weapons (1 MT) when compared on a per unit fission yield basis. The reason is that the nuclear debris of low yield airbursts is confined within the troposphere, whereas most of the nuclear debris from high yield airbursts enters the stratosphere.

5. Increasing the local fallout decontamination effectiveness to residual levels below 0.1 will not materially decrease the total number of long-term latent health effects because the local fallout post-shelter population dose constitutes only a small

---

*5 million worldwide cancer deaths over a period of 40 years represent an increase of about 2 to 3 percent of the current cancer death rate.

61

fraction of the total population dose when the fallout levels are reduced by a factor of 0.1 by decontamination.

6. The use of low yield weapons in the surface burst mode rather than high yield weapons as air bursts would increase the long-term latent adverse health effects in the country attacked and decrease the number of the effects in the rest of the world.

7. For massive nuclear attacks (Scenario 5a and 5b), although the number of early fatalities are sensitive to the shelter protection provided the population, the projected total number of latent health effects are relatively insensitive to the shelter protection provided.

REFERENCES

1. The Effects of Nuclear Weapons, Compiled and edited by S. Glasstone and P. J. Dolan, Third Edition, U.S. Department of Defense and U.S. Department of Energy, 1977.

2. Report of the United Nations Scientific Committee on the Effects of Atomic Radiation, General Assembly, Official Records: Seventeenth Session, Supplement No. 16 (A/5216), United Nations, New York, 1962.

3. H. Lee, P. W. Wong, and S. L. Brown, SEER II: A New Damage Assessment Fallout Model, DNA3008F, SRI International, Menlo Park, California, May 1972.

4. (Classified Report)

5. G. R. Crocker and T. Turner, Calculated Activities, Exposure Rates, and Gamma Spectra for Unfractionated Fission Products, USNRDL-TR-1009, U.S. Naval Radiological Defense Laboratory, San Francisco, California, 28 December 1965.

6. N. C. Rasmussen et al., Reactor Safety Study: An Assessment of Accident Risks in U.S. Commercial Nuclear Power Plants, Appendix VI, Calculation of Reactor Accident Consequences, WASH-1400, Nuclear Regulatory Commission, October 1975.

7. H. Lee, W. L. Owen, and C. F. Miller, General Analysis of Radiological Recovery Capabilities, SRI International, Menlo Park, California, June 1968.

8. The Effects on Populations of Exposure to Low Levels of Ionizing Radiation, Advisory Committee on the Biological Effects of Ionizing Radiations, National Academy of Sciences, Washington, D.C., November 1972.

9. R. A. Armistead et al., Analysis of Public Consequences from Postulated Severe Accident Sequences in Underground Nuclear Power Plants, Advanced Research and Applications Corporation, Sunnyvale, California, December 1977.